To
Rea King

Best Wishes
from
The West Torrington
Garden Club.

The Electric Epicure's Cookbook

By the author

POPPY
CANNON

⊕ *The*

Electric Epicure's

Cookbook

THOMAS Y. CROWELL COMPANY
ESTABLISHED 1839   NEW YORK

Designed by Edwin Kaplin

Manufactured in the United States of America
by the Vail-Ballou Press, Inc., Binghamton, New York

Library of Congress Catalog Card Number 61-7611

This book is for
my treasured friend

Alice B. Toklas

one of this century's
most accomplished gourmets,
whose imaginative experiments
with the electric blender
opened my eyes to a
new world of cooking

Acknowledgments

It is a joy to be able to express my grateful thanks and deep appreciation to the companies and the warm-hearted people who made available to me the electric appliances necessary for my experimenting and aided me immeasurably with information, guidance, and encouragement. Among those who have been particularly helpful are Corning Glass, Dominion Electric Company, General Electric, Hamilton Beach, Iona Food Blender, Knapp-Monarch, Munsey Oven Toaster, National Blenders, Nutone, Oster, Presto, Redi-Baker, Roto-Broil, Salton, Silex, Sunbeam Corporation, Thermo-Tray, Toastmaster, Universal, Waring, West Bend, and Westinghouse.

And—

A very special thank-you to Ann Seranne and Mable Stegner, Frances Borden and Ann Williams-Heller, to the Garveys (both Agnes and Pat), to Sally Chackow, Dorothy Bergman, and Betty Mudge.

Contents

The Electric Epicure's Cookbook

Introduction

KITCHEN REVOLUTION

To say that there has been a major revolution in cooking is an understatement. Today fine cooking is being accomplished by inexperienced cooks. It is being done by the book. There is practically no apprenticeship. And what makes life even more confusing, it would be impossible to reproduce the recipes of our grandmothers jot for jot, measure for measure, even if they were accurate, which they weren't . . . and even if we had all the skills and experiences of the past, which few have.

The old recipes for cakes and pastry simply will not work because the ingredients have changed so much—especially the character of our flour. Call ours better; call them worse. Censure or praise is irrelevant. The fact remains that the recipes of the past must be altered. Of course the great flour companies hesitate to make such admissions. But even in the home economics divisions of our great food companies recipes are retested constantly over the years and altered in order to produce uniform results.

Knowledge is power and in some cases, knowledge gives power even in electricity.

If you have an electric blender, an automatic fry pan or skillet or pressure cooker, a broiler or an electric hot tray, you can work miracles. Very few people realize how many and how varied these miracles can be. Not only the beginner, but even experienced

1

cooks can find their repertory widened and their prowess increased. With the blender, for instance, perfect Hollandaise and its tarragon-scented kin, Bearnaise, can be achieved not only without fear but even without any actual cooking other than melting the butter.

A dozen variants of mayonnaise come almost as effortlessly out of the blender as from a jar, offering to you not only freshness but the widest possible choice of oils, lemon juice or vinegar, as well as flavorings.

An electric ice crusher and a blender together make it possible to serve within three to five minutes a delicious Bavarian cream that only a short time ago would have required a half dozen operations and at least several hours to set.

Elaborate purées, tortes, whips, all sorts of long time-consuming processes—scraping, chipping, chopping, grating—become effortless if you have the right appliance. But what is just as important, you must understand the capabilities of that appliance, know what it can and can't do. The manufacturers' booklets will tell you a part of the story, but only a small part.

We live, all of us, in the midst of waves of recipes. It is not the purpose of this book merely to add to the sometimes delightful, often bewildering, welter.

This book does not attempt to cover the world. It is instead intended to be a guide to translating fine cooking into new methods. It is an introduction to the use of tools so new that even the experts find themselves, in the course of one recipe, ricocheting back and forth between the old ways and the new ways.

The chafing dish, the double boiler, the bain-marie as well as the asbestos pad, and constant stirring and constant watching are no longer necessary if you have a thermostatically controlled saucepan and *if* you know the principles of using it to full advantage.

A great deal of what you will find in this book is pioneering. It is a first attempt to correlate the findings of the scientist with the requirements of culinary artists. Every month, practically every week, there are improvements and discoveries. The realm of the electric epicure is ripe for your discovery.

KITCHENS BIG AS ALL OUTDOORS

Suddenly your kitchen and your dining room become as big as all outdoors. For electric appliances can be used wherever there is an electric outlet. The use of portable appliances makes outdoor cooking more convenient, more available to many more families than ever before. Foods can be cooked and served far away from the kitchen.

Not only the roaster and the automatic skillet, but the blender, the pressure cooker, and the Dutch oven can go along with the family on trips to the beach or to summer cottages, so that the convenience of the most modern cooking is available at all seasons and on all occasions.

VERSATILE CONTROLS

A great boon to electric cookery has been the invention of the removable probe or temperature control which fits a whole family of appliances. Generally these controls are designed to be used with a skillet, a saucepan, a griddle, or sometimes, with a pressure cooker of the same brand name. They cost only a few dollars and represent a considerable saving. Since all the electric parts except the heating elements, which are sealed, are enclosed within the probes, the utensils themselves can be treated like any other pans—completely immersed in water, or even placed in the dishwasher.

Such temperature control has been called the heart of good cooking. It measures heat so exactly that there is no sticking, burning, boiling over, constant watching or stirring. The heat is measured and maintained pretty much as it is done in the oven. There is an indicator light to tell you when you attain or when you simply maintain the proper temperature. Various brands provide varying temperatures, but as a general rule the popular controls permit you to set any temperature from about 150° F., just about enough to keep foods warm without drying them out, to a high temperature of 400° F.

Now with these thermostatic controls it is possible to be accurate about everything. You can measure the degree of heat as well as the flour and milk and butter. The heat has always been crucial in many recipes—sauces, omelets, scrambled eggs.

With control of temperature the milk or the cereal will not boil over. The ragout will not boil dry or burn. The rice will not stick to the bottom of the pan; the vegetables will not be dull and lifeless, overcooked.

THE UTENSILS

The Electric Blender

The possibilities of the blender have scarcely been touched. Already some of the ideas and principles expounded a few years ago have been proved incorrect. In the beginning we were told that neither cream nor egg whites should go into the blender. Now we have many recipes where we flout such warnings.

The trick of flicking the blender on and off quickly has made it possible to chop various foods coarsely or to dice or grate or scrape them without using liquid or reducing them to a powder.

A word of warning. Not all blenders are alike. Some appliances, billed as blenders, are actually not much more than drink mixers. The blades are so small, the construction so fragile that it would be folly to use them for other purposes.

In the most costly de luxe blender the blades are practically twice as large and probably four times as strong as in lighter, inexpensive models. In some blenders the container is made of heatproof plastic. Several use Pyrex and a number of them have markings on the container to simplify measuring. The bigger, better blenders are equipped with much more durable motors and generally the container is larger too, making it easier to work with sizable amounts. In several instances the same base comes with a blender attachment and a mixer attachment—a brilliant solution to the problem of having both blender and mixer when space is limited.

In your first flush of enthusiasm it will seem to you that the blender can do anything. But it won't remove the stringy part of asparagus stalks or the sharp little spikes that may get into a purée of artichokes unless you are careful.

It is impossible here to begin to uncover all the blender magic.

You will make any number of discoveries—all your own. When in doubt why not try a small amount? Incidentally, doing a small amount at a time is the key to success in many blender operations. In general it is a safe rule to put liquids into the blender first, at least enough to cover the blades.

Be sure to equip yourself with a couple of rubber spatulas, ordinary size and long and slender. You will certainly need them to scrape the materials off the sides into the center and also you will often find that it is necessary to break the surface of the mixture to let in the air and get a proper whir going.

Whatever you do, never use a metal or a wooden spoon. The wooden spoon will shatter and splinter into thousand pieces; the metal may break the blades.

Your blender is a valuable aid in the making of creamy frostings and dessert sauces. It grates chocolate and, with the addition of a little hot liquid, blends it to a smooth consistency. It chops nuts quickly and efficiently and it purées fresh, canned or frozen fruits into flavorful ice cream or pudding toppings.

CAKE MIXES PREPARED IN THE BLENDER

Some cake mixes but not all of them can be done in the blender. The ones that are best for blender mixing are close-textured cake, like ginger bread, spice cake, pound cake and fudge cake mixes.

Place in the blender the eggs, if eggs are required, and half the liquid. Add the contents of the package of cake mix, then the remaining liquid. Cover and turn on blender. Run 5 seconds, stop blender and stir down cake batter with a rubber spatula. Now blend 15 seconds longer. Stir down again if necessary. Pour into pans and bake according to package directions.

ELECTRIC BLENDER AND CHILLED SOUPS

The biggest chilled soup news of the decade is the role of the electric blender. Amazing how it whirs together, from canned soups, within seconds, delicious prototypes of some of the world's most elaborate and time-consuming specialties with no cooking at all.

Because it does such an extraordinary job of distributing and incorporating ingredients, the blender makes it unnecessary to "mellow the soup for several hours in a cold place" as the old recipes suggest. Not only does the blender make the finest of purées, but a single minute in the blender merges the flavors as effectively as hours of standing and gives the effect of simmering.

No problem about where you'll find the ingredients for these notable soups. All are made with condensed soups, which are well known everywhere throughout the country. Some of these are comparatively new, while a few are improved versions of old favorites. As for the herbs, many will be growing in your dooryard. Probably many more than you dream are at your grocer's and even chopped chives are being put up by one of the herb houses.

RECIPES USING THE BLENDER

Appetizers
  Caviar of Eggplant
  Avocado Dip

Soups
  Curried Shrimp Bisque
  Cream of Clam Soup
  Vichyssoise
  Gazpacho
  Cucumber Soup
  Chilled Beet Top Soup or **Botvina**
  Frosted Bisque
  Emerald Soup
  Cream of Avocado Soup
  Cream of Chicken Senegalese

Fish and Sea Food
  Poached Rainbow Trout with Green Mayonnaise

Fish and Sea Food
  Fish Fillets in Silver
  Salmon Mousse
  Sweden's Finest Fish Mousse
  Grilled Shrimp with Curry
  Sautéed Scallops
  Lobster and Rice au Mayonnaise
  Timbale of Crabmeat

Poultry
  Chicken and Almond Mousse
  Chicken Mousse
  Chicken and Carrot Loaf Nivernaise
  Boned Indonesian Chicken Breasts

Meats
  Glaze for Roast Pork
  Jellied Ham Loaf
  Jellied Ham Mousse
  Mousse of Ham and Chicken Livers

Vegetables
  Asparagus Duet Amandine
  Cauliflower with Sauce Aurore
  Potato Pancakes
  Spinach with Sesame Dressing

Sauces and Seasonings
  Exotic Salt
  Heung New Fun Spices
  Cracked Black Pepper
  Sauce Bearnaise
  Hollandaise Sauce
  Barbecue Sauce
  Chinese Duck Sauce
  Sauce Mayonnaise
  Old-Fashioned Cooked Salad Dressing
  Mayonnaise Chaud-Froid
  Gregorian Relish
  Cranberry and Kumquat Relish

Sauce à la Ritz
Sweet Whipped Butter
Instant Vanilla Custard Sauce
Instant Butterscotch Sauce
Instant Chocolate Sauce
Uncooked Hot Fudge Sauce
Fruit Sauce
Vanilla Sugar
Lemon Sugar
Anise-Flavored Sugar
Orange Sugar

Eggs and Cheese
Cheese Soufflé
Cottage Cheese Mold

Breads and Cereals
Garlic Bread
Old-Fashioned Whole Wheat Bread
Superior Corn Bread
Popovers from a Mix
Crêpes from a Popover Mix
Blini
Home-Ground Cereal

Fritters
Fritter Batter
Very Special Fritter Batter

Desserts
Mabel Stegner's Apple Sauce
Tart Green Apple Sauce
Chocolate Soufflé
Ginger Soufflé
Dinner Table Soufflé
Soufflé Flambé
Zabaione
Unforbidden Egg Nog
Crème Brulée (Broiled Cream)
Easiest Crème Brulée

Desserts
    Creamless Crème Brulée
    Cantaloupe Sherbet
    Watermelon Sherbet
    Instantaneous Fruit Sherbet
    Another Old-Fashioned Vanilla Ice Cream
    Vanilla-Flecked Ice Cream
    Strawberry, Raspberry, Banana, or Peach Custard Ice Cream
    Puerto Rican Coconut Ice Cream
    Banana Ice Cream
    Georgia Peach Ice Cream
    Green Gage Plum Ice Cream
    Strawberry Ice Cream
    Strawberry Bavarian Cream
    Bittersweet Chocolate Bavarian Cream
    Spanish Cream
    Apricot Mousse
    Snow Pudding
    Lemon Snow Pudding
    Lime Whip
    Orange Chiffon Pie in Crumb Crust
    Instant Cheese Cake
    Orange Chiffon Cake
    Banana Chiffon Cake
    Hazelnut Torte with Fruit
    Pecan Torte
    Almond Torte
    Almond Torte for a Party
    Fruit Meringue
    Bourbon Balls

Coffee
    Coffee for Gourmets

The Electric Beater or Mixer

The blender and the beater are entirely different things. The blender with its small high-powered blades does a mechanical job on the food. The function of the beater is, in general, to incorporate air.

As a rule of thumb the blender works best on egg yolks and on thin batters. The beater should be your choice for egg whites and whipping of cream. For some peculiar reason, the mixer is better also for creaming butter.

There are two principal types of mixers. One is lightweight, portable, not so highpowered. The other is stationary and capable of doing a number of hefty jobs which would prove too demanding for the lighter, less expensive mixer. The words "beater" and "mixer" are used interchangeably.

Many traditional cooks are skeptical about mechanical beaters. For angel cake, for instance, they prefer a wire whisk. Excellent results can be obtained through the use of the mixer if you do not use too high a speed.

When in doubt, it is better to err on the side of the lower speed. It may take a few seconds longer, but you are less likely to have dry, dull-looking egg whites and a dry, dull cake or soufflé. The same thing is true with cream. Different speeds produce somewhat different results. If you whip the cream at a low speed, you will have less volume but a more luscious result. After all, flavor and texture are more important to the epicure than volume.

Egg whites should be beaten only long enough to stand up in a little horn when the beater is withdrawn. At the point of perfection, they should have a glossy, shiny look.

Overbeating is the biggest problem with the electric beater, because it works so fast. So, when in doubt, use the lower speeds and be sure.

RECIPES USING THE BEATER OR MIXER

Sauces and Seasonings
  Sauce Aurore
  Frozen Mousse of Horseradish, Epicure
  Homemade Whipped Butter
  Lingonberry Butter
  Whipped Honey Butter
  Creamy Sauce

Breads and Cereals
  Cottage Bread
  Mixer Buns
  Sally Lunn
  Brioche from a Hot Roll Mix
  Whole Wheat Batter Bread
  Sour Dough Pumpernickel
  Virginia Spoon Bread
  Popovers
  Yorkshire Pudding

Desserts
  Dinner Table Soufflé
  Soufflé Flambé
  Unforbidden Egg Nog
  Chilled Orange Bavarian
  Sauterne Bavarian
  Charlotte Russe
  Charlotte Russe Imperiale
  Russian Paska
  Concord Grape Parfait

Apple Snow
Tipsy Snow Pudding
Coeur Flottante à la Ritz
Egg Nog Pie
Lime Chiffon Pie
Nesselrode Pie
Wisconsin Refrigerator Cheese Cake
Ginger or Chocolate Rolls
Orange Chiffon Cake
Banana Chiffon Cake
Banana Glaze
Hazelnut Torte with Fruit
Pecan Torte
Almond Torte
Almond Torte for a Party
Meringue
Williamsburg Pecan Confections
Meringue Torte
Lumberjacks
Fraulein's Brandy Wafers

The Electric
Roaster Oven

Asking around over a period of months reveals that there is an extraordinary number of electric roasters resting mournfully in hall closets and attics. It seems that a great many of them were bought some years ago, for it was a beguiling thought to be able to roast or bake or cook up stew for fifty people without reference to location except that the roaster had to be at the end of a plugged-in electric cord.

Sadly, though, the roaster was done in by dullness. Each one came equipped with a set of inset pans and was accompanied by lugubrious menus for oven meals. Who wants stuffed breast of lamb and steamed rutabagas or salmon loaf and scalloped corn?

Another feature that terrified and finally stymied many people was the automatic timer clock, alleged to turn itself on and then turn itself off again automatically. Detailed diagrams in the instruction books failed to give a glimmering. They merely confused most people (including this author).

FALLING IN LOVE WITH A ROASTER

But forget the dreary little oven meals. Throw away the measly inset pans. Disregard, if you like, the timer clock. It's high time to get reacquainted with the electric roaster—on different terms.

Realize that now, at long last, you have a kettle big enough to do almost anything you want to do. Poach a whole salmon, cook a country ham. Pre-soak it too in the same pan.

With an electric roaster you have an oven thermostatically controlled. No matter how hot and breathless the day you can still have staunch, well-cooked appetizing meals. The roaster is divinely amenable. Set it out on the terrace. Plug it in if you're lucky enough to have a plug beside the swimming pool—if you're lucky enough to have a pool. Wherever there is an electric outlet you are equipped for the most grandiose cooking.

Your roaster is ideal for steaming lobsters or clams; in fact, for steaming anything.

When you're giving a party, cooking for a crowd, it is no longer necessary to run around the neighborhood borrowing kettles. In the roaster all at once you can cook for 50 people. If you set the thermostat at 150° F., you can keep your food at exactly the right temperature until you're ready to eat it. If you feel that your roaster is too shiny white and unwieldy to adorn a festive setting, try banking it with leafy boughs. Incidentally, you will find that it is more comfortable to set the roaster on a low stand or table so that the top is just about waist high, the right height for easier ladling.

For preserving and pickling or making apple butter, the electric roaster is a dream. Because it is shallow, more surface is exposed to heat; you can cook twice as large a quantity as in the usual preserving kettle, and cook it more evenly.

You are doomed to disappointment, however, if you do not know the shortcomings as well as the virtues of the electric roaster. Because it is engineered to operate on regular house current rather than electric stove current, the roaster does take a long time to heat. You must remember to get it going at least an hour before you want to use it. On very low voltage, it may take longer. For foods like baked beans and cassoulets that require long, slow cooking but need not be too carefully timed, you can put the dish into the cold roaster, but you must allow an extra hour or so of cooking time.

For stocks, soups, and all the dishes that belong to the stew family you need heat, not merely on the bottom of the pan but up the sides. All of the top brands of thermostatically controlled electric appliances are made of materials that do conduct and hold heat, and for this reason you will discover that this type of food tastes better than when cooked in an ordinary light-weight pan.

Beans baked in an electric roaster or a Dutch oven will have much of the same taste as those that are baked in a hole in the ground heated with coals. You get the same effect in a roaster with the heat coming from the five sides as you do in a pit full of coals. The roaster is a perfect utensil for a clambake or a lobster bake.

The roaster, as you may have gathered, is not intended for speed. It does provide you with ease, comfort, convenience, and amazing versatility.

RECIPES USING THE ROASTER OVEN

Fish and Sea Food
  Salmon Imperator Baked in Clay
  Whole Poached Salmon
  Cold Poached Salmon
  Steamed Fish, Chinese Style
  Steamed Lobster
  Clam Bake

Poultry
  Chicken Brunswick Stew
  Chicken-in-Clay

Meats
  Kentucky Burgoo
  Crown Roast of Pork
  Baked Virginia Ham
  Blue Grass Ham

Coffee
  Coffee for a Throng

The Electric
Portable Oven

The small portable ovens or a Dutch oven, a saucepan or even a preheated skillet with a rack can be used to thaw quickly or even to thaw and bake frozen foods. These appliances will thaw frozen foods approximately five times faster than at room temperature, and two to three times faster than thawing in warm water. Many frozen foods, such as frozen pies, may be thawed and baked to a tempting golden brown in these ovens.

CHART FOR BAKING FROZEN FOODS

Frozen Food	Amount	Preheat for baking to:	Time (Minutes)
Fruit Pie	10½ ounces	425°	40 to 50
	1½ pounds	"	60 to 70
Meat Pie	8 ounces	"	40 to 50 *
Sweet Potatoes, candied	12 ounces	"	35 to 40
Macaroni and Cheese Casserole	8 ounces	"	40 to 45 *
Pizza (8 to 9 inches in diameter)	14 ounces	"	20 to 26

* Allow 5 to 10 minutes additional time when baking several frozen foods at a time.

The great convenience about small table ovens is the speed at which they reach baking temperature. Even the large size, big enough to hold a dozen rolls or biscuits, is ready to bake in 5 minutes.

When rolls or toast are done, they may be kept warm by turning the dial to less than 200° F.

TO THAW STEW MEAT

Formerly we believed that stew meats were difficult to cook frozen "because the pieces stick together and can't be browned." However, you can get around this difficulty very easily. Simply brush the meat fore and aft with fat or oil. Place in a very hot oven or under a broiler. In the heat the pieces will drop apart. You may separate them with a fork and spread them out for even browning, turning once or twice. This method saves any spattering. It is easy and quick. Less smoke in the kitchen. And you proceed from this point on just as if you were cooking fresh meat. You will probably find that the cooking time will be only a little longer.

RECIPES USING THE PORTABLE OVEN

Appetizers
Piroshki
Glamorized Hot Dogs

Fish and Sea Food
Connecticut Coquilles

Meats
A Glamorous Meat Loaf
Rack of Lamb
Whole Ham Baked in Foil

Vegetables
Spinach Soufflé
Soufflé de Tomates à la Napolitaine

Breads and Cereals
Onion Rolls
Deviled Bread
Bacon Bread Baked in a Casserole
Homemade Bread from a Mix

Old-Fashioned Whole Wheat Bread
The Grant Loaf
Anadama Bread
Sour Dough Starters for Rye Bread
Sour Rye Ponies

Sandwiches
Baked French Toast Sandwiches
Riviera Loaf

Desserts
Apple Croûtes
Apple Sauce
Pecan Pie from Kings Arms Tavern
Eclairs
Profiteroles au Chocolat

The Electric Rotisserie

There are a number of advantages to cooking roasts with the bone in on the rotisserie. First of all, they taste better. It is quite true that the sweetest meat is next to the bone. The meats are juicier and, quite surprisingly, the cooking time is considerably shortened, for the bone acts as a conductor of the heat.

As in so many other methods of cookery, one of the most common faults of the novice is overcooking. It takes longer to roast meat in the oven than it does on the rotisserie . . . at least 25 per cent more time. A rib roast of beef cooked on the rotisserie requires only about 12 minutes per pound for very rare; it would take at least 16 minutes per pound in an oven at 375° F.

Many women complain that chicken is dry on the rotisserie. Generally this is because it is overcooked. A very good way to judge is to use a meat thermometer and take the temperature of your roast. You can't, of course, do this while the rotisserie is in motion, for the thermometer would be ruined by direct heat. Simply stop it, place the thermometer in the center of a meaty portion, make certain that it is not against bone or fat and allow the thermometer to stay in place for 3 or 4 minutes. On the dial of the meat thermometer there are markings for poultry, pork, lamb, and beef at various stages—rare, medium, well done. If you like lamb slightly pink in the Parisian fashion, you will probably want it at about 140° F. rather than 160° F. as marked on most dials. Really, rare roast beef should be, in my opinion, about 130° F. rather than 140° F.

Here is a brief chart of timing for the rotisserie:

ROTISSERIE TIME CHART

	Weight in Pounds	Internal Meat Thermometer Temperature	Total Cooking Time in Hours
BEEF (*boneless*)			
Rolled rib or sirloin roast	4–5	130° F. (rare) 160° F. (medium) 170° F. (well-done)	1¼ to 1½ 1½ to 1¾ 1¾ to 2¼
Standing rib with bones	6–7	130° F. (rare) 160° F. (medium) 170° F. (well-done)	1½ to 1¾ 1¾ to 2¼ 2¼ to 2¾
	8–9	130° F. (rare) 160° F. (medium) 170° F. (well-done)	1¾ to 2¼ 2¼ to 2½ 2½ to 3
Rolled chuck or eye of round	4–5	130° F. (rare) 160° F. (medium) 170° F. (well-done)	1¼ to 1½ 1½ to 1¾ 1¾ to 2¼
	6–7	130° F. (rare) 160° F. (medium) 170° F. (well-done)	1¾ to 2 2 to 2½ 2½ to 3
LAMB			
Rolled leg	3–4	140° F. (medium) 175–180° F. (well-done)	1¼ to 1½ 1¾ to 2¼
With bone	7–8	140° F. (medium) 175° F. (well-done)	2¼ to 2¾
PORK			
Loin (boned, tied)	4–5	185° F. (well-done)	1¾ to 2½
	6–7	185° F. (well-done)	2¾ to 3¼
Spare ribs	1½–2	"	¾ to 1
Ham (ready to eat)	8–12	130° F.	2 to 3
Picnic ham (ready to eat)	3–4	"	1 to 1¼
	5–6	"	1½ to 2

ROTISSERIE TIME CHART (continued)

	Weight in Pounds	Internal Meat Thermometer Temperature	Total Cooking Time in Hours
POULTRY			
Chicken (drawn weight)	2–2½	190° F.	1 to ¼
Roaster (drawn weight)	3–4	"	1 to 1¼
	5–6	"	1¼ to 1½
Capon (drawn weight)	5–6	"	1½ to 1¾
Duck (drawn weight)	5–6	"	1¾ to 2¼
Rock Cornish Hens		"	
(drawn weight)	¾–1	"	¾ to 1
Turkey (drawn weight)	7–9	"	2¼ to 2¾
	10–12	"	3 to 3½
	14–16	"	3¾ to 4½
Chicken (unstuffed)	2–2½	190° F.	1 to 1¼
(stuffed)	4–5	165° F. (temperature of stuffing is taken)	1½ to 1¾ (stuffing adds about ½ hour to cooking time)
Turkey (stuffed)	10–12	165° F. (temperature of stuffing)	3½ to 3¾

NOTES ON THE USE OF THE ROTISSERIE

Always use compact or well-tied food. Be certain that the meat is well balanced on the skewer, that wings or ends do not flop about.

Insert the two removable forks firmly into the food. When roasting two large pieces of food, such as two chickens, it may be necessary to tie or skewer them together at the center so that they turn as a unit.

Place the dripping pan without a rack on the shelf below the meat to catch the delicious drippings.

Leave the door open. Ignore those directions which tell you to pull down the glass. Don't be afraid of spatter. It is highly important that as much air as possible gets to your food as it turns. It is air, most experts are convinced, and not charcoal or any other fuel, which imparts that luscious flavor to food cooked outdoors.

Be careful about overcooking. Food cooks anywhere from one-third to one-fourth faster on the spit than it does in the oven.

It is wise to check food occasionally while it is cooking to make sure that it is turning evenly. Every once in a while you may want to stop the motor and readjust the forks.

When food is done, the heat can be turned to low, about 180° F., and allowed to remain on the skewer until serving time. Or food may be removed from the skewer immediately and allowed to stand on a warm platter on an electric hot tray. It is always better for meat or poultry to rest anywhere from 15 to 30 minutes before slicing.

Cooking on a spit gives a miraculously different flavor to meat because the meat is sealed behind a rotating wall of its own juices and it does not dry out. Very little juice is lost; all the flavor is in the meat. Whatever juices do drop out can be used for basting the meat or as the bases of miraculous sauces. You can achieve endless variations by putting herbs, chopped onions, shallots, spices, wines or spirits, or condiments into the juices in the drip pan.

RECIPES USING THE ROTISSERIE

Poultry
Stuffed Birds
Peking Duck

Meats
Roast Beef au Poivre
Spring Lamb on a Spit
Baron of Lamb
Grilled Rack of Lamb
Lamb on Skewers, Grecian Style
Barbecued Canadian Bacon

Vegetables
Rotisserie Potatoes

Desserts
Dinner Table Soufflé
Soufflé Flambé

The Electric Broiler

There are on the market almost as many electric as charcoal broilers, which means they are legion. Some are known as infra red; some of the newest and most expensive are made of ceramics and are supposed to impart a special outdoor flavor to the food. At the risk of being an illusion shatterer, we must admit that we have never been able to taste any special virtue from the source of heat.

As we point out also in our discussion of the rotisserie, one of the most important factors in broiling is *air*. Broiling requires lots of oxygen, the more the better.

Because open coils are easily injured, it is important that the coil on the broiler should be protected. And it is a good idea to be able to regulate the amount of heat. Many of the less expensive broilers, however, are not equipped with thermostatic controls, and the amount of heat is regulated by distance. In some cases, however, the places where the food can rest are few and far between. These are points to bear in mind when selecting a broiler.

Although broiling is generally considered one of the easiest ways to cook, it is in fact one of the most ill-used techniques. Broiling does not mean burning or charring. There is a bitter, acrid taste to burned meat which is completely different from the crisp or crusty browning that you want.

The best types of broilers, in my opinion, are those in which the heat is either above or behind the food. With this construction it is impossible for the fat to drip onto the hot grids and burn. Pristine and unbothered, the drippings are there for a sauce or a gravy.

GENERAL DIRECTIONS

Broiling with electricity is no different from broiling by any other method, except that in most instances you have better control. Opinions vary, but it is my belief that it is best to preheat the broiler. Grease the broiling rack well so that the food will not stick to it. Unless you are specifically told not to do so, it is usually best to cook the food briefly on one side, turn and cook about half the total time required, and then turn again to the original side to complete the cooking.

RECIPES USING THE BROILER

Appetizers
Souffléed Canapé
Tongue Tartars

Fish and Seafood
Broiled Fish Japanese
Broiled Fish
Grilled Shrimp with Curry

Poultry
Boned Indonesian Chicken Breasts
Chicken Livers Saté
Broiled Chicken with Wine and Tarragon
Cornish Game Hen

Meats
Broiled Chuck or Round Steak
Teriyaki-Steak Sticks
Broiled Hamburgers
Broiled English Cutlets
Lamb Shish Kabob
Quick Ham Croustades

Vegetables
Grilled Vegetables

Desserts
   Grilled Fruits
   Grilled Fruits Afire
   Crème Brulée (Broiled Cream)
   Easiest Crème Brulée
   Quickest Crème Brulée
   Singed Angel Wings

The Electric Skillet

With an electric skillet or saucepan it should be possible to dispense with the chafing dish, the double boiler, and the bain-marie.

When you use a skillet to do deep fat frying, you may find that there is a problem with foaming. The fat may bubble over the edge of the skillet and for this reason the skillet should not be filled more than half way; and foods should be patted dry with paper toweling to get rid of excess moisture before they are placed in the pan.

NONCALORIC FRYING

There are on the market now certain products that enjoy some popularity with dieters, especially those who are particularly calorie-conscious and fat-conscious. The best known are made from a vegetable product which has been known for a long time to the scientists and to makers of fine chocolate candies. It is lecithin, a vegetable product which has been used by doctors in the treatment of nervous disorders. This product is sprayed on a cold pan and keeps food from sticking to the pan. It can be used alone or in conjunction with a small amount of butter or oil. In some cases we found that these sprays do interfere with browning, especially the browning of meats. They work very well on griddles and in the automatic skillet when you are making an omelet or thin pancakes where sticking is often a problem and where browning is not too desirable. (Pan Dry-Fry is one of these products.)

29

SHALLOW BUT DEEP

Shallow deep fat frying may sound like a contradiction in terms but actually it refers to the use of just enough oil to cover the largest pieces with at least half an inch to spare. For this type of frying pan you can use a skillet instead of a deep fat fryer or saucepan. However, it is well to remember that when you have a wider surface and less fat you have also more heat loss and it is a little more difficult to maintain a perfect temperature.

FRENCH FRIED FROZEN FOODS

Package directions persist in spreading the idea that frozen French fried potatoes, French fried onions, sea food and the like can be properly reheated in the oven or under the broiler. This simply isn't so. Despite the reluctance of the manufacturers to suggest the use of some sort of deep fat frying method, there is unfortunately no other way to make these foods palatable. Of course it is not necessary to use a great deal of oil. French fried potatoes can be taken solid frozen straight out of the freezer and heated a handful at a time in oil about an inch deep. The whole operation done at about 375° F. takes about 60 seconds per handful.

RECIPES USING THE SKILLET

Fish and Sea Food
   Filet of Sole Amandine
   Sole Amandine with Bananas
   Fiddler Crab à la Nero

Poultry
   The King's Chicken

Meats
   Steak Maxim
   Steak Flambé

Family Steak au Poivre
Steak au Poivre Flambé
Steak Diane
Economical Steak Diane
California Sukiyaki
Flaming London Broil
Syrian Stuffed Grape Leaves
Veal Kidneys Flambé
Noisettes of Lamb

Vegetables
Escarole with Pine Nuts
Spinach with Pine Nuts

Sauces and Seasonings
Ham Gravy—Red or Red-Eye Gravy
Clarified Butter

Eggs and Cheese
Poached Eggs
French Omelet
Omelet Fines Herbes
Omelet Fines Herbes from Dried Herbs
Special Scrambled Eggs
New York Style Egg Sandwich

Breads and Cereals
Brown 'n' Serve Rolls
Skillet Spoon Bread

Sandwiches
Heroes Trinacria
Denver Sandwich

Desserts
Skillet Custard

The Electric Deep
Fat Fryer

Whether you use a deep pan or a skillet, you can often dispense with the fry basket and use instead a slotted spoon or a strainer. If you do use a fry basket, be sure to heat it along with the fat. Do not put the food into a dry cold fry basket or it will very likely stick to the basket; and if you put a chilly basket into hot fat the temperature will take a nose dive. Best results are obtained when you fry small amounts at a time. A heaping basket full of raw potatoes will cause a drop in temperature, generally resulting in a sad and soggy situation.

WAIT FIVE MINUTES

In deep fat frying it is good policy to wait for five minutes after the light has gone off before putting the food into the hot oil. In this way you can be sure that the whole quantity of fat or oil has come up to the desired temperature.

THE BEST FATS FOR FRYING

For sautéing or pan frying, butter or bacon drippings are widely used because they give such fine flavor. Lard was formerly popular and margarine is often suggested as a substitute for butter. From the point of view of the gourmet, however, margarine has its limitations. When heated to comparatively high temperatures many brands do develop an off flavor. Butter smokes and breaks down

32

at a lower temperature than any of the other popular fats, which means that it changes its taste readily. A listing of fats in the order of their smoke points would run something like this: butter, margarine, olive oil, lard, solid shortenings, vegetable or peanut oils. Oils vary slightly in their smoking point, and different brands will vary also. Cottonseed, soy, and corn oils all have about the same smoke point. Peanut oil has a slightly higher smoking point. This means that margarine and olive oil are *least* desirable for deep fat frying and certain types of vegetable and nut oils most desirable.

RECIPES USING THE DEEP FAT FRYER

Appetizers
  Indian Pappadums
  Monte Benito
  Lazy Pommes Soufflés

Fish and Sea Food
  Fish Tempura
  Shrimp Tempura
  New Orleans Oyster Loaf

Poultry
  Chicken Martinique
  Cotelettes Kiev
  Twentieth-Century Cotelettes Kiev

Vegetables
  Pommes de Terre Soufflés
  French Fried Sweet Potatoes

Timbales
  Timbale Shells

Breads and Cereals
  Rosettes
  Rosettes Poivrades

Fritters
    French Style Fritters
    Creole Rice Calas
    Banana Fritters
    Pineapple Fritters
    Apricot or Peach Fritters
    Orange Fritters
    Apple Fritters
    Tangerine Fritters
    Squash Flower Fritters
    Flower Fritters
    Glazed Fritters
    Japanese Tempura
    Vegetable Tempura

Desserts
    Half-Moon Pies of Mincemeat
    Crullers from Ready-to-Bake Biscuits

The Electric
Saucepan

HOW HOT IS RIGHT?

(A *Discussion of Thermostatic Cooking*)

Judging the right temperature for the right food at the right moment is the very heart of fine cooking. Ever since the first cave man or his mate speared a piece of meat on a stick and held it to the fire, judgment of temperatures has been crucial. Generally such judgment has come only with experience or apprenticeship. Our grandmothers knew that a griddle was right for pancakes when drops of water danced a certain jig over the surface.

The ancient Chinese cooks could see at a glance how the oil wrinkled on the surface. Oven temperatures even a generation ago were calculated by the number of seconds it took a film of flour to brown, and deep fat for frying was tested by the number of seconds required to brown a cube of bread. A lady on the West Coast who is famous for her potato pancakes showed us once how to judge the temperature of the fat by the appearance of a necklace of bubbles that formed at the proper moment around a thick slice of onion. Time after time her observation was as accurate as any thermometer.

But now this type of wisdom through doing has become more and more rare especially among the younger, book-taught and self-taught cooks. That is why the thermostatically controlled electric appliances fill a vast need.

A generation ago recipes for oven cookery began to be written in a new way. Instead of merely specifying a slow, moderate or very hot oven, we started speaking of a moderate oven (350°) or a very hot oven (450°). But up until now few of the directions for surface cooking have suggested temperatures although most of the new appliances enjoying vast popularity are equipped with controls showing various degrees of heat. This work is still in the pioneer stage. Surface cooking by degrees of temperature appears to be a great deal more complicated than oven cookery. In laboratories all over the country experiments are being carried on. There is a remarkable lack of unanimity. On the handle of most of the popular equipment like skillets, saucepans, and Dutch ovens you will find suggested temperatures for frying eggs, hamburgers and omelets, French toast, cooking bacon, braising, stewing, simmering. No two makers agree. Eggs, for instance, are listed anywhere from 250 to 375°; bacon has as wide a range. Some of the differences can only be ascribed to stupidity or carelessness but others stem from differences of opinion, different likes and dislikes, different settings.

Despite the current vogue for low temperature in egg cookery, especially among the home economists, some people still like their fried eggs to have a lacework of golden brown around them which is easier to achieve at higher temperatures and less cooking time. Some people like their French toast crisp and brown, others like it soft and custardy. Some people are wildly enthusiastic about the benefits of low temperature cooking in meats while others are just as stubborn about their enthusiasm for a crisp charcoal crust. All this makes the writing of a cookbook like this one almost as hazardous as betting on the races.

In a number of instances we give a wide range of temperatures, and insofar as it is possible with mere words to describe textures, looks, and taste, we have attempted to warn the reader about the varying results to be expected from the use of these different temperatures.

In order to help you translate your favorite recipes into thermostatically controlled cookery, we have prepared a list of cooking terms and the approximate temperature or range of temperatures which they require.

Let's begin at the beginning.

How to boil water. We were all taught in our eighth-grade science classes that water boils at 212° F. Undoubtedly the teacher pointed out that this is true only at sea level. The boiling point changes with higher altitudes. The engineers at the General Electric Laboratories calculate that this boiling point goes down five degrees with every thousand feet of altitude. On a mountain peak, a thousand feet above sea level, the boiling point of clear water without any salt, sugar, or fats added to it would be about 207°.

Braising is a technique most often applied to meats and includes first browning the meat at high temperature, about 400°, and then simmering with a small amount of liquid at about 200°.

Pan frying is another method of dealing with tender meats that do not require long cooking. It differs from regular frying inasmuch as it is done with the minimum of fat and for this reason it is often called pan broiling. All broiling implies dry heat and is always done in the presence of air. The pan is never covered. There has been a general tendency to pan fry or broil at low temperatures but, since many people like a crisp surface and rare meat in the center, the temperatures may range anywhere from 300 to 375°.

Searing, which is generally the initial stage in all brown stews and pot roasts, is traditionally done at high temperatures, about 375°, but it can be done with much less heat at anywhere from 275° on up. A lower temperature takes longer, of course, but there is less shrinkage and sometimes the high heat hardens the meat too much.

Browning is another name for searing and here again you have your choice of moderately low or high temperatures.

A steady, uninterrupted boil such as you will want for steaming will require about 230°, or about 30° higher than the simmering point on your utensil.

NEW TIMING

Up until now there is no thermostatically controlled utensil on the market which can be considered completely automatic. It is true that foods are less likely to boil dry, less likely to stick, less likely to burn. They need a lot less watching, a lot less stirring, but there are definite limitations to automation in the kitchen. Having voiced this warning, we can go on to say that most women do not take full advantage of the automatic features that are available to them. For example, it is no longer necessary to switch the theromstat back and forth when you are defrosting and cooking frozen vegetables. If you add the required amount of liquid, very little liquid, or butter or oil into the bottom of the automatic saucepan or skillet, set your thermostat at 200°, *i.e.*, simmering temperature, leave the lid on and the steam vent closed, you will in the requisite number of minutes have a perfect result. All kinds of frozen foods cooked and uncooked can be prepared in this fashion with no wiggling of the thermostat.

As for timing, automatic electric saucepans and skillets take no more and no less time than utensils of equal weight and similar materials. However, cooking times will be more uniform because you are using the same pan constantly, not switching from one to another.

At the present writing there are few timers and automatic shut-offs. We have found that a portable timer or even a wrist watch alarm is most practical. With your timing device on your arm, you are not permitted to forget the stew in the pressure cooker or the vegetables in the saucepan.

BOIL-IN-THE-BAG FROZEN SPECIALTIES

A variety of cooked frozen foods is now available in small-size plastic bags which, according to package directions, need only to be dropped into boiling water for a few minutes, then cut open and served. These specialties include a number of sauced vegetables and stews, ragouts, goulash, meat balls. They range from mediocre to excellent in taste and texture and, of course, the automatic saucepan or skillet is ideal for heating them. However, there are problems involved in this boil-in-the-bag vogue. The brief heating period advised is usually too brief for proper heating and also, it lengthens considerably if more than one bag goes into the pot. Once or twice in our house the bags broke leaving meat balls to wander disconsolately in a hot brown water. This does not happen often. Even once is too often. But always these hot bags are difficult to handle. They must be removed from the hot water with tongs. You need a cloth or a potholder to hold them and a pair of sharp kitchen scissors to cut them open. Portions are exceedingly meager.

We suggest that it is much simpler to remove the food from the bag or bags. Provide a spare package or two. Add 2 tablespoons of some appropriate liquid, water, milk, bouillon or wine for each package of food and heat, covered, at 200°.

FREE BUT CONTROLLED

Probably one of the first of the electrical appliances was the old-fashioned electric hot plate—flimsy and inefficient as compared with the carefully engineered, thermostatically controlled equipment of today. But they did have one important feature. You could use on a portable unit your own favorite cooking pots and pans. At the present writing there is only one shallow automatic saucepan (or you might possibly call it a skillet) which is separate from the unit and can be used as a serving dish or put in the refrigerator or even the freezer or set upon the broiler or in the oven.

No doubt there will soon be many such for they do fill a definite need. In using them, however, it is well to remember that the thermostatic settings must be at least 25 degrees higher than those you would use in the saucepan where the unit is integrated.

You can use the lower heating part of this particular unit like a hot plate with other pans as well, but you must allow then for considerable heat loss.

CHART FOR THAWING FROZEN FOODS IN AUTOMATIC SKILLET OR SAUCEPAN *

Frozen Food	Amount	Preheat Skillet to:	Time (Minutes)
Cherries, red, pitted	1 pound, 4 ounces	250°	25 to 30
Chicken à la King	10 ounces	300°	30 to 35
Chicken livers **	8 ounces	"	" " "
Chicken, cut up	1 pound	"	" " "
	2 pounds	"	40 to 45
Chow Mein	1 pound	"	30 to 35
Cranberry-Orange Relish	10½ ounces	250°	15 to 20
Crabmeat, flaked	6 ounces	"	20 to 22
Fish-Steaks	1 pound	"	20 to 35
Fillets	12 ounces	"	20 to 25
	1 pound	"	30 to 35
Fruit (Blueberries, Peaches,	10 ounces	"	15 to 20
Mixed Fruit, Strawberries,	12 ounces	"	20 to 25
Raspberries, Rhubarb)	1 pound	"	25 to 30
Grapefruit Sections	13½ ounces	"	20 to 25
Lobster Tails **	10½ ounces	"	25 to 30
Meats (to thaw enough to separate)			
Ground meat patties, liver, etc.	1 pound	300°	20 to 25
Steaks, chops	1 pound	"	15 to 20
	2 pounds	"	20 to 25
Melon Balls	12 ounces	250°	25 to 28
Oysters	8 ounces	"	25 to 30
	12 ounces	"	35 to 40
Pie, baked	1½ pounds	"	30 to 35
Pineapple Chunks	13½ ounces	"	20 to 25
Rolls, browned (to heat)	6	"	12 to 15
Squash	12 ounces	300°	30 to 35

* Can also be done in a portable oven at temperatures 50° higher.
** Remove from freezer carton and place in shallow baking pan to thaw.

The times and heat settings recommended are based on frozen foods stored in a true food freezer maintaining a temperature of zero degrees. If foods are stored at a higher temperature or are partially thawed, allow less time than recommended.

When thawing more than one package at a time allow approximately five minutes longer time for each additional package. Thawing is usually done in the unopened freezer carton or container. Don't use plastic containers as they might melt.

WHAT IS A SIMMER?

One would assume that all the experts would agree on a simple matter like what is a simmer. But no! Some people say it is the point at which there is a rim of little bubbles around the edge and an occasional big bubble breaking in the center. Other people say that there should be no bubbles, just the gentlest kind of continuing activity. One thing is certain: If you have a critical dish on the fire, like a sauce which might curdle, you must always make certain to set the thermostat well *below* the simmering point because, and this is a crucial admission, thermostats do overshoot and undershoot. They go up 5, 10, sometimes as much as 25 degrees before they turn off, and, on the other hand, they go down 5, 10, or even 25 degrees below the point at which you have set them. Of course the better the thermostat the more carefully engineered the appliance, the less overshoot and undershoot there will be.

A certain amount of variation must be expected. But if your appliance does not seem to be functioning as it should, if you have trouble maintaining a gentle boil or a simmer, don't be docile. It is possible that the fault lies not in you but in the utensil or the control. Ask your dealer to take a look at it.

Since the boiling point of water is affected by differences and altitudes and since there is a difference in thermostats as well, it is a wise idea to determine for yourself the simmering temperature of your own appliances. Use this simple home test.

Put 4 cups water in your saucepan, skillet or whatever. Cover and allow the steam vent to stay open. Set the control at 250° F. After 10 minutes during which time the water will have been steadily boiling turn the control knob slowly back until the light goes off. The point is your simmering temperature. It may be 200°. It may be as low as 185° F. In any case, it is a very important point for you to remember. In one of the big laboratories the ladies mark this point on the control knob with a bit of red nail polish. The gentlemen hoot, of course, but the idea is a good one. Or if you prefer you can make a note of this simmering temperature with an indelible marking pencil on the utensil or on the handle.

HOW AND WHEN TO SCALD MILK

Many classic recipes call for scalded milk and this has been a hurdle for innumerable cooks. Hundreds of times we have been asked,
"Just what do you mean by scald but don't boil?"
Actually scalding is a stage at the very beginning of a boil. At this point slight bubbles appear around the edges of the pan and there is a shimmer on top of the milk. This occurs at about 195°. However, I like to dispense with scalding milk in many recipes. I find that cold milk can be used just as well and in some cases the results are even better when you make custards or sauces with the cold milk. However, it does add a little extra cooking time but the custards are glossier, the sauces are smoother, and the extra time needed is brief compared to the bother of an extra pan and an extra process.

RECIPES USING THE SAUCEPAN

Appetizers
    Anchovy Buttered Popcorn

Soups
    Charleston Crab Soup
    Court Bouillon for Fish
    Aspic
    Cucumber Soup

Fish and Sea Food
    Salmon Poached in White Wine

Poultry
  Chicken Poulette

Vegetables
  Risotto au gras

Sauces and Seasonings
  New England Butter Sauce
  All-Purpose Barbecue Sauce

Breads and Cereals
  Home-Ground Cereal
  Whole Grain Cereals
  Automatic Cereals

Desserts
  Tart Green Apple Sauce
  Crème Brulée (Broiled Cream)
  Creamless Crème Brulée
  Another Old-Fashioned Vanilla Ice Cream
  Mrs. Pennington's Boiled Custard Ice Cream
  Even Richer Custard
  Strawberry, Raspberry, Banana, or Peach Custard Ice Cream

The Electric
Pressure Cooker

GOURMET COOKING UNDER PRESSURE

Let this chapter begin with confession. There was a time
not too far back when I feared, mistrusted and generally loathed
the pressure cooker, considering it a contrivance only slightly
less devilish than a tommy gun and not much more closely
related to gracious eating.

Like many others, I had my first introduction to pressure
cooking during World War II, when yielding to pressures of a
different sort—enthusiastically, patriotically, but not too efficiently, I attempted to can a crop of green beans. For some
peculiar reason still unexplained, the cooker, the jars and the
beans blew up. So at the same time did I. For years, as far as
the pressure cooker was concerned, I stayed in a state of seethe.
For years our pressure cooker was kept in dusty disuse at the
back of the deepest, darkest cupboard in our house in the
country.

From time to time I read about pressure cooking. I delved at
times into recipe booklets and even books but nothing kindled
my interest. Far more depressing than the literature were certain
soupy, generally soggy and soppy vegetables and stews served to
me on various occasions and usually by someone in the mood for
saving something—either time or effort or fuel or vitamins.

Then a distinguished gourmet friend, Ann Williams-Heller,
offered to share with me a recipe for Hungarian goulash which
had won her a thousand-dollar prize. This was, without doubt,

the most perfectly balanced, the most knowingly seasoned, the most authentically Magyar goulash I have ever encountered and it called for a pressure cooker (see page 152). Unconvinced, I tried the recipe two ways. First I simmered it on top of the stove in the traditional fashion and then I tried it her way under pressure in one-fourth the time. The pressure-cooked goulash was, in the opinion of all who tasted it, equal and, in certain subtle ways, even a little better, richer, more "married."

But the big wave of excitement came with the homemade soup stocks. These were a revelation, a glory, untold riches. As every cook and cookbook reader knows, hundreds, even thousands and tens of thousands of recipes call for some sort of stock—beef, veal, chicken or mushroom or fish fumet. Certainly one can substitute canned broths and consommé. Many of these are excellent. Bouillon cubes, meat glazes, and various concentrates can also do yeoman service in the kitchen. Some of them have good flavor; others have no flavor other than salt.

We found that with the pressure cooker, bones and scraps of meat, dibs and dabs of almost anything could be transmuted with very little effort into rich, highly concentrated stocks, broths, bouillon, consommé and aspic bases. Since comparatively little liquid is used, the broths came from the kettle already concentrated. No long cooking or reducing is necessary. All the meat juices, the marrow and gelatins from the bones, all the lovely glisten of homemade soup, comes forth in a rush. The stock can be skimmed if you insist, but it isn't necessary. The so-called scum that rises to the top is nothing more nor less than precious protein and albumin. Although it may not look too pretty, these proteins give a right fine taste.

The miracle of broth takes place in a pressure cooker in half an hour or less. It doesn't take a day or "a day and a night" as Escoffier requires. Even if the stock had to be used immediately or within hours, it would still be worth making in the pressure cooker. But nowadays you can team your pressure cooker with another wonder worker, the freezer. Pour the stock into ice cube trays. Next morning remove any fat that has collected on the top. Store the cubes in plastic bags; close with rubber bands.

Tag and date them. Use the fat that has been removed for browning meats or seasoning all sorts of soups and sauces. Whenever
you want stock, add one or two of your cubes to a cup of water,
simmer for a few minutes.

Not since the days when our grandmothers gloated over their
treasure troves of homemade jams, preserves, and jellies has
there been such house-proud feelings of accomplishment and
luxury as you will experience when you see in your freezer plastic
bags filled with frozen cubes of your own gourmet stock. Craig
Claiborne, food editor of *The New York Times*, makes it clear
that if anyone cares to give him a present, he would like, please,
some frozen cubes of concentrated fish fumet (see page 88).
Something different, certainly, in the way of a gourmet gift!

FROM POTS AU FEU TO POTS DE CREME

Stocks and soups are only one small part of the pressure cooker
saga. All sorts of stews and ragouts, pots au feu and boiled New
England dinners, smoked tongue, oxtails, elaborate steamed
puddings, and the most delicate custards and pots de crême
emerge from this gently hissing genie. Even the timbales, a
coterie of elegant Edwardian dishes, are being revived because
now they no longer require elaborate equipment, baths of hot
water, or endless watching. Hundreds of epicurean specialties go
nonchalantly under pressure and with startling rapidity emerge
triumphant.

PRESSURE ELECTRIFIED

Now the whole subject of pressure cooking has been electrified.
The pressure cooker has been equipped with thermostatic controls that make it not quite, but almost, automatic; not quite, but
almost, foolproof.

Once again there is danger that the pressure cooker will be
damned by overenthusiasm—that it will be used in many ways
for which it was never intended. Whether electric or nonelectric,
the pressure cooker is not all things to all dishes. It has great

possibilities but, in spite of the claims of two zealous manufacturers, it has also some very definite limitations. It is ideally suited to foods that require slow and fairly long and steamy treatment. Never, never, never should it be used for roasting or broiling or any dry heat type of cookery. You will find recipes and timetables for cooking pastas and various fresh vegetables under pressure. Theoretically, there is no reason why this should not be done. Practically, it is almost impossible not to overcook such foods under pressure.

The small books that come with your pressure cooker should be carefully read and studied. Pay the strictest attention to all the mechanical directions. Obey the instruction that the cooker must never be more than half full of liquid, never more than two-thirds full of liquid and solids. There is one exception to this rule: bulky foods, like artichokes and corn on the cob, can be piled a little higher.

Use the manufacturers' timetables as a guide but only as a guide. In most cases we have found that the given times are too long. Most foods are tastier and better textured if you cut the cooking time under pressure. It is much better to cook too little than too long. If the meat, for instance, should not be quite tender enough to suit you, it can be finished on top of the stove. This holds true of vegetables, too. A combination of pressure cooking and top-of-the-stove simmering gives you the best of both techniques.

Custards, timbales, and other egg dishes are an exception to this rule. The time given on most of the charts that accompany your cooker should be followed exactly.

The recipes included in this book do not, of course, embrace the entire field of pressure cooking. They are only the beginning to use as guides, to act as incentives, to become door-openers to the mind and imagination.

You will find as you go along that a great many recipes can be adapted to the pressure cooker. It is distressingly easy to overcook with this type of utensil. So if the booklets suggest that meats may be cooked, for example, one third as long in a pressure cooker, you may find, as we have, that one-fourth the time is preferable; *i.e.*, a pot roast that would ordinarily take three hours to cook might be pressure cooked 45 minutes.

Another point in which I am inclined to disagree is the addition of vegetables to stews or corned beef. Standard pressure cooking recipes suggest that the meat be cooked first, then the pressure lowered, the vegetables added and more pressure cooking. Aside from turnips, beets, lima beans and artichokes, most vegetables, I believe, have a superior flavor and texture when simmered on top of the stove. One possible exception is corn on the cob, which is actually steamed rather than pressure cooked inasmuch as the pressure cooking time itself is or should be less than a minute.

A great many pressure cookers do not allow for a choice of pressures. Most of them are set to operate at 15 pounds because the manufacturers consider that this is most satisfactory for all purposes. However, if your cooker does permit you to make your own decisions, you will probably use a low pressure, 5 pounds, for fruits and frozen vegetables; a medium pressure, 10 pounds, for meats, dried peas and beans, and a higher pressure, 15 pounds, for other uses. The highest pressure is best, by the way, for making rich stocks and all sorts of soups, for it drives the goodness into the broth.

The amount of water that you use is important. If too little is used, the food will dry up, burn, and stick. On the other hand, it is desirable, especially with vegetables, to use a minimum amount of water. As a rule of thumb, you might use in the cooker just enough water to cover the bottom of the pan to a depth of one-half inch if you're cooking up to 10 minutes. Use another quarter-inch for 10 to 20 minutes. When you're steaming puddings, which take rather a long time, you will need at least 2 cups of water. For stews and soups, fill the pan not more than half full of liquid. Remember that the stock that you make in the pressure cooker will be much richer than that made on top of the stove so that you can use less water and will not find it necessary to reduce the liquid by further boiling.

It is not necessary to learn new ways of making your favorite dishes in the pressure cooker. They can easily be adapted simply by cutting the cooking time anywhere from one fourth to one third of the usual period. For soups and broths of various types use only one half the usual amount of liquid and, if necessary, add more liquid after the pressure has been reduced. In any case, simmer for a while on top of the stove and correct the seasoning. Do not attempt to season before pressure cooking, for the balance of flavors has a way of changing.

SHOW PROPER RESPECT

While the new pressure cookers—whether electrified, thermostatically controlled or made to use with other forms of heat—are amiable and fairly docile, it is unwise to allow familiarity to breed carelessness. Do follow the rules. Don't overload the cooker. Adjust the cover properly so that it fits tightly in place. Begin the cooking at high heat with the thermostat set at 400° F. When the steam begins to come forth in a steady column or when, on the electric models, it begins to snort around the gauge, turn the heat or the thermostat down to between 210° F. and 225° F. There should be just enough heat to induce some slight wiggling of the valve and a cozy whisper from time to time.

Begin to time the cooking not from the moment when the food starts cooking, but from the second heat stage.

A timer of some sort is a practical necessity for pressure cooking, preferably a device with some sort of alarm. Most convenient is a portable timer, or even a watch that calls you back.

BIGGER IS BETTER

Most of the popular pressure cookers come in the four- and six-quart sizes. Choose a large size, for you can cook as small a quantity as you wish, but you must use the full amount of liquid called for in the recipe. Most of the books and booklets give recipes adjusted to a four-quart cooker. For a six-quart cooker you may add half again as much. Allow the same amount of time for a small amount of food as for the full quantity.

The crucial interval in pressure cooking occurs after the cooking is over. When the prescribed interval is over, then it's time to decide whether the pressure should be allowed to drop naturally or should be brought down immediately. Generally the recipe will tell you. Nevertheless, it is not too difficult to figure it out for yourself. Allowing the pressure to drop naturally continues the cooking. If you're making stock, this will not matter. If, however, you are cooking any meats that might easily break down into loose ribbons, naturally you must take care. Usually it is safer to set the pressure cooker into cold water or allow a stream of cold water to run down the side of the pan immediately after the cooking period is over. Never let the water get down into the valves.

A four-quart, thermostatically controlled electric pressure cooker is a utensil with many uses. It will serve you as an automatic saucepan, as a deep fat fryer, as a steamer, as a Dutch oven. Preheated, it becomes a small oven for baking potatoes, apples, and the like. And incidentally, it's a corn popper, too.

SOME MYSTERIES OF PRESSURE COOKING

Perhaps a physicist—a gastronomically minded Einstein—could explain why it is that certain foods are most perfectly cooked either at very high temperatures for brief periods or at very low temperatures for a long time. The French classic cooks prepare an omelet on a blazing hot pan with constant manipulation within a few seconds. The conservative American cook can get almost the same results by using very gentle heat and letting the uncooked portion run down under the omelet. The same phenomena hold with the soufflé, although the end results are different. You can bake a soufflé at 475° F. and it is soft and saucy in the center and with a standup glory that passes quickly. Or you can, if you set it in a pan of hot water, keep it at low to moderate heat for an hour or longer. Evidently there is some basic relationship, some relativity between time—or rather the passing of time—and degrees of heat.

The philosophical implication of this time and heat relationship is even more interesting in its application to the pressure cooker and the use of steam. Since water boils at sea level at

212° F., it does not matter how high you turn the heat, you cannot possibly raise the temperature of water above 212° F. Steam, however, is much hotter, and steam under pressure is hotter still. Consequently, it does seem passing strange that a custard that will cringe and curdle unless it is babied by being put into a water bath even in a moderate oven will, on the other hand, acquire a perfect texture, a perfect smoothness, in three minutes under pressure.

It is equally curious that boiled beef, which the Viennese insist is irreparably ruined if the water even for one minute begins to bubble wildly, can be done to perfection under pressure. The same holds true for any number of stewed and braised meats.

THESE ARE UNSUITABLE

There are some products which simply are not suited to pressure cooking. Cranberries are one of them. Inevitably, no matter what you do, bits and pieces of them get caught in the valves. Dried beans are risky too, and so are many other dried legumes which have a way of foaming. Potatoes get waterlogged, and develop an odd flavor and a gluey texture.

RECIPES USING THE PRESSURE COOKER

Soups
  Brown Stock
  Your Own Consommé
  White Veal Stock
  Chicken Stock, Broth, or Bouillon
  Mushroom Broth
  Jellied Mushroom Broth
  Duck Soup from Bones
  Essence of Lobster, Shrimp or Crab
  Fish Stock or Fish Fumet
  Japanese Soup
  Chilled Beet Top Soup or Botvina

Soups
  Kentucky Hambone Soup
  Oxtail Soup

Meats
  The World's Easiest Stew
  Beef Stew with Carrots
  Boiled Beef
  Viennese Boiled Beef
  Beef Stew
  Hungarian Beef Goulash
  Swiss Steak
  Corned Beef and Cabbage
  Lamb Dolmades
  Szekely Gulasch
  Gulasch of Spareribs

Vegetables
  Artichokes
  Italian Artichokes

Timbales
  Chicken Timbales
  Ham Timbales
  Spinach Timbales
  Broccoli Timbales

Desserts
  Miracle-Easy Plum Pudding
  Plum Duff
  Pressure-Cooked Custards

The Electric Griddle

The electric griddle is unsurpassed for the preparation of hot cakes, crêpes, grilled sandwiches and meats.

HOW TO MAKE THE FINEST HAMBURGER

Get acquainted with the goodness of economical chuck and neck meat. Remove the sinews, clots, cartilage and all excess fat.

Cook meat as soon as possible after grinding. Immediately, if possible.

Cook on a very lightly greased thermostatically controlled griddle or surface unit at 350° F. Turn only once.

Do not overcook hamburgers. Five to 15 minutes are the usual limits, depending on thickness of the burgers, the degree of doneness desired and, of course, the temperature used.

Add salt after cooking—never before.

Try hamburgers without extraneous seasoning of any kind just once. Then you can, if you like, return to your old ways. Many never do.

GRILLING OR PAN BROILING FROZEN MEATS

Hard-frozen steaks or chops may be grilled on a griddle or in a heavy frying pan by exactly the same method you use for fresh meat. Merely increase the time and take the temperature.

Steaks, chops and thick patties which are hard-frozen at the start of cooking sometimes cook unevenly when pan broiled. Unexplained irregularities occur. That is the reason for this slightly different technique.

Heat the electric griddle or pan to about medium heat, about 350° F. Then cook the meat 3 to 6 minutes covered on each side. This period is too brief to steam or stew the meat. Then remove the cover and cook meat in the usual way. By this quick-thaw method a solid-frozen sirloin steak 2 inches thick is cooked in about 36 minutes.

As a general rule, however, meats should be cooked in an uncovered pan without foil. Covering produces steam and acts like a Turkish bath, opens the pores so that the juices stream forth. Wonderful for the gravy! Not too good for the meat itself!

RECIPES USING THE GRIDDLE

Meats
>   Russian Bitki
>   Frozen Hamburgers on the Griddle
>   Hashburgers de Luxe

Breads and Cereals
>   Corn Cakes or Corn Oysters
>   Peter Pan Pancakes
>   Sour Dough Hot Cakes
>   Crêpes on the Griddle
>   Blini
>   Homemade English Muffins

Sandwiches
>   Sunday Morning Sandwiches
>   French Toast Sandwiches
>   Sweet and Sour Pork Sandwiches

The Electric Hot Tray

To the present-day hostess, the electric hot tray is one of life's essentials. It takes the place of the old-fashioned warming oven and the old-fashioned waitress. With an electric hot tray by her side, the lady in charge can serve every dish at the desired temperature. Second helpings are just as accessible and just as delicious as first servings.

The modern hot tray when correctly used does not dry out the food nor change its original texture, taste, or appearance. Few people, however, understand the nature of the hot tray or how to make full use of its possibilities.

There are various types of electric hot trays. Some are set at different temperatures. A few are adjustable. Ordinarily they are not marked in degrees, but you will find on inquiry that they are set at about 220° F., which means that they will hold the food at about 200° F. This means just about twelve degrees below the boiling point at sea level, which, as you will remember, is 212° F. This is well within the range of a well-mannered chafing dish or double boiler. It is safe for Hollandaise and other delicate sauces.

If your hot tray has a number of settings, such as low, medium and high, it probably means that you have steady heat ranging all the way from 180° F. to 230° F. A little experimentation will show you just where the setting should be in order to permit a low holding heat or a gentle simmer. It is impossible to say offhand just what your setting should be. A great deal depends upon the type of utensil that you are using. For example, a heavy cast-iron pan will hold a simmer much more readily than a lightweight aluminum pan. A very flat dish or pan with a wide bottom will be much more efficiently heated than one with a small surface. The old-fashioned china coffee pots that stand either on legs or on a china rim above the surface are practically impossible to keep warm on an electric hot tray, because the layer of air underneath acts as insulation against the heat.

TWICE BLESSED

Not only when the meal is served but also while it is being prepared, the electric hot tray is a blessing. Hundreds of recipes lose their terror for the not-too-experienced cook if there is some easy and practical way to keep one thing warm while another part of the recipe is in process. Reheating is not the answer. Often foods do not taste the same if they are chilled and then reheated. The hot tray enables you to go from step to step at your own pace and without worrying.

In most cases when foods are to be kept warm, the hot tray should be preheated for two or three minutes, and the hot food in a warm receptacle set on the tray and loosely covered. Aluminum foil is an excellent covering.

A surprising number of foods can be laid directly on the hot tray either on foil or without foil—pancakes, for example, and French toast and fritters. Anything crisp or deep fat fried should be covered *ever so lightly*; if it is too closely covered, it may become soft or even a little soggy.

Steaks and chops and roasts are much easier to slice and mellower in flavor if they are cooked about 75 per cent done and then placed on the hot tray for 20 to 30 minutes. These meats can be placed directly on the trays. Most of the new models are sealed to prevent the juices from entering the "works" and are designed so that they can be easily cleaned.

The imaginative epicure will discover dozens of ways in which the steady, dependable, low heat of the electric hot tray can be used to make meals more epicurean. A number of these uses are illustrated in the recipes in this book. Here you will see that butter may be melted without any danger of browning. Spirits can be brought to exactly the right temperature for a perfect flambé. Soft-boiled eggs and poached eggs can be kept at the point of perfection, not merely for minutes but for hours, in warm water on the hot tray.

Pancakes, French toast, and the like cannot be cooked on the hot tray, of course, as they require a much higher heat. They can, however, be kept in perfect condition if laid flat on the tray; once again, either directly on the surface or on the foil. If you like, you may stack them two or three deep and cover lightly with foil. Bacon, hamburgers, and sausage cakes can be kept hot in the same fashion.

The Electric Slicer

The charms of the electric slicer are perhaps less obvious than those of other electric appliances, but it is amazing what a difference they can make in your cooking. What joy not to be forced to have cold meats sliced by the butcher or delicatessen and run the risk of their drying in the refrigerator! It is bliss to be able to slice cooked meats and cheeses thin or thick as befits your mood and the dish.

All sorts of delicacies become possible, even the almost forgotten pleasure of good smoked bacon cut a quarter of an inch thick so that it really tastes like smoked meat and not like warm, flavored paper.

The whole world of Chinese cookery opens when you have a slicer. Vegetables like carrots and beets and turnips take on the most extraordinary interest when they are sliced in the raw state. And they do cook faster. Suddenly the sandwich becomes an epicurean thrill when the breads as well as fillings are elegantly thin and uniform.

These few recipes are intended merely to open the flood gates of inspiration. In addition to some favorite recipes for Beef Stroganoff, which is having such a vogue among hostesses, we have included a glorious version of Potatoes Anna and full directions for Pommes Soufflés.

Then, for further gaiety, you will find here directions for slicing beets, turnips, or carrots and making them into full-blown flowers to decorate a buffet platter of cold meats or fish.

Also, the best of the slicers have serrated cutting edges. This means that they will work efficiently on foods as soft as a ripe tomato or on well-cooked meats. And, believe it or not, they are now easy to clean.

In case you are nervous about having an electric slicer around the house and the children—as I admit I was a few years ago—it is reassuring to know that the top brands of electric slicers have a variety of safety features which make them even more suitable to family living than some of the older models that were hand-turned.

Never, if you want to get the good out of your slicer, store it away. It won't seem worthwhile to pull it out of purdah for any single job. Keep it ready for use and you will use it constantly.

Roses Made From Beets

The trend in general is away from prettiness in food, but here is a rose that is a rose that is a rose that is lovely enough to eat —and eatable if you insist. Red roses are made from beets. Pink or pale yellow roses or pink-touched tea roses can be made from white turnips very lightly brushed with vegetable coloring.

YOU WILL NEED:

1 or 2 firm white turnips	parsley or watercress
1 or 2 firm young beets	toothpicks or needle and thread

Beets or turnips should be removed from refrigerator several hours before use so as to be more pliable. If they are too cold or crisp, the slices tend to break.

See illustrated directions page 61.

When flower is complete, it may be touched lightly here and there with a bit of raw beet to give a natural blush pink. Or, try coloring the turnip with vegetable color after peeling and before slicing. This gives an interesting colored edge to all petals.

Carrot Flowers

Carrots cut lengthwise may be made into flowers. Long, thin shreds may be tied together and crisped in cold water.

Calla Lily Sandwiches

Bread sliced very thin on slicing machine may be shaped the same way—spread with softened cream cheese and fastened with toothpick. Stamen is made from American cheese. A pretty sandwich, tasty, too. Feeling very merry? Try tinting the cheese spread with vegetable color.

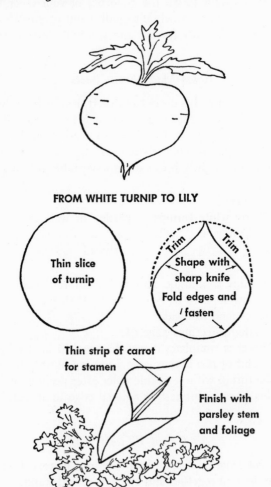

FROM WHITE TURNIP TO LILY

Thin slice
of turnip

Trim   Trim

Shape with
sharp knife

Fold edges and
fasten

Thin strip of carrot
for stamen

Finish with
parsley stem
and foliage

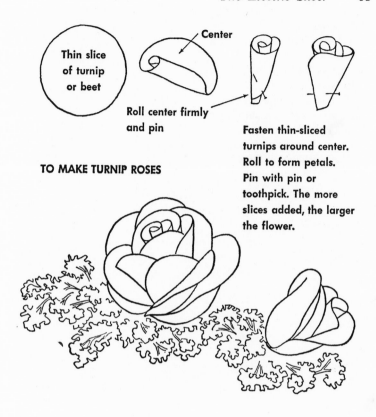

Thin slice of turnip or beet

Center

Roll center firmly and pin

TO MAKE TURNIP ROSES

Fasten thin-sliced turnips around center. Roll to form petals. Pin with pin or toothpick. The more slices added, the larger the flower.

RECIPES USING THE SLICER

Appetizers
Yam Chips
Saratoga Chips
Green Banana Chips
Plantain Chips
Texas-Style Potato Chips

Meats
Beef Stroganoff
Lamb Cutlets in Jackets

Vegetables
  Baked Sliced Beets
  Cole Slaw
  Carrots Vichy
  Russian Scallions
  Pommes de Terre Soufflés
  Pommes de Terre au Grùyere
  Scalloped Potatoes
  Pommes de Terre Anna
  Chrysanthemum Turnips

The Electric
Ice Crusher

It is amazing how much cachet seems to be added to your food presentations when you have plenty of crushed ice on hand. You can nestle grapefruit into cracked ice, or set a dish of butter balls in cracked ice, or color the ice with vegetable tints and use it as a little mountain on which to arrange pieces of fruit or olives and celery. You can set bowls of fresh sea food in cracked ice, or serve almost any kind of fruit juice or clam juice or vegetable cocktail as a frappé in a champagne glass or a wine glass filled with crushed ice. There are, in fact, endless ways to use the luxury of ice.

Cracking or crushing ice has always been a bore and a chore, but not any more. Various ice-crushing machines have been on the market for several years. Only recently, however, have they become really practical and easy to use. Now most of the top-name electric blenders can be equipped with ice crushing attachments that are nothing short of miraculous. In moments one ice tray full of cubes is transformed into three heaping cups of shimmering crushed ice. Many of the ice crushers have gauges which enable you to crush ice fine, medium, or coarse. Some have as many as eight different gauges—though we must admit that there really are just about three recognizably different sizes when they come forth.

To prevent spattering, hold your hand over the top of the opening. And secure a plastic bag around the mouth of the ice crusher with a rubber band. The bag works better than a bowl set under the crusher. Also, it saves washing an extra bowl and enables you to store your crushed ice in the same plastic bag in the freezing compartment of the refrigerator or the freezer. Crushed ice in these bags can be kept for several hours under these conditions. If stored too long, however, the ice will freeze into a mass and will have to be recrushed or broken apart.

CRUSHED ICE COOKERY

Brillat-Savarin once said that the discovery of a new dish was at least as noteworthy as the sighting of a new star in the heavens. What would he say about the discovery of an entirely new technique such as has been developed by one of the most imaginative gourmets of our generation? Experimenting with the manifold possibilities of the electric blender, Ann Seranne discovered that a wide variety of foods made with cream and gelatines could be prepared and ready to serve in less time than it took to go through one of the many steps required by the classic recipes that she adapted.

The secret lay not only in the blender, but also in the use of crushed ice as a basic ingredient in the recipe.

As the result of Ann Seranne's revolutionary gastronomic discoveries, you can now make light-as-a-breeze fruit-flavored desserts, rich and elaborate Bavarian creams, fluffy chiffon pie fillings and puddings. All of them are made without cooking. They are blended and ice-set in less than two minutes.

These desserts may be poured into a mold and then unmolded in three to five minutes. Or they may be turned into baked pie shells or crumb crusts. They can also be piled in glass serving dishes or chilled serving glasses and eaten immediately.

This book contains a number of recipes adapted from Ann Seranne's originals. In each case it is important that the ingredients be added exactly in the order given. Do not, at least in the beginning, tamper either with the technique or with the amounts suggested.

RECIPES USING THE ICE CRUSHER

Soups
Vichyssoise
Cream of Avocado Soup

Fish and Sea Food
Salmon Mousse

Meats
Jellied Ham Mousse

Desserts
Instantaneous Fruit Sherbet
Strawberry Bavarian Cream
Bittersweet Chocolate Bavarian Cream
Spanish Cream
Lime Whip
Orange Chiffon Pie in Crumb Crust
Instant Cheese Cake

The Electric Ice-Cream Freezer

There seems to be not a shadow of doubt that ice cream made in a freezer that turns has a different flavor, a different texture. There are purists who insist that the old-time freezer turned by a small boy makes the best ice cream. And it is within the realm of possibility that there is a shade of difference between ice cream that is turned slowly at first and then more eagerly as the ice cream stiffens. An electric freezer and electric ice crushers now make it possible to have freezer ice creams almost any time and without the cooperation of a large family.

There are two types of electric ice-cream freezers. The first is the more usual. It is exactly like the old-fashioned crank ice-cream freezer with the wooden tub. The only difference is in the turning, which is done by electricity rather than arm power. One strong point in its favor: the electric freezer turns itself off automatically when the ice cream is properly frozen, so there is no need to keep investigating.

The second type of freezer is one that fits into the ice-cube compartment of the refrigerator or into your freezer. It comes equipped with a flat cord so that you attach it to a plug nearby and shut the door of the refrigerator on it. These freezers dispense entirely with the need for ice or salt. You simply put a couple of tablespoons of water on the bottom of the grid and put the freezer in place. The dashers are generally made of nylon material. These keep turning until the ice cream is properly frozen. Then they turn off automatically and you may, if you wish, remove the dashers, cover and keep the ice cream in the freezing tray to ripen until you are ready to serve it. Generally the capacity of these freezers is less than that of the regular ice-cream freezers. But the trouble is much less too. The product is not quite the same, but it is infinitely better than commercial ice cream and much, much better than refrigerator ice cream.

GENERAL DIRECTIONS FOR FREEZER ICE CREAM

Prepare the mixture according to your recipe. Make certain that the can is not more than two-thirds full, for you must allow for expansion during freezing. It is possible to make smaller quantities in a large freezer but it does seem wasteful, for any extra ice cream can be packed away in the freezer. It will keep at top quality for three to four weeks.

Crushing the Ice

The new electric ice crushers solve this problem admirably. A single tray of ice cubes makes about three cups of crushed ice. Or, if you like, you can crush ice in a canvas bag with a wooden mallet or rolling pin. In some places, you can buy a bag of crushed ice almost as easily as you can buy ice cubes. In any case, the ice should be crushed small enough so that the pieces will not jam as the freezer turns.

Salt for the Ice-Cream Freezer

Table salt will not do for your ice-cream freezer. You must get a bag of rock salt, now often called ice-cream salt. (In the winter time in some places it is called sidewalk salt, for it is used for melting ice on sidewalks.) Generally you can find it in the most modern chain stores and the most old-fashioned hardware stores and groceries.

Generally 8 parts of crushed ice are used to 1 part of salt. The more salt you use the faster your cream will freeze, but it will not be so smooth and velvety.

Packing the Freezer

Scald the freezer can and rinse it with cold water. Put the can in the tub and fit the dasher in place. Pour the chilled ice-cream mixture into the can making certain, we repeat, that it is not more than two-thirds full. Adjust cover and crank. Turn once or twice to be sure that everything is in order. Fill the tub one-third full of coarsely crushed ice. Then add a layer of salt and a layer of ice, alternating salt and ice until it stands just about level with the mixture in the can. It should never get close to the top of the can, for the salty water might seep in. Pack the ice down with a wooden spoon; allow to stand 5 minutes before starting the motor. When the ice cream is frozen, the motor will automatically turn itself off.

After the motor stops, drain off the water through the hole provided. Wipe the lid of the can carefully. Take off the cover and lift out the dashers. Scrape off the ice cream.

Pack the ice cream down solidly with a spoon. Cover with aluminum foil. Replace the lid and repack, using 4 parts of ice to 1 part salt. Or place in covered bowl in the freezer.

Allow to ripen at least ½ hour before serving.

RECIPES USING THE ICE-CREAM FREEZER

Desserts
Cantaloupe Sherbet
Watermelon Sherbet
The Simplest Old-Fashioned Vanilla Ice Cream
Richer Ice Cream
Another Old-Fashioned Vanilla Ice Cream
Mrs. Pennington's Boiled Custard Ice Cream
Even Richer Custard
Strawberry, Raspberry, Banana, or Peach Custard Ice Cream
Puerto Rican Coconut Ice Cream
Banana Ice Cream
Georgia Peach Ice Cream
Green Gage Plum Ice Cream
Strawberry Ice Cream

THE RECIPES

Appetizers

Caviar of Eggplant BLENDER

This is a superlatively delicious way to prepare eggplant. It seemingly turns the vegetable into an entirely different species and is always a great success with my guests. It used to be quite a lot of work to grill the eggplants, scrape out the pulp and pound it, but not when you use your electric blender.

YOU WILL NEED:

eggplants	coarsely ground black
lemon juice	pepper
olive oil	onion juice (optional)
	hard-boiled eggs

Cut two large or three medium eggplants in halves lengthwise. Cut the pulp out of the shells of the two most beautiful halves and brush the hollowed shells immediately with lemon juice to keep them from discoloring. Cut both the peeled and the unpeeled eggplant into slices about an inch thick. Broil until soft. Cut into half-inch cubes and measure.

Measure out ½ cup fine light French olive oil for each 2 cups of eggplant. Blend 10 seconds. Then while the blender is still running, keep adding olive oil and eggplant alternately. After you have used 2 cups of eggplant and ½ cup olive oil, empty the blender and start afresh. Season with 1 teaspoon salt (more if you like salty caviar) in each batch, plus ¼ teaspoon coarsely ground black pepper. You may also add lemon juice and onion juice to suit your own taste.

AT SERVING TIME:
Chill very well. Pile into hollowed eggplant, lined, if you like, with fresh grape leaves. Instead of quartered eggs, you might use chopped eggs as a garnish—whites and yolks separate—or you could use sliced eggs. Iced caviar of eggplant keeps for days in the refrigerator, but don't leave the eggs on it. Add them just before serving or the eggplant will turn them a disagreeable green.

Pass any of the classic caviar accompaniments, such as quartered lemon. Finely chopped onion or sour cream is very good. This particular version of eggplant caviar really does look and taste remarkably like the fabulous beige caviar, so much prized in the Near East.

Avocado Dip   BLENDER

YOU WILL NEED:
avocados
lemon juice
olive oil
garlic

chives or green onion tops
dill weed
chili sauce
Tabasco

Place each of the following ingredients into the container of the blender: 2 peeled, seeded, and sliced avocados; 2 tablespoons lemon juice; 4 tablespoons olive oil; 1 clove garlic; 1 tablespoon chives or green onion tops; 1 teaspoon salt; 1 teaspoon dill weed; 2 tablespoons chili sauce, and a dash of Tabasco. Cover and blend these ingredients on high speed until smooth. If necessary, turn off motor and stir ingredients with rubber spatula once or twice. Store in refrigerator, covered, until ready to serve. Yield of dip is 1 pint.

AT SERVING TIME:
Use as a spread for tea sandwiches, closed or open face, or pile into an avocado shell or small bowl.

Souffléed Canapé   BROILER

It's amazing how much drama you can achieve with so little effort.

YOU WILL NEED:
    bread   egg white
    meat spread   mayonnaise

Cut thin-sliced bread into circles, diamonds, squares, fingers. Toast or sauté lightly on one side. Cover the other side generously with your favorite meat spread—deviled ham, tongue—whatever you fancy. At the last moment make the topping. Beat 1 egg white until stiff and gently fold it into 1 cup mayonnaise. Place a spoonful on each canapé. Set under the broiler just long enough to puff up and gild.

AT SERVING TIME:
Keep warm on an electric hot tray.

VARIATION: *TONGUE TARTARS* are excellent. Instead of a spread, use canned sliced tongue. Cover with tartar sauce. You can buy it ready made or make it by combining equal parts drained India relish and mayonnaise. Place a spoonful on each canapé. Sprinkle very lightly with grated cheese and set under broiler 1 or 2 minutes.

Piroshki   PORTABLE OVEN

The French have their "tartelettes" of puff paste, the English their "pasties." The Spaniards and Brazilians call them "empados." In the West Indies, pepper hot, they become "patés." In Slavic lands they take unto themselves a variety of different shapes, sizes, and fillings. The big one, "pirogen"; the small ones, "piroshki." All are admirable accompaniments to any soup. We use for the crusty part a package of ready-to-bake biscuits; and for the filling, strained canned beef or some finely chopped left-over beef.

YOU WILL NEED:

biscuits	eggs
strained canned beef or	butter
finely chopped cooked	onion
meat, chicken, or sea	
food	

Ten biscuits already rolled and cut are in the package. Cut each in half crosswise. Flatten with the hand so that they are about 3 inches in diameter. On one side of each place a teaspoonful of filling made by combining 3 ½-ounce cans strained beef for in-fants, or use about ½ cup finely chopped cooked meat, chicken or sea food, 2 coarsely chopped hard cooked eggs, 2 tablespoons softened butter, 1 small onion very finely chopped. Add salt and pepper to taste. Mix well. Fold dough over to make half moons and press down the edges with a fork. Brush with a beaten egg. Bake about 10 minutes at 450° F. Makes 20.

AT SERVING TIME:
Serve hot with soup or salad.

Yam Chips   SLICER AND DEEP FAT FRYER

YOU WILL NEED:
yams or sweet potatoes   oil for deep fat frying

Slice yams crosswise as thin as possible, using your slicer. Heat fat to 375° F., fill fry basket a quarter full, separating the slices. Shake basket or stir chips several times to keep chips from sticking together. Fry 3 to 4 minutes. Drain on paper towels. Sprinkle with salt and freshly-ground black pepper.

Saratoga Chips

SLICER AND
DEEP FAT FRYER

Incredibly good, easy cocktail snacks.

YOU WILL NEED:
white potatoes   oil for deep fat frying

Slice white potatoes crosswise as thin as possible. Soak in cold water one hour. Dry between paper towels. Heat fat to 375° F., fill fry basket a quarter full, separating the slices. Shake basket or stir chips several times to keep chips from sticking together. Fry 3 to 4 minutes. Drain on paper towels. Sprinkle with salt and freshly ground black pepper.

Green Banana Chips

SLICER AND
DEEP FAT FRYER

YOU WILL NEED:
green bananas   oil for deep fat frying

Slice green bananas crosswise as thin as possible. Heat fat to 375° F. Fill fry basket a quarter full, separating the slices. Shake basket or stir chips several times to keep chips from sticking together. Fry 3 to 4 minutes. Drain on paper towels. Sprinkle with salt and freshly ground black pepper.

Plantain Chips

SLICER AND
DEEP FAT FRYER

YOU WILL NEED:
plantains   oil for deep fat frying

Slice plantains crosswise as thin as possible, using a vegetable slicer. Heat fat to 375° F., fill fry basket a quarter full, separating the slices. Shake basket or stir chips several times to keep chips from sticking together. Fry 3 to 4 minutes. Drain on paper towels. Sprinkle with salt and freshly-ground black pepper.

Texas-Style Potato Chips   SLICER AND DEEP FAT FRYER

In Texas where everything is giant size, they have a special way with potato chips.

YOU WILL NEED:
large baking potatoes   oil for deep fat frying

Slice the potatoes very thin, but lengthwise rather than crosswise and proceed as for any other potato chips.

AT SERVING TIME:
These chips are at their best served warm and scattered with coarse salt.

Indian Pappadums   DEEP FAT FRYER

Sometimes you'll see it spelled Popads. These are wafers thin as gauze, made from lentil meal and other grains, a perfect accompaniment to cocktail spreads and dunks. They are traditional with curries, rijstafel, and all such Oriental dishes. You can get them in cans at any number of specialty shops and department stores in New York and other cities.

YOU WILL NEED:
can of pappadums   oil for deep fat frying

Drop 3 or 4 at a time into hot fat, 380° F. and fry for only about 1 minute until puffed and ever so slightly browned. Drain on paper towels. Be careful not to overcrowd the fryer, or they will push each other out of shape. One 6-ounce package contains about 4 dozen pappadums.

Glamorized Hot Dogs   PORTABLE OVEN

The lowly little sausage is welcome at any party, especially if it's the dainty canned Vienna sausage nestled into small finger rolls.

YOU WILL NEED:
Vienna sausage   chili powder
finger rolls   butter

Drain and grill sausages. Split finger rolls. Spread with butter into which you have incorporated a bit of chili powder.

AT SERVING TIME:
Serve piping hot. If you want to make them ahead of time, wrap in foil, freeze and reheat—still in the foil—in the oven or under the broiler.

Anchovy Buttered Popcorn   SAUCEPAN

Imaginative and delicious cocktail accompaniment.

YOU WILL NEED:
salad or peanut oil   anchovy paste
canned popcorn   parsley or chives
butter

Place 2 tablespoons salad or peanut oil into automatic saucepan or deep-fat fryer. Heat to 375° F. Pour in 1/3 cup canned popcorn —enough to cover the bottom of the pan 1 kernel deep. Cover;

within a minute or so the popping will start. Let it continue until all the kernels have popped. Meanwhile, melt 3 tablespoons butter; add 1 teaspoon anchovy paste. Stir until well blended.

AT SERVING TIME:
Pour anchovy-butter mixture over popcorn and sprinkle with chopped parsley or chives. Serve piping hot.

Monte Benito   DEEP FAT FRYER

A most interesting canapé. This is a miniature version of the Monte Cristo and Monte Carlo sandwiches of San Francisco which have achieved great popularity for lunches and suppers. Double deckers all. A Monte Cristo is made with sliced chicken or turkey and sliced cheese—Monterey Jack, Swiss, or cheddar. Monte Carlo has a layer of tongue or ham along with cheese.

YOU WILL NEED:
bread
butter
flour
milk
eggs

Sandwich fillings:
chicken, turkey, cheese,
tongue (optional)

Butter and remove crusts from 9 slices of bread; the middle slice should be buttered on both sides. Fillings should be very thinly sliced and placed in several layers. Cut into strips or squares; hold together with toothpicks. Dip into batter made of 1 cup flour, 1 cup milk, 2 eggs, slightly beaten. Fry in deep fat at 370° F. one or two minutes until golden brown. Drain, place on paper towels. Makes 24.

AT SERVING TIME:
Serve immediately or keep hot in warming oven, 200° F.

Lazy Pommes Soufflés   DEEP FAT FRYER

Probably the most dramatic short-cut to gastronomic drama is provided by the quick-frozen *pommes soufflés* which you can buy in a tin box. They have been given a special secret treatment which makes them more than ever inclined to puff into hollow, airy cushions.

At the present writing the distribution of this product is limited to the gourmet shop attached to the Chambord restaurant (803 Third Avenue, New York) but undoubtedly they will become more widely available as time goes on. You could write for information, or for the *pommes* themselves, to the Chambord restaurant. About twenty slices cost about $1.25. At least ninety per cent of them should puff—a considerably higher proportion than the most experienced chefs can count on.

YOU WILL NEED:

quick-frozen pommes   oil for deep fat frying
    soufflés

Heat salad oil until very hot, at least 450° F.

Allow frozen slices to thaw at room temperature about 10 minutes. Drop a handful at a time into the hot fat. They should explode instantly and gild properly in about 2 minutes. Remove with a skimmer and drain on brown paper.

AT SERVING TIME:

Sprinkle with salt and serve either as a cocktail accompaniment or with steak or chops. One package should serve four.

Soups

Making Your Own Stocks

These homemade stocks made in the pressure cooker have a richness and depth of flavor that is impossible to achieve in any of the soups or stocks commercially available. If you want to use them for cooking, they need not be skimmed or cleared. The so-called scum that rises to the top contains valuable and delicious proteins and albumins. The recipes given here are highly concentrated and very lightly seasoned. You will notice that we are very chary about using herbs, for if the stocks are to be frozen into cubes and kept in bags you may discover that herbs change flavor, develop slightly off tastes.

The strength of your homemade stock will necessarily vary according to the materials on hand. Generally you will find that two of your own ice-cube-size blocks can be diluted with 1 cup of water. For the best taste add the cubes to cold water, bring to a boil, simmer 2 or 3 minutes, then season to taste.

Choosing Meats for Stock

The best choice of meat is a middle cut of beef shin or brisket. However, many other soup meats will do. The bones must be cracked. Better ask for two-thirds lean meat and one-third bone and fat.

Add to the stock pot any bones or bits of cooked meats—cooked beef or veal chops or bones from roast beef, lamb, or fowl. Your choice is almost limitless. For an all-purpose stock, smoked or corned meats are not used nor is lamb or mutton because each has such distinctive flavor of its own.

To Clear Stock

Remove fat from stock and place quantity to be cleared in pan. Taste and if further seasoning is needed, add at this point, not after clearing. For each quart add 1 egg white, beaten slightly with fork and mixed with 2 teaspoons cold water. Add egg shell broken in small pieces.

Bring to boiling point, about 210° F., stirring constantly, and boil 2 minutes. Reduce heat to 150° and let stand. Strain through fine strainer, lined with double thickness of cheesecloth.

To Remove Fat from Stock

Chill the stock and refrigerate until the fat rises. Run a knife around the edge of the bowl and carefully lift off the fat. Any small quantities of fat that remain may be removed by passing over the broth a cloth wrung out in hot water. The fat will cling to the cloth.

If you want to serve the stock immediately, you can remove the fat from the stock while it is still hot by using a spoon and get at some of the remainder by passing a crumpled paper towel over the surface, being very careful that the paper doesn't get into the soup. Or better still, in my opinion, drop a few ice cubes into the stock and take them out as soon as the fat has collected on them. Reheat the stock, of course, to get rid of the chill.

Brown Stock   PRESSURE COOKER

One of the basics of fine cooking, this recipe gives you a highly concentrated broth almost like what the French chefs call a demi-glaze. We suggest browning the meat so that the stock will have a deep brown color and added richness of flavor. However, you can get by without browning the meat. The flavor will be a little different. The color can be deepened by adding a few drops of Kitchen Bouquet or Gravymaster.

YOU WILL NEED:

shin of beef and bones including marrow bones if possible	bayleaf
	parsley
	carrot
peppercorns	onion
cloves	celery

Remove lean meat from 4 pounds shin bones of beef and cut into 1-inch cubes. Brown one half of the cubes in 3 tablespoons melted suet or marrow from the bones. This can be done in the pressure cooker kettle, which should in this case be set at high heat, close to 400°. Add more marrow if needed. Put the fat, the bones and the remaining meat cubes into the kettle. Cover with cold water, using 1 cup water to each pound meat. Add 1 teaspoon salt. The cooker should never be more than two-thirds full. Add 1 small onion stuffed with 3 cloves, a sprig of parsley, a small handful of celery tops or a teaspoon celery flakes, ½ bayleaf, 1 carrot sliced. Allow to stand 1 hour at room temperature to draw out the juices. Cook under pressure 20 minutes. Let the pressure go down normally so that more and more essence will be drawn from the bones. Strain, remove fat (see page 81).

AT SERVING TIME:

Dilute to the strength required, correct the seasonings and serve as a broth. Or freeze in ice trays. Remove fat. And keep in plastic bags in freezer to be used in innumerable recipes that require brown stock. This recipe makes a little over a quart of highly concentrated stock, about 2½ quarts of broth.

Your Own Consommé   PRESSURE COOKER

This consommé has a marvelously subtle flavor because it is made of beef, veal, and chicken cooked together under pressure. A glorious mélange!

YOU WILL NEED:

cubed lean beef	butter or fat
a marrow bone	peppercorns
a knuckle of veal	cloves
bones from a chicken or	parsley
chicken wings	bayleaf
carrot	marjoram or thyme if
celery	consommé is to be
onion	served immediately

Have 2 pounds lean beef cut into 1-inch cubes. Brown half of the meat in some of the marrow from the marrow bone, at 400° F. Add this to the remaining beef cubes along with 3-pound knuckle of veal cut in pieces, 1 pound of marrow bones, the carcass of a chicken broken up in small pieces or a pound of chicken wings. Cover with enough cold water to fill the pressure cooker two-thirds full. Allow to stand ½ hour. Cook under pressure 20 minutes.

Meanwhile cook ⅓ cup each of diced carrot, celery and onion in 2 tablespoons butter or chicken fat 5 minutes at 370°. Add to the soup with 1 teaspoon salt, ½ teaspoon peppercorns, 2 cloves, 2 sprigs parsley, ½ bayleaf. If consommé is to be served immediately add 1 sprig marjoram and 2 sprigs thyme or ¼ teaspoon each of the dried herbs. Add to the pressure-cooked stock. Simmer 1 hour at 200°. Strain, cool quickly, remove fat and clear the soup if desired.

AT SERVING TIME:

Correct the seasoning, flavor to taste with sherry or Madeira and add whatever garnish you please. For future use, freeze in ice cube trays.

White Veal Stock   PRESSURE COOKER

Many French recipes owe some of their traditional flavor to this type of stock which can be made with a knuckle of veal or a combination of veal and lean beef.

YOU WILL NEED:

knuckle of veal or veal and beef	carrot
	mace
peppercorns	bayleaf
onion	thyme
celery stalks	cloves

Have the meat cut off a 4-pound knuckle of veal or use a 3-pound knuckle of veal and about a pound of lean beef cut into small pieces. Add enough cold water to fill the pressure cooker two-thirds full. Add 8 peppercorns, 1 medium size onion cut into quarters, 2 celery stalks, a small carrot cut into slices, a blade of mace or, if you have no mace, use a few grains of nutmeg instead. Add ½ of a bayleaf and 3 cloves. Cook under pressure 20 minutes. Allow pressure to come down naturally. Simmer at 200° at least 30 minutes or as long as feasible.

AT SERVING TIME:

Pour through a strainer lined with a double thickness of cheese-cloth. Flavor with Madeira or sherry if desired, correct the seasonings and garnish to suit your fancy. Or for future use, freeze in ice cube trays.

Chicken Stock, Broth or Bouillon
PRESSURE COOKER

For superior flavor and a darker color, some of the pieces of chicken may first be browned in chicken fat or butter. This can be done in the pressure cooker kettle at 370°.

YOU WILL NEED:

fricassee type chicken or	onion
legs, backs, necks, etc.	bayleaf
carrot	peppercorns
celery	

Clean and wipe 4 pounds of cut-up chicken or use a package of frozen fricassee chicken or 4 pounds of legs, backs, wings, etc. Add 4 cups cold water, 1 sliced carrot, 2 stalks celery, 1 sliced onion and ½ bayleaf, ¼ teaspoon peppercorns, 1 teaspoon salt. Cook under pressure 20 minutes. Let the pressure go down naturally. Cool slightly. Remove fat. Bring back to boiling point again. Strain and correct the seasonings. The cooked chicken can be used in many ways—creamed or in salad or to make sandwiches.

AT SERVING TIME:

Though good and rich, this soup is not always deeply golden in color. If you like, you may enhance the hue by adding 2 or 3 drops of yellow vegetable coloring. A benign deception. It works on canned soups too.

This recipe makes 1 quart of very rich stock which can be diluted to taste.

Mushroom Broth   PRESSURE COOKER

One of the richest and meatiest-tasting of meatless broths is that which you make in your pressure cooker. It is, by the way, one broth that to the best of our knowledge can't be bought. You may use the stems and peelings of fresh mushrooms or what is even more convenient, dried mushrooms.

There is a sad sameness in the pretty white and fairly tasteless mushrooms in the fresh state at markets in our country. If you want to become initiated into the delightful varieties from other lands, you can get dried mushrooms from Japan, China, Czechoslovakia, France, Tuscany, Morocco.

All can be transformed into broths by this same method. An ounce of dried mushrooms equals a full pound of fresh mushrooms.

YOU WILL NEED:
>dried mushrooms or
>>stems and peels of
>>fresh mushrooms
>instant onion

celery flakes
parsley flakes
sherry or Madeira

Cover an ounce of dried mushrooms with 4 cups warm water. Add ½ teaspoon instant onion, ½ teaspoon celery flakes, ½ teaspoon parsley flakes. Let stand at room temperature at least an hour or longer. Cook in pressure cooker, beginning at 400° F. until valve rocks, turn down to between 200 and 250 so that there is some slight movement of the valve, but nothing too violent. Cook 7 minutes. Reduce pressure immediately.

AT SERVING TIME:
If you want a clear consommé, strain and serve. If you like bits of mushrooms in the broth, strain anyhow to remove parsley, etc. and place the mushrooms together with 1 cup of the broth in the blender. Blend just about 1 second; on then off again, and return the mushrooms to the broth. Flavor to taste with sherry or Madeira. Garnish with thin slice of lemon or lime. Makes 1 quart.

VARIATION: *JELLIED MUSHROOM BROTH*   Soak 1 envelope unflavored gelatine in ¼ cup water, then dissolve in 1 cup of the heated broth. Add remainder of broth and cool in the refrigerator. Break the jellied soup into pieces with a fork or a spoon and serve in chilled consommé cups, garnished with chopped chives, and serve sections of lemon or lime for squeezing. This recipe makes 1 quart.

Duck Soup from Bones   PRESSURE COOKER

Duck soup is duck soup to make with an electric pressure cooker. So is a delicious soup of chicken or turkey bones. The pressure cooker seems to draw all the flavor out of the bones and scraps. If the color is not bright enough to suit you, use a mere touch of Kitchen Bouquet or Gravymaster. Or you could use a little yellow coloring or a touch of tomato paste.

YOU WILL NEED:

duck, chicken, or turkey bones	celery tops
	leftover broth or gravy,
onion	optional
carrot	

Place in the pressure cooker the bones from a duck, chicken or turkey. Broilers, roast fowl or fricasseed can be used. Add 1 small sliced onion, a carrot also sliced and a handful of celery tops. The amounts of each can vary to suit your taste. Add any leftover broth or gravy and enough liquid, water or tomato juice to make about 3 cupfuls. Cook under pressure 20 to 30 minutes. Bring the pressure down immediately or let it go down of its own free will. It doesn't matter. Strain broth and season to taste.

AT SERVING TIME:

Add any desired garnish or freeze in cubes and store in plastic bags.

Essence of Lobster, Shrimp or Crab
PRESSURE COOKER

When you serve steamed lobster or shrimp or crabs, don't throw away the shells or the bits and pieces. They make the most delicious essence to flavor your sauces or your bisques. Canned or frozen soups will be completely transformed by the addition of such essences.

YOU WILL NEED:
 shells and bits and pieces of lobster, shrimp or crabs

Place the sea-food shells and whatever leavings are handy in the pressure cooker. It should be not more than two-thirds full. Add 1 pint to 1 quart of water, depending upon the amount of shells, using about ½ cup water to cup of shells. Cook under pressure 20 to 30 minutes, once again depending upon amounts. Generally I do not add any flavorings to the stock at this stage. Bring pressure down immediately or allow to come down naturally. This method drives every bit of flavor and richness out of the shells. It is not necessary to cool the sea food. Simply pour into refrigerator trays, freeze, and next day place cubes in plastic bags and keep frozen.

AT SERVING TIME:
This stock adds ineffable distinction to any sea-food dish.

Fish Stock or Fish Fumet   PRESSURE COOKER

This broth made from fish bones and scraps will form the basis of glittering aspics or the most delectable sauces.

YOU WILL NEED:
fish heads, bones, and scraps	clove
carrot	bayleaf
onion	lemon juice
stalk of celery	egg white (optional)
parsley	yellow vegetable coloring,
peppercorns	saffron or curry powder
	(optional)

Place 3 pounds of fish heads, bones and scraps into a 4-quart pressure cooker. Add a cup of water to each pound of fish. Make sure that the cooker is not more than two-thirds full. Then add 1 carrot, 1 onion, a stalk of celery cut into small pieces, a sprig of parsley, 3 peppercorns, 1 clove, a bit of bayleaf, 2 tablespoons lemon juice. Cook under 15 pounds pressure about 20 minutes. Allow the pressure to go down naturally. This method will exact every bit of flavor and gelatine from the bones and fish.

Strain the stock. Clarify with egg white if you wish (see page 81) and use immediately or pour into ice cube trays, freeze and store the cubes in plastic bags.

If you want to add a lovely golden glimmer to your stock or aspic, use a bit of yellow vegetable coloring or flavor with saffron or a touch, but only a touch, of curry powder.

Japanese Soup   PRESSURE COOKER

Chawan-Mushi, which often takes the place of clear soup on a Japanese menu, is a delicate custard served in exquisitely designed cups with an overhanging lid. Ingredients vary with the season and the individual's preference.

YOU WILL NEED:

- clam broth, soup stock or chicken or beef bouillon cubes
- eggs
- chicken
- shrimp
- ginkgo nuts, chestnuts or green peas
- mushrooms
- bamboo shoots
- soy sauce
- stock
- sugar
- dry sherry or vermouth

Canned clam broth, soup stock, or chicken or beef bouillon should be cooled and an equal amount of beaten eggs should be added (1 average egg slightly beaten equals about ¼ cup).

The mixture is then poured over the ingredients already arranged in the cups, which are as follows: 2 small pieces of raw breast of chicken sliced thin, 3 small or 1 large shrimp with head, shell and vein removed, 6 ginkgo nuts or several chestnuts or 12 fresh or canned green peas, 1 dried mushroom softened in water or substitute canned mushrooms, 2 slices of bamboo shoots. The bamboo shoots, mushroom and chicken and shrimp should have been covered for 15 minutes in: 2 tablespoons soy sauce, 1 cup stock, 1 teaspoon sugar, ½ teaspoon dry sherry or vermouth.

Place the ingredients in the cup arranging them with vegetables and chicken first and mushroom, shrimp or bamboo shoots on top. After pouring in the custard cover the cups with waxed paper. Tie in place with string. Steam for about 20 minutes or until it sets. Or a pressure cooker works like a charm. Follow the usual method for making custards. Cook at 15 lbs. pressure for 3 minutes and reduce pressure immediately.

AT SERVING TIME:
Serve piping hot, preferably with a porcelain spoon.

Some prefer a more soupy custard. For this type use three or four times as much soup stock as beaten egg. That is: 1 egg to ¾ or 1 cup broth. This delicate custard-like soup can be made in Pyrex custard cups or in pot de crème cups. Instead of a lid you may use two thicknesses of aluminum foil pressed close around the edges and tied with string.

Charleston Crab Soup   SAUCEPAN

One of the great delicacies of Charleston, South Carolina, is crab soup most delicately flavored with mace and sherry. She-crabs are much more prized than he-crabs, for the eggs add a special savor. However, if you are far away from Charleston, you can come very close to the real soup if you'll crumble into the bottom of the tureen the yolks of eggs cooked hard.

YOU WILL NEED:

cream of celery soup	crabmeat
milk	whipped cream
mace	paprika (optional)
Worcestershire sauce	sherry
eggs	lemon peel

To 2 cans condensed cream of celery soup add 2 soup cans milk, ½ teaspoon mace, ½ teaspoon Worcestershire sauce, the chopped whites of 4 hard-cooked eggs, 2 cups crabmeat. Set thermostat at 180° and allow to stand 10 minutes. Serves 4 to 6.

AT SERVING TIME:

Crumble the yolk of a hard-cooked egg into each bowl. Ladle soup into bowls. Top each portion with slightly salted whipped cream, which may be made pink by the addition of paprika.

Pass a small silver pitcher of warmed sherry and a small dish containing wisps of lemon peel which each person will twist and drop into his soup as you do when you make a Martini.

Court Bouillon for Fish SAUCEPAN

YOU WILL NEED:

white wine or cider	bayleaf
vinegar	onion
peppercorns	celery
parsley	

Bring to a boil and cook for 20 minutes at 250° F. 2 quarts water, 1 cup white wine or cider vinegar, 8 peppercorns, 3 sprigs parsley, ½ bayleaf, 1 onion sliced, 2 stalks celery, 1 teaspoon salt. Put through a strainer. Cool the bouillon before using it for fish. Shell fish, however, are plunged into the boiling-hot court bouillon.

If you are doing a large fish in the roaster, you will need at least 1 gallon of court bouillon.

Curried Shrimp Bisque   BLENDER

YOU WILL NEED:
shrimp soup   parsley clusters
milk   curry

Place 1 can frozen shrimp soup, 1 can measure of milk, ¼ cup parsley clusters and ½ teaspoon curry into the container of your blender. Cover and blend on high speed for 10 seconds. Heat at 200° F.

AT SERVING TIME:
Garnish with whole cooked shrimp. Serves 4.

Cream of Clam Soup   BLENDER

YOU WILL NEED:
minced clams   cream
chicken stock

Blend 1 can (7½ ounce) minced clams with 1 cup chicken stock and ½ cup cream.

AT SERVING TIME:
Serve well chilled or heated. Garnish with chopped parsley. Makes 4 servings.

Aspic   SAUCEPAN

The aspic used here is quickly made and, although it contains tomato juice to give it flavor, it has a golden clarity. The color and opaqueness of the tomato liquid is removed by beaten egg whites and egg shells, which are boiled with the aspic before it is strained through flannel.

YOU WILL NEED:
chicken or fish stock	egg shells
tomato juice	egg whites
gelatine	cognac
sugar	

In the saucepan combine 3 cups chicken or fish stock with 1 cup tomato juice, 4 envelopes unflavored gelatine, salt to taste, freshly ground black pepper to taste, 1 teaspoon sugar, 2 egg shells crushed and 2 lightly beaten egg whites and heat at 200° F., stirring constantly until the mixture boils up in the saucepan. Cut off heat entirely—let stand 2 minutes. Stir in 2 tablespoons cognac.

Strain the mixture through a sieve lined with a flannel cloth that has been rinsed in cold water and wrung out. Yields about one quart.

Vichyssoise ICE CRUSHER AND BLENDER

There are thousands of recipes. This one is really fine.

YOU WILL NEED:
onion	crushed ice
chicken broth	cream or milk
potatoes, cooked	

Slice ½ small onion into the blender. Add about ½ cup chicken broth or enough to cover the blades. Cover and blend on high speed for 6 seconds. Add ½ teaspoon salt, ⅛ teaspoon pepper, 1½ cups cooked diced potatoes and 1 cup chicken broth. Cover and blend for 8 seconds. Add 1 cup crushed ice and about ½ cup milk and blend for 10 seconds longer. Serves 6.

AT SERVING TIME:
Garnish with chopped chives.

Gazpacho   BLENDER

A perfect summer soup.

YOU WILL NEED:
tomatoes	garlic
green pepper	olive oil
onion	wine vinegar
cucumber	

Quarter 4 ripe tomatoes, seed and slice ½ large green pepper, peel and slice ½ small onion and 1 cucumber and place in blender. Add 1 clove garlic, 1 teaspoon salt, ¼ teaspoon pepper, 2 tablespoons olive oil, 3 tablespoons wine vinegar and ½ cup ice water. Cover and blend just 2 seconds. Chill in refrigerator.

AT SERVING TIME:
Pour into serving plates and serve with an ice cube in the center of each serving. Serves six.

Cucumber Soup   BLENDER AND SAUCEPAN

Something delightfully different!

YOU WILL NEED:
cucumbers	flour
butter	chicken stock
onion	cream or milk

Wash 2 cucumbers and peel 1. Cut both cucumbers into chunks and put them into a saucepan with the butter, water and onion. Cover and simmer for 10 minutes or until vegetables are tender. Empty vegetables and juice into container of your blender. Add 2 tablespoons flour, ½ teaspoon salt, ⅛ teaspoon pepper and 1 cup chicken stock. Cover and blend on high speed. Remove cover and, with motor on, gradually pour in ½ cup cream or milk. Pour into a saucepan and heat at 180° F. This recipe serves six.

AT SERVING TIME:
Garnish with thin slivers of cucumber peel.

Chilled Beet Top Soup or Botvina
PRESSURE COOKER

This is a Polish variant of the popular cold beet soup, a wonderful summer delicacy to serve mixed or topped with sour cream and garnished with boiled potatoes, sliced cucumbers and sliced cooked eggs.

YOU WILL NEED:

beet tops and beets	lemon juice or sour salt
white onion	sour cream

Cut beet tops and stems into ½ inch pieces. Place 1 cup water in blender. Add 2 medium size or 4 small peeled young beets, 1 small white onion cut in pieces. Blend about 5 seconds. Place in pressure cooker along with cup of beet tops. Add 4 cups water, adjust cover and turn thermostat to high (400° F.). When a continuous steam appears, turn down to 200° or 250°, just enough to keep the valve moving slightly, not rocking violently. Cook 2 minutes. Disconnect and allow cold water to pour down the side to reduce pressure immediately.

Season to taste with salt, about 2 teaspoonfuls; about ¼ teaspoon white pepper, 2 or 3 tablespoons lemon juice or ½ teaspoon sour salt (which is citric acid). Chill in refrigerator or with ice cubes.

AT SERVING TIME:
Add 1 half pint sour cream and ice cubes if necessary. Ladle into soup plates or bowls. Pass in separate bowls fluffy hot boiled

potatoes cut in halves, sliced eggs, sliced cucumbers or kosher dills, all of which go into the soup. Pumpernickel finger sandwiches made with sweet butter go very well. Serves 6 to 8.

Frosted Bisque   BLENDER

Around this interesting bisque you can plan an inspired meal at summer dusk or a luncheon underneath the trees.

YOU WILL NEED:
   cream of tomato soup   Tabasco
   milk   cucumber
   tarragon vinegar   green pepper
   beet juice

Combine a can of cream of tomato soup chilled, 1 soup can (1⅓ cups) milk, 2 tablespoons tarragon vinegar, 1 cup juice from canned beets, dash of salt, pepper, 3 or 4 drops Tabasco. Blend 1 minute. Add 1 unpeeled cucumber, 1 green pepper cut in pieces. Blend 15 seconds. Make 6 to 8 servings.

AT SERVING TIME:
Serve in chilled plates. Sprinkle generously with finely minced parsley, chives, or chopped onion tops, celery leaves, dill or fennel.

Emerald Soup   BLENDER

Mary Frost Mabon invented and named this soup. Says she, "It sprang full-grown, like Minerva from the brain of Zeus, the moment I tasted some miraculous fillets of sole with a green spinach sauce, raw-made in the blender." She uses raw spinach, however, which takes washing. And one can't always find the tender young leaves. Mature spinach has strings and won't do at all. I use frozen chopped spinach, same recipe as Potage aux Herbes.

YOU WILL NEED:

    frozen chopped spinach   garlic
    cream of chicken soup   Tabasco
    milk

Defrost 1 package frozen chopped spinach. Place spinach in blender with 2 cans cream of chicken soup and 1 soup can milk. Press ½ clove garlic; add to other ingredients with one dash Tabasco sauce. Blend thoroughly and chill, or simmer at 200° F. about 15 minutes. Serves 8.

AT SERVING TIME:

Serve with sour cream and plenty of freshly ground black pepper from the grinder.

Cream of Avocado Soup   ICE CRUSHER AND BLENDER

A delicate and delightful chilled soup.

YOU WILL NEED:

    avocado   crushed ice
    chicken broth   cream
    garlic   chives or parsley
    cayenne pepper or   green coloring (optional)
      Tabasco

Peel, seed and slice 1 large avocado. Then place in blender. Add 1½ cups chicken broth, 1 clove garlic, ⅛ teaspoon cayenne pepper or 3 drops Tabasco. Cover and blend on high speed for 15 seconds. Add 1½ cups crushed ice and ½ cup cream. Cover and blend for 10 seconds longer. If too thick, thin with more broth or cream. If desired, a drop or two of green coloring may be added. Serves six.

AT SERVING TIME:

Sprinkle with chopped chives or parsley.

Cream of Chicken Senegalese   BLENDER

Several famous restaurants in New York serve in summertime a soup very much like this one—delicate, creamy, subtly but only subtly "curried."

YOU WILL NEED:
cream of chicken soup	curry powder
milk	lemon juice

Blend 1 can cream of chicken soup, 1 soup can of milk with 2 teaspoons curry powder and 3 tablespoons lemon juice. Serves 3 or 4.

AT SERVING TIME:
Serve ice cold or hot, and pass a variety of curry accompaniments such as coarsely chopped, thinly sliced green or sweet red peppers; chutney; very thinly sliced, unpeeled tart red apple; scallions cut into ½ inch pieces; peanuts or pistachio nuts, and small amount of flaky rice.

Kentucky Hambone Soup   PRESSURE COOKER

What do you do with the bone and scraps after you've served the ham? This soup is a robust answer.

YOU WILL NEED:
ham bone and scraps or a	canned tomatoes
ham hock with a little	cabbage
meat on it	potatoes
onions	

Cover a ham hock or a ham bone and about a pound of scraps with a quart of water. Add 3 sliced onions. Cook at 15 pounds pressure 25 minutes, if the ham has been previously cooked;

45 minutes if the ham has not been cooked beforehand. Bring down the pressure. Add 4 medium potatoes sliced, 1 medium size head cabbage shredded, 1 large can tomatoes, and simmer until the potatoes are tender. Add salt and pepper, if any is needed. Keep hot at about 160° for as long as you please—the longer the better.

AT SERVING TIME:
Skim off any excess fat. Serve with smoking hot corn bread and wilted greens.

Oxtail Soup   PRESSURE COOKER

With oxtails handily packaged and quick frozen, this great delicacy can now be enjoyed without killing an ox. A quarter of a cup of Madeira wine is a pleasing addition and tradition.

YOU WILL NEED:

an oxtail	onion
flour	celery
fat	lemon juice
brown stock or consomme	Worcestershire sauce
carrot	Madeira wine optional
turnip	

Have a small oxtail weighing approximately 2 pounds cut into pieces about an inch long. Wipe with a damp cloth if it comes from a butcher. If the oxtail is quick frozen it will already be cut into pieces and clean. Sprinkle with 1 teaspoon salt, ½ teaspoon pepper, 2 tablespoons flour.

Melt 3 tablespoons lard, butter or other fat in the pressure cooker. Add the oxtail and brown at about 375° F. about 10 minutes. Add 1 quart brown stock or water. Cook under 15 pounds pressure 45 minutes. Bring down pressure immediately. Add another quart of hot water and also ½ cup each of diced carrots, turnips, onions, celery. Simmer at 200° until vegetables are tender. Add 1 teaspoon lemon juice, 1 teaspoon Worcestershire sauce and, if desired, ¼ cup Madeira wine or New York State sherry. Keep warm at about 180°.

AT SERVING TIME:
Serve garnished with thin slices of lemon and coarsely chopped parsley. This recipe serves six.

Fish and Sea Food

Salmon Imperator Baked in Clay
ROASTER OVEN

At the Forum Restaurant in New York, banker-gourmet Stanton Frederick of Seattle was served a chicken baked in clay. Since a bird is so good cooked in this manner, why not a salmon, he asked. He began to experiment. So did the Forum's Director Chef, Albert Stockli. This recipe represents their combined efforts.

YOU WILL NEED:

salmon, bass, rock fish or trout	milk or white wine
lemon	white bread
butter	fresh or dried basil
canned salmon	thyme
eggs	clay

To serve a party of six or eight, get a fine whole salmon, weighing at least 6 to 8 pounds. (You may also use striped bass or sea bass, rock fish or a large trout.) Rub the fish inside and out with a cut lemon and with butter. Sprinkle with salt and pepper. Roll out a large piece of double-duty foil. Brush it with salad oil or butter. To keep the fish moist and to prevent the whole production from collapsing under the clay as it might when the bones get soft, make a stuffing of canned salmon, preferably Chinook. Drain a pound of canned salmon; beat 6 eggs in a blender with ¼ cup milk or white wine until pale and airy.

Soak for about 2 minutes 8 slices of white bread with crusts removed in this mixture. Add salmon and ¼ cup fresh basil or a tablespoon dried basil, ¼ teaspoon dried thyme, 1 teaspoon salt, a pinch of pepper. Blend until very smooth. Stuff the fish lightly. Do not press down. Wrap in buttered aluminum foil.

Now the fun part. Encase the fish in moist modeling clay.* Roll the clay about a half-inch thick with your hands or a rolling pin. Press edges together tightly, turn upside down and mark with a fork or knife to simulate the markings of a fish. Place on a large cookie sheet, or improvise a large sheet from aluminum foil. Bake in a hot oven 500° F. 50 to 60 minutes.

AT SERVING TIME:

Bring the fish to the table in its own clay casing, wreathed with leaves. At the Forum Restaurant they use a large basket but a tray will do. Provide a mallet for breaking the clay shell. Serve with Hollandaise sauce.

* The clay used must be odorless. After a good deal of experimentation, we found at *House Beautiful* that Grumbacher's moist modeling clay No. 753 seemed to do the job best. This may be bought at art supply stores, in hobby shops, or in large department stores. It costs about $1.00 for 5 pounds —an adequate amount to cover a large fish.

Whole Poached Salmon   ROASTER OVEN

This is one of the lordliest of gastronomic creations, but before the advent of the roaster oven it was difficult to achieve without a special yard-long fish kettle equipped with a rack. Our grandmothers with large houses and acres of shelf space could keep such a receptacle on hand for the salmon season.

In addition to the kettle and rack, considerable knowledge and care were required to make sure that the court bouillon did not boil hard; otherwise the salmon would fall apart in strings. But with the thermostatic control of the roaster oven there is no problem whatsoever.

YOU WILL NEED:
    whole salmon   cheesecloth (optional)
    court bouillon (see
      page 91)

Choose a fish which will fit on the rack of your roaster oven with the head and tail intact. This is the ideal way. However, if you prefer, you may remove the head and tail. Wrap the fish, if you like, in a layer of cheesecloth. Add sufficient court bouillon to cover the fish and set the thermostat to 350° F. When the red light goes off, turn the thermostat to 250° and simmer, covered for about 15 to 20 minutes.

AT SERVING TIME:
If you wish to serve the fish hot, simply lift it on the rack, remove cheesecloth and serve with any favorite sauce. Hollandaise is one of the most revered accompaniments to salmon, as are boiled new potatoes and baby peas.

VARIATION: *COLD POACHED SALMON*   Allow salmon to cool in the court bouillon, then remove and serve with mayonnaise, or decorate with Chaud-Froid sauce (see page 202).

Broiled Fish Japanese   BROILER

A fish dish, teriyaki, which is tasty and easily prepared, is broiled salmon decorated with fresh grated horseradish or a turnip made into the shape of a flower. Here is a recipe for six:

YOU WILL NEED:
    salmon steaks   mirin or sherry
    shoyu

Salt 3 salmon steaks cut in half through the center and broil until light brown. Dip in sauce made of shoyu and mirin or sherry and broil again. Turn and pour sauce over both sides, broil until fish is well glazed and flakes easily when touched with a fork.

AT SERVING TIME:
Serve on individual dishes with a turnip flower (pages 60–61).

Salmon Poached in White Wine   SAUCEPAN

This is epicurean treatment for fresh or quick-frozen salmon steaks, halibut steaks, or fillets of flounder. Even canned salmon heated in this court bouillon, is elegant.

YOU WILL NEED:

salmon, halibut, or flounder	peppercorns
carrot	cloves
celery	bayleaf
onion	vinegar
butter	white wine
parsley	lemon juice

Cut up 1 medium-sized carrot, 1 onion, a couple of stalks of celery, and cook all together in 2 tablespoons butter along with 2 sprigs of parsley for about 3 minutes. Add 4 or 5 peppercorns, 2 cloves, ½ bayleaf, 1 tablespoon salt, 2 tablespoons vinegar, 1 tablespoon lemon juice, and 2 quarts white wine. Boil uncovered about 10 minutes.

Lay the fish gently into the court bouillon. Turn down the heat and simmer 6 to 10 minutes per pound. The exact time depends upon the thickness of the fish. When done, fish will have lost its transparent look and will flake off easily at the touch of a fork. Allow to cool in its own broth.

AT SERVING TIME:
Provide mayonnaise or Hollandaise sauce and boiled potatoes.

Poached Rainbow Trout
with Green Mayonnaise BLENDER

YOU WILL NEED:

trout

basil-flavored white wine
vinegar and white
vinegar

mayonnaise

egg

spinach leaves

dry mustard

olive oil

salad oil

Poach or steam whole trout in water to which you may add a little basil-flavored white vinegar. Cool. Drain.

Cover with the following green mayonnaise: Place 1 egg, 6 spinach leaves, 2 tablespoons white wine vinegar, 1 teaspoon salt, ½ teaspoon dry mustard, ¼ cup olive oil in blender. Blend about 5 seconds. While blender is running, gradually add ¾ cup salad oil. Stop as soon as all oil has been incorporated.

AT SERVING TIME:

Nestle trout on crisp spinach leaves preferably on a fish-shaped platter.

Fish Fillets in Silver BLENDER

YOU WILL NEED:

frozen fish fillets

aluminum foil

onion

green pepper

tomato

olive oil

lemon juice or vinegar

garlic

Defrost and separate 1 package frozen fillets. Place each fillet on a separate piece of aluminum foil and pat dry with a paper towel. Place in your blender 2 slices onion, ½ green pepper which has been seeded and sliced, 1 medium tomato which has been quartered, 2 tablespoons olive oil, 1 tablespoon lemon juice or vinegar, 1 clove garlic. Season to taste with salt and pepper. Cover and blend for 6 seconds. Spoon sauce over the fish, dividing it between the 6 fillets. Fold the aluminum foil over the fish like envelopes, sealing in the sauce. Place packages on baking sheet and bake in a 350° F. oven for 15 minutes.

AT SERVING TIME:
Cut a slit in the foil envelope. Fold back foil and serve accompanied with vegetables and boiled potatoes or rice.

Salmon Mousse   ICE CRUSHER AND BLENDER

For the most tremendous drama you could make this mousse at the table and serve it immediately, mounted on crisp lettuce for individual portions, or even more dramatically, inside a large spread-out heart of Boston lettuce or Romaine.

YOU WILL NEED:

gelatine	cayenne pepper or
onion	Tabasco
canned salmon	crushed ice
egg yolks	cream
lemon juice	peanut oil
pepper	red coloring (optional)

Put ½ cup hot water into the blender with 2 envelopes unflavored gelatine. Cover and blend 40 seconds. Add ¼ of a small onion cut in pieces, 1 8-ounce tin of canned salmon, 2 egg yolks or 1 whole egg. Cover and blend for 5 seconds. Add 1 tablespoon lemon juice, ⅛ teaspoon pepper, a few grains of cayenne pepper or 2 drops Tabasco. Blend 5 seconds longer. With motor on, remove cover, add 1 cup finely crushed ice, 1 cup cream, and if desired, a couple of drops of red color. Continue to blend for 40 seconds or until mousse begins to thicken. Serve immediately as suggested above. Or have ready a quart size mold, which should be cold and rinsed with cold water or lightly painted with peanut oil. Quick chill in the freezing compartment 5 minutes or in the refrigerator about an hour.

AT SERVING TIME:
There should be plenty of crisp greens, quartered tomatoes, sliced cucumbers, and if you're feeling extremely elegant, some slices of truffles.

Sweden's Finest Fish Mousse BLENDER

As contrasted with the "simple everyday" fish soufflés made in Scandinavia from cooked fish or leftovers, this mousse is "a real party dish for discriminating guests." "And the beauty of it," according to Anna Olsson Coombs, author of several Scandinavian cookbooks, "is that this mousse does not suffer from a little overcooking." So the hostess can enjoy her cocktail in peace and then go to the kitchen and unmold this work of art. It looks like a wonderful cake and tastes like something a French gastronome might have conceived in a moment of divine inspiration.

YOU WILL NEED:

quick-frozen fillets (haddock, flounder, perch or cod)	anchovy fillets or paste
	white pepper
	dash of cayenne
milk	butter
eggs	heavy cream
flour	bread crumbs

Defrost ½ pound quick-frozen fillets (haddock, flounder, perch or cod). Place in blender ½ cup milk, the fish diced, 2 egg yolks, 1½ tablespoons flour, 1 or 2 anchovy fillets or ½ teaspoon anchovy paste, ½ teaspoon salt, ⅛ teaspoon white pepper, dash of cayenne. Blend at high speed about 2 minutes, stopping to stir down every 30 seconds. When the fish is very fine, keep the blender running and add, little by little, ¼ pound soft but not melted butter. With electric beater, using separate bowls, beat until stiff 2 egg whites, ½ cup heavy cream. Combine, add the fish mixture and fold in with a few deep motions.

Brush a quart mold with melted butter or salad oil, making sure that you reach every crevice. Sprinkle thickly with tiny bread crumbs (these are easy to make in your blender). Pour in the fish mixture, adjust a tight-fitting lid greased on the inside or cover closely with greased aluminum foil or waxed paper. Set in hot water, which should not come more than halfway up the side of the mold. Bake at 350° F. 1 to 1½ hours, till the soufflé is firm and a toothpick inserted in the center comes out clean. If you like, you may use a steamer on top of the stove. One quart mold makes 4 to 6 servings. If you double the recipe, use 2 molds rather than 1 large one. Smaller molds cook faster, are easier to unmold.

AT SERVING TIME:

Do not unmold until ready to serve. Garnish with watercress, a green vegetable, and tiny boiled potatoes. Pass separately mushroom sauce or, better still, a regal lobster sauce. This last is fast as a flash if you use 1 can concentrated lobster bisque, ½ soup can light cream. Heat, add 1 tablespoon sherry, 1 tablespoon brandy.

Broiled Fish   BROILER

Thin pieces of fish do not need to be turned at all. Be careful when you are broiling fish not to overcook it. Don't try to get it very brown. The lightest of tanning should suffice. Cook 4 inches from the source of heat if the broiler is on full force, or at moderate temperatures and only until the fish flakes off easily when touched with a fork and does not have any transparent look.

Small whole fish such as smelts or brook trout may be broiled. Blue fish, mackerel, pompano or scrod are often merely split and broiled flesh side up without turning. Fillets of fish or salmon steaks or halibut steaks may be broiled also and they are turned only if they are quite thick.

Rinse the fish in cold running water. Pat dry with paper towels. Brush with olive oil or salad oil.

Preheat broiler. Place fish on a well greased rack. Sprinkle with salt and pepper. Dot with bits of butter or brush with olive or salad oil.

If you have trouble moving the fish without breaking it, try using 2 pancake turners or 2 broad spatulas.

Filet of Sole Amandine   SKILLET

A delightful dish to make and serve at the table.

YOU WILL NEED:

fillets of sole, fresh or frozen	dry cocktail sherry or dry table wine
paprika	lemon juice
flour	slivered almonds
salad oil	

To serve 4, use 4 fillets of sole or 1 pound package of frozen fillets which need not be completely thawed—just enough to separate.

Add 1 teaspoon salt, ¾ teaspoon pepper, ¾ teaspoon paprika to 4 tablespoons of flour. Coat the fish on both sides with the seasoned flour.

Heat ¼ cup salad oil to 370° and brown the fillets. Remove fish to a hot platter and keep warm on the hot tray. Add to the oil in the skillet ½ cup very dry pale cocktail sherry or dry white table wine, 2 tablespoons lemon juice. Simmer at about 200° for 3 minutes, replace fish in sauce and keep warm at about 150° to 180°. Do not cover the skillet or the fish will lose its crispness.

AT SERVING TIME:

Sprinkle with ¼ cup toasted slivered almonds and serve with lemon sections.

VARIATION: *SOLE AMANDINE WITH BANANAS*   An extraordinarily interesting combination—bananas and a delicate, fine-textured fish! Peel 4 small bananas, cut into halves lengthwise and simmer in the wine sauce above. One half teaspoon ground ginger may be added also.

Steamed Fish, Chinese Style   ROASTER OVEN AND BLENDER

YOU WILL NEED:

peanut or salad oil	dried mushrooms
sherry or Madeira	white fish
soy sauce	chopped chives or scallion
white onion	tops

Place in blender 2 tablespoons peanut or salad oil, 1 tablespoon dry sherry or Sercial Madeira, 1 tablespoon soy sauce, half of a small white onion cut into pieces, 6 small dried mushrooms that have been soaked in warm water for at least a half hour. Blend 2 or 3 seconds.

Rub fish on all sides with white pepper and sprinkle the sauce on all sides of the fish. Then sprinkle the top with chopped chives or scallion tops. Set roaster oven at 400° F. Pour into roaster 2 inches of boiling water. When water is steaming at a lively fashion, place the fish on a platter and lower onto the rack set above boiling water. Cook covered 10 to 15 minutes for a fish 2 inches thick; cook 4 to 6 minutes for fish fillets or small fish steaks.

AT SERVING TIME:

Serve with rice.

Fish Tempura   DEEP FAT FRYER

Fish should be cleaned and scraped. Slice into pieces two to three inches in size and three-eighths of an inch thick. Smelts are often split, the heads and bones removed, leaving tails. Fifteen minutes before frying, sprinkle fish lightly with salt.

YOU WILL NEED:
    fish, smelts or shrimp   oil
    tempura batter (see
        page 257)

Heat oil (about 2 inches deep in fryer) to 300° F. to 350° F. A tempura chef makes the testing of the temperature quite a ceremony, tossing a bit of the batter from the end of his long cooking chopsticks into the oil with a dramatic gesture, listening to the spatter and noting the time it takes to brown.

Dip fish into the batter, and drop gently into the oil.

AT SERVING TIME:
Drain on paper and serve immediately with Dashi tempura sauce (page 200).

Shrimp Tempura   DEEP FAT FRYER

Shrimp make the most widely known tempura. Remove all shells and heads but leave tails. Crosscut the belly side to prevent curling when frying.

YOU WILL NEED:
    shrimps   tempura batter (page 257)

Use fresh or green shrimp unpeeled. Shell shrimp except for the tail and adjoining segments. Devein. Remove the tendon which is between the tail. Spread the tail apart and pull tendon out with your fingers. Press each shell between the thumb and forefinger to flatten it and push the water out. Bend the shrimp backward until it will lie straight when released. Wash and dry on paper towels.

Dip shrimp into tempura batter (page 257). Drain off excess. Drop a few at a time into salad oil at 360° F. Shrimp must be fried back first to keep them straight. When one side is brown, turn over. They cook very rapidly. When nicely browned drain on paper towels. Two dozen shrimp should serve 4 to 6 people depending on the size of the shrimp and the appetites.

AT SERVING TIME:
Serve hot with Dashi tempura sauce (page 200) or hot mustard.

Grilled Shrimp with Curry   BROILER
AND BLENDER

Fresh cooked, canned, or quick-frozen shrimp may be used to make this delicate dish. It can be served as an hors d'oeuvre or with rice for lunch or supper.

YOU WILL NEED:
cooked peeled shrimp
herb-flavored French
   dressing
curry powder

For dunk:
sour cream or yogurt
chopped chives
cracked black peppercorns

Make an herb-flavored French dressing by blending 1 cup peanut oil or salad oil with ¼ cup white wine vinegar, ½ teaspoon salt, ¼ teaspoon cracked black peppercorns, ¼ teaspoon each of dried parsley and chervil, 1 clove garlic. Add to the dressing 1 teaspoon curry powder. Pour the dressing over 1 pound cooked peeled shrimp. Allow to stand covered with this mixture several hours. Overnight is better.

Drain, string on skewers or place well separated on greased

aluminum foil. Broil only about 1 minute or just long enough
to heat through. Be very careful not to overcook.

AT SERVING TIME:
Provide toothpicks and a dunk made by combining 1 cup sour
cream or yogurt with 1 tablespoon fresh chopped chives or 1
teaspoon dried green onion tops and ½ teaspoon cracked black
peppercorns.

Connecticut Coquilles   PORTABLE OVEN

Scallops baked in their shells are a favorite dish in France where
generally they are dressed in an ultra rich creamy sauce. This is
a New England version which is light, delicate and blessed with
herbs.

YOU WILL NEED:

butter	garlic salt
onion or chives	lemon juice
parsley flakes	bay scallops
tarragon leaves	soft bread crumbs

With a wooden spoon soften 3 tablespoons butter. Add ½
teaspoon instant minced onion or dehydrated chopped chives,
½ teaspoon parsley flakes, ¼ teaspoon tarragon leaves, ¼ teaspoon garlic salt, 1 teaspoon lemon juice, a pinch of black pepper.

Wash 4 dozen fresh little bay scallops or thaw 2 dozen sea
scallops cut in halves. Place 6 pieces in each of 8 scallop shells
or small ramekins. Top each portion with 1 teaspoon softened
herb butter and buttered crumbs, using about ½ cup bread
crumbs mixed with 3 tablespoons melted better. Bake in a
preheated oven 500° F. 5 minutes. Makes 8 servings.

AT SERVING TIME:
Serve in the scallop shells.

Sautéed Scallops   SKILLET AND BLENDER

Each year in New Bedford, Massachusetts, home of the whalers, there is in the late summer a scallop festival, at which time, under green-striped tents, are consumed tons of the sea food that the French call the *coquille* or shells of St. Jacque. Many people still harbor the illusion that scallops are punched-out pieces of fish. Never so! There are two kinds of scallops, the tiny bay scallops (comparatively scarce and seasonal) and the larger sea scallops that can be obtained either fresh or frozen almost everywhere any time. The trick about cooking scallops—like most sea food—can be expressed in two words: *don't overcook.*

YOU WILL NEED:
    fresh or frozen scallops   garlic
    flour   parsley
    olive oil

If frozen scallops are used, they need not be completely thawed. If they are large sea scallops, they should be cut into pieces about ¼ inch in diameter. Wash and dry the scallops on paper towels. Roll in flour just enough to make a very thin coating.

Meanwhile place in blender 6 tablespoons olive oil and 2 or 3 cloves garlic. Blend till garlic disappears.

In the frying pan heat olive oil to 390°, very hot. When light goes off, add the scallops and cook very quickly, tossing them lightly in the hot oil. Sprinkle with ½ teaspoon salt, ⅛ teaspoon pepper.

AT SERVING TIME:
(which should be immediately) Add ½ cup chopped parsley. Toss parsley around so that scallops are nicely coated with it. Serve with lemon wedges and heated potato chips or julienne potato sticks. Makes 4 to 6 servings. Parsley is most easily chopped by snipping it with a scissors or can be done in the blender.

Lobster and Rice au Mayonnaise   BLENDER

YOU WILL NEED:

lobster chunks
cooked rice
cooked green peas
tomatoes

For Sauce Aurore:
mayonnaise
fresh tomato pulp
lemon juice

Mix chunky pieces of lobster meat with firm, cold, cooked rice, cooked green peas and a few sections of peeled red tomatoes. Dress with a Sauce Aurore (to 2 cups homemade mayonnaise, add ½ cup fresh tomato pulp; season with lemon juice and pepper; blend). Mix gently with two forks to avoid breaking the lobster and squashing the vegetables.

AT SERVING TIME:

Serve very cold. Shape neatly and garnish with some extra peas and tomato.

Steamed Lobster   ROASTER

An electric roaster is ideal for an old-fashioned New England lobster bake. Six or eight or even ten small lobsters may be steamed at once. If you can get some rock weed, place it on top of the lobsters. It does give a delightful flavor. Rock weed, by the way, can be kept in plastic bags in your freezer and re-used two or three times.

YOU WILL NEED:

lobsters, whole fresh live
(1 to 1½ pounds is
considered ideal size for
flavor and tenderness)

rock weed (optional)
New England Butter
Sauce (see page 195)

For each person allow 1 lobster weighing from 1 to 1½ pounds. They should be moving about in a lively fashion. If you must keep the lobsters around the house for a few hours, place them in a bag with ice in the refrigerator.

Preheat roaster to 350°. Cover the bottom of the roaster with boiling water 1 inch deep. Place live lobsters on the rack. Cover and steam from 15 to 18 minutes or until lobster turns pink. Count the cooking time after the steaming starts.

AT SERVING TIME:

Remove lobster from the kettle onto a wooden board and place on its back. Split lengthwise with a heavy sharp knife or Chinese cleaver, running it from the mouth through the body and tail. Remove the dark vein and intestinal sack. Frequently the under-developed spawn or coral which is a deep coral pink in color will be found in the lobster and this is, in most people's opinion, the very best tidbit of all. Do not remove it. Crack the large claws. Serve lobster in the shells with New England Butter Sauce (page 195).

New Orleans Oyster Loaf   DEEP FAT FRYER

In New Orleans several generations ago husbands who stayed out too late of an evening brought home these oyster-filled loaves as peace offerings—hence the name, La Mediatrice (Peace-maker).

YOU WILL NEED:

brown 'n serve French loaf

butter

oysters

cracker meal, bread crumbs, or corn meal

eggs

Cut a half-inch top off brown 'n serve French loaf. Remove soft insides. Brush both loaf and lid with butter and toast in the oven or drop for a minute into hot fat, 370° F. until light brown.

Open and drain or thaw and drain 1 pint of oysters (about 12), saving the liquor. Sprinkle with salt and pepper, roll in cracker meal, bread crumbs, or corn meal; dip in a mixture of 2 beaten eggs, ¾ cup oyster liquor. Fry at 360° F. two or three minutes. Drain on paper towels. Pile into hollowed loaves. One oyster loaf serves two.

AT SERVING TIME:
Serve with pickles, mayonnaise, ketchup or tartar sauce.

Timbale of Crabmeat   BLENDER

A luscious luncheon or buffet supper specialty.

YOU WILL NEED:
gelatine	celery
sherry	onion
chicken broth	parsley clusters
eggs	dry marjoram
crabmeat	cream
Tabasco	

Into the container of the blender put 2 tablespoons gelatine, 2 tablespoons sherry and ½ cup hot chicken broth. Cover and blend on high speed for 1 minute. Add 2 egg yolks, 6½ ounces crabmeat, 5 dashes Tabasco, ½ stalk sliced celery, 1 slice onion about ¼ inch thick, 1 tablespoon parsley clusters, ¼ teaspoon dry marjoram. Cover and blend for 10 seconds. Remove cover and pour in ½ cup cream. Stop motor. In mixing bowl beat 2 egg whites until stiff. Pour blended mixture over egg whites and fold gently until mixed. Pour into a 4-cup mold and chill until set, about 1 hour. Serves 6.

AT SERVING TIME:
Unmold and garnish with celery tops and red onion slices. Serve with green mayonnaise (see page 105).

Fiddler Crab à la Nero   SKILLET

The Forum Restaurant prepares this dish in a copper skillet over a charcoal brazier. It works just as well in an electric skillet.

YOU WILL NEED:

butter or margarine
fresh, frozen or canned
  crab
pimientos

paprika
brown gravy
heavy cream
cognac

Melt ¼ pound butter or margarine in electric skillet. Set at 350° F. Arrange 1 pound lump crab (fresh, frozen or canned) around edge of pan. Put drained whole pimiento slices (1 4-oz. can) in center and sprinkle with ¼ teaspoon paprika. Cook a minute or two, forking the crab gently so that lumps remain unbroken. Add ½ cup homemade or canned brown gravy and ½ cup heavy cream and heat through.

AT SERVING TIME:

Warm ⅓ cup cognac in a separate pan on your electric hot tray, ignite with a match and pour into crab mixture. When flame dies away, serve to four.

Clam Bake   ROASTER OVEN

A quantity of clams may be steamed in the roaster oven. Be sure to ask for the large steamer clams. Little cherry stones or little-necks will not do. The only tricky part of the preparation is cleaning the clams. You must brush each clam twice under running water to remove all traces of sand.

YOU WILL NEED:

clams for steaming

New England butter sauce
(see page 195)

Supply a dozen clams per person. Sounds like a lot but you'll be embarrassed if you don't have enough.

Clams must be alive, which means tightly closed and smelling sweetly of the sea. With a vegetable brush or any other stiff brush go over each clam separately twice. Meanwhile preheat roaster oven to 350°. Cover bottom of pan with boiling water ½ inch deep. Heap the clams on a rack and steam 8 minutes or until shells pop open wide. This will happen all of a rush.

Strain the hot clam broth in the roaster through a double thickness of cheesecloth or a napkin to remove any bits of sand or sediment.

AT SERVING TIME:

Serve clams in a large bowl or basket, lined, if you wish, with a snowy linen towel or linen napkins. It is customary to serve New England melted butter sauce and cups of clam broth.

Poultry

Chicken Martinique

There are many ways with batter-fried chicken. This is one of the most delightfully flavored, an exceptionally fine way to prepare quick-frozen frying chickens or chicken breasts.

YOU WILL NEED:

chicken	lemon juice
chives and parsley	biscuit mix
thyme	eggs
cayenne pepper	milk

To serve 6, you will need about 5 pounds of chicken. Thaw and rub well with a mixture of 2 teaspoons salt, ⅛ teaspoon pepper, 1 tablespoon each finely chopped chives and parsley, 1 teaspoon thyme, ⅛ teaspoon cayenne pepper, 1 tablespoon lemon juice. Let stand at least one hour to absorb seasonings.

Make a batter of 2 cups biscuit mix, 2 eggs, 1⅓ cups milk, 1 teaspoon powdered thyme, 1 tablespoon finely chopped parsley. The batter must be thick enough to stick to the pieces of chicken. Turn pieces around in batter until they are completely covered; let excess batter drip off. Fry, a few pieces at a time, at 350° F., about 12 minutes, until delicately browned. Drain on paper towels.

AT SERVING TIME:

Serve with lemon sections and rice cooked in chicken broth instead of water.

120

Chicken and Almond Mousse BLENDER

YOU WILL NEED:

gelatine

onion

almonds

eggs

chicken stock

cream

boned chicken or leftover

chicken (diced)

tiny peas

Put 2 envelopes gelatine, ½ cup very hot water, ¼ teaspoon pepper and 1 thinly sliced medium onion into the container of the blender. Cover and blend on high speed for 40 seconds. Add ½ cup blanched almonds and 2 eggs, cover and blend on high speed for 20 seconds. Add 1 cup chicken stock and 7 ounces canned boned chicken or leftover chicken meat (diced), cover and turn motor on high. Remove cover and pour in 1 cup heavy cream. Turn off motor. Pour mixture over 1 can (14 ounces) tiny peas in a mixing bowl and mix gently. Pour into a 4-cup loaf pan and chill until set.

AT SERVING TIME:

Unmold and garnish with sliced cucumbers.

Chicken Mousse BLENDER

YOU WILL NEED:

gelatine

dry vermouth

lemon juice

chicken broth

eggs

mayonnaise

Tabasco

cooked or canned chicken

cream

chopped almonds (op-

tional)

Into the container of the blender put 2 tablespoons gelatine, 2 tablespoons dry vermouth, and 1 teaspoon lemon juice. Add ½ cup hot chicken broth, cover and blend on high speed for 1 minute. Add 2 egg yolks, ½ cup mayonnaise, 5 dashes Tabasco, ¾ cup (6½ ounces) cooked or canned chicken and ¼ cup cream. Cover and blend on high speed for 3 seconds only. In a mixing bowl beat egg whites until stiff. Pour blended mixture over 2 egg whites and fold gently until mixed. Pour into a 4-cup mold and chill until set, about 1 hour. Serves six.

AT SERVING TIME:
Unmold. Sprinkle with chopped almonds. Garnish with watercress.

Chicken and Carrot Loaf Nivernaise
BLENDER

YOU WILL NEED:
gelatine
onion
boned chicken
nutmeg
tarragon
garlic powder

chicken stock or bouillon
  cubes
heavy cream
carrots
mayonnaise

Into the container of the electric blender put 1 envelope gelatine and ⅓ cup very hot water. Cover and blend on high speed for 40 seconds. Add half of very small onion, 7 ounces boned chicken or 1 cup, plus any leftover chicken meat you may have on hand, ¼ teaspoon nutmeg, ¼ teaspoon pepper, ½ teaspoon salt, ¼ teaspoon dry tarragon, ¼ teaspoon garlic powder, 2 teaspoons chicken stock base or 2 bouillon cubes, 1 cup heavy cream. Cover and blend on high speed for 10 seconds. Pour mixture into a large loaf pan and chill until set.

Into container of electric blender put 1 envelope gelatine and ⅓ cup *very* hot water. Cover and blend on high speed for 40 seconds. Add 1 pound sliced carrots, 2 tablespoons mayonnaise and ⅛ teaspoon pepper. Cover and blend on high speed for 10 seconds. Pour mixture into loaf pan over the chicken mousse and chill until set.

AT SERVING TIME:
Unmold on cold serving platter and garnish with salad greens and small cut-outs of cooked sliced carrot.

Chicken Brunswick Stew   ROASTER OVEN

A party dish—the recipe makes 40 to 50 portions.

YOU WILL NEED:

roasting chickens or hens	tomatoes
onions	okra
potatoes	Worcestershire sauce
lima beans	butter
corn	

Cut 4 roasting chickens or young hens each into pieces as for frying, season with salt and pepper and place in the inset pan of the roaster oven. Add 3 quarts of water. Cover the roaster and set temperature control at 350° F. Steam the chicken until ready to fall from the bones. Then remove bones from chicken, if desired. Add 8 medium-sized onions sliced and 12 medium-sized potatoes cut in quarters, and if fresh vegetables are being used, add 8 cups lima beans, 8 cups corn, 12 medium-sized tomatoes, 4 cups okra sliced crosswise. Cook until potatoes are tender. If canned vegetables are used, cook onions and potatoes until partially tender, then add 4 cans (No. 2) lima beans, 4 cans (No. 2) whole kernel corn, 4 cans (No. 2) tomatoes and 2 cans (No. 2) okra or 4 cups fresh okra, sliced crosswise and cook until thoroughly heated and potatoes are tender. Season to taste, with salt and pepper. Add 3 tablespoons Worcestershire sauce and 1 cup butter for additional flavor. If fresh vegetables are used, it may be necessary to add additional water, but care should be taken to maintain consistency by not adding too much liquid.

AT SERVING TIME:
Serve hot, in heated soup plates or shallow bowls, with smoking hot cornsticks or corn bread.

Chicken-in-Clay   ROASTER OVEN

As served at the Forum Restaurant in New York. Drama incarnate for your most elegant entertaining!

YOU WILL NEED:

chicken	shallot
butter	cognac
garlic	heavy-duty foil
parsley	moist, odorless modeling
chives	clay *

Place 2½- to 3-pound chicken on heavy-duty foil. Sprinkle skin and cavity of chicken with salt. Mix ½ cup softened butter with 1 clove minced or crushed garlic, a few sprigs of finely chopped parsley, a few chopped chives, 1 chopped shallot and ¼ cup cognac until creamy. (All this can be done in the blender if you put cognac in first.) Spread the seasoned butter between wing joints, leg joints, over breast bone, and in body cavity. Wrap securely in foil.

To roll the chicken in clay, pat the clay or roll it with a rolling pin into a large circle about ½ inch to ¾ inch thick. Put the

---

* Use Grumbacher's Moist Modeling Clay, No. 753. Available thoughout the country in artists' materials stores or art supply stores. About $1.00 for 5-pound can. (Allow 1 can per chicken.)

foil-wrapped bird in the center of the clay circle. Now mold the clay around the chicken so that all areas are completely covered. Preheat your oven to 500° F.—or *very* hot. This very high temperature is extremely important. Bake chicken for 80 minutes. One chicken will serve 2 generously.

AT SERVING TIME:
Serve chicken in clay on a napkin. Tap clay gently with a little mallet or hammer, peel off the foil, then carve.

Boned Indonesian Chicken Breasts   BROILER AND BLENDER

If you use quick-frozen chicken breasts they should be thawed. Then remove the bone and cut crosswise into pieces about an inch wide. If you are serving this dish as an entree, the strips should be left intact, but if you want to serve it as an hors d'oeuvre, cut the chicken meat into cubes a little less than an inch square.

YOU WILL NEED:

quick-frozen chicken breasts	coriander seeds ⎫ or curry
peanut oil	cumin seeds ⎰ powder
soy sauce	brown sugar or honey
monosodium glutamate	ginger
salt	onion or shallots

Make a marinade by placing in the blender 1 cup peanut oil, ¼ cup soy sauce, 1 teaspoon monosodium glutamate, 1 teaspoon salt, 1 teaspoon ground coriander seed, 1 teaspoon cumin seeds or you may use 1 tablespoon curry powder instead of the coriander and cumin. Add also 1 tablespoon brown sugar or honey, ¼ teaspoon ginger, 1 medium onion or 3 or 4 shallots. Blend about 30 seconds or until onion disappears. Pour marinade over the chicken breasts. Allow to stand at least 1 hour at room

temperature. Place the pieces on greased aluminum foil. Broil
4 inches away from the heat until the meat looks opaque. Count
on 1 chicken breast to serve 1 person as an entree.

AT SERVING TIME:

Serve with finely chopped nuts, almonds, peanuts, hazelnuts,
toasted Brazil nuts and another little bowl of toasted sesame
seeds. The broiled chicken is sprinkled to taste or dipped first
into the nuts and then into the sesame seeds. Thin slices of
homemade or old-fashioned type white bread make an ideal
accompaniment.

Chicken Livers Saté   BROILER

This recipe was originally intended for charcoal hibachis but I
have discovered that it can be done just as well on an electric
broiler. This makes a delightful hors d'oeuvre.

YOU WILL NEED:

chicken livers	sugar
dry sherry or vermouth	ginger (optional)
soy sauce	

Bring close to a boil but do not boil (if you use a thermostat set
it about 180°) 1 cup dry sherry or vermouth, ½ cup soy sauce,
2 tablespoons sugar—or use a sweeter sherry or vermouth and
omit sugar. Cool 5 minutes. Pour over 1 pound chicken livers
cut into small ¾-inch pieces. Allow to stand covered for about an
hour at room temperature or several hours in the refrigerator.
Place on skewers or well separated on a piece of greased aluminum foil. Brush livers with peanut oil. Broil 5 minutes or less
if need be. Liver must not be overcooked.

AT SERVING TIME:

Keep warm on preheated electric hot tray. If desired, sprinkle lightly with ginger. Spear with toothpicks or serve on Melba toast rounds.

VARIATION: Chicken livers for luncheon prepared in exactly the same way but serve with rice and a green vegetable. One pound of livers should serve 4 persons.

Broiled Chicken with Wine and Tarragon
BROILER

White wine, herbs, plenty of butter and slow cooking are the secrets of this exquisite food.

YOU WILL NEED:

broilers or fryers	fresh or dried tarragon
butter or salad oil	or rosemary
white wine	chives and parsley

Sprinkle quartered broilers or fryers with salt and pepper and rub well on all sides with butter. Arrange on well greased broiler grid, flesh side up toward the heat. Place at least a tablespoonful of butter on each piece. Broil 5 or 6 inches from the heat. This will take about 20 to 25 minutes on each side. Finish the broiling with the skin side up.

Meanwhile, prepare a basting sauce, using ¼ cup butter, ½ cup white wine, ½ teaspoon dried tarragon or rosemary and 2 tablespoons each of chopped chives and parsley. Baste the chicken as it broils with this sauce. Count on 2 broilers or fryers to serve 4 people.

AT SERVING TIME:

Garnish with bouquets of parsley or watercress.

VARIATION: CORNISH GAME HEN split for broiling can be prepared in the same way.

Chicken Poulette   SAUCEPAN

YOU WILL NEED:
   chicken fricassee, canned   lemon juice
      or homemade   nutmeg or mace
   eggs

Heat slowly in saucepan at 180° F. 4 cups of chicken fricassee
from which the bones have been removed.

Beat 2 egg yolks or one whole egg slightly and add to the egg
yolk a little of the sauce from the chicken. Stir and add 1 tablespoon lemon juice and a ¼ teaspoon mace or nutmeg. Add the
mixture to the warm chicken and keep warm at about 160° F.

AT SERVING TIME:
Serve on pieces of toast that have been buttered before toasting
or on mounds of flaky rice. Garnish with sautéed mushrooms or
drained, canned broiled-in-butter mushrooms which have been
heated. A bouquet of watercress is a fine addition. Serves six to
eight.

The King's Chicken   SKILLET

When the young King Badouin of Belgium was in New York
after a tour of the United States, we had an opportunity to
interview him on the subject of American eating. What did he
remember most vividly about his meals in the United States?

"Chicken," he answered, without a moment's hesitation.
"Chicken, chicken, everywhere."

His aides agreed that the King had been deluged with chicken
in all forms—Southern-fried, barbecued, roasted, fricasseed. His
favorite among all of them was (though we admit it does
sound almost too pat) chicken à la king that was served to him
in Texas. It seems to have been a very special à la king, for according to the description by members of his entourage, the
dish was richly gilded with egg yolks and had a lively taste of
onion and the sparkle of lemon juice.

Standard cookbooks contain many classic recipes for dishes of this type. But here is a new way to achieve a dish that is wondrously similar to the one that made the King's eyes shine.

YOU WILL NEED:

chicken à la king, canned	instant onion
or frozen	egg
mushrooms	lemon juice

Begin with a package of quick-frozen chicken à la king. Add 1 (4 oz.) tin of sliced, broiled-in-butter mushrooms complete with liquid and ½ teaspoon dehydrated instant onion. Heat at 200° F. Turn thermostat off. Wait 2 minutes.

Beat 2 egg yolks or 1 whole egg slightly with a silver fork. Add 1 teaspoon of lemon juice to the egg and beat again. Stir a couple of tablespoons of the hot sauce from the chicken into the egg. This method will prevent the egg yolks from curdling. Then add the egg to the chicken à la king and stir. Turn thermostat to 150° and heat again but never allow to boil after the egg has been added. Keep warm at 150°.

AT SERVING TIME:

Place on toast, or over rice. Or, better still, serve on flaky-hot baking powder biscuits. (Could be the ready-to-bake type.) This amount makes 2 king-size servings.

Stuffed Birds   ROTISSERIE

Although the instruction books have always insisted that one should not stuff the birds that you cook on the spit, that is not so. You can use any of your favorite stuffings but just be careful not to overstuff. If you feel the need of extra stuffing, simply place it in a shallow pan under the rotisserie where it will be beautifully flavored with the drippings. Do this during the last hour of cooking.

Cotelettes Kiev   DEEP FAT FRYER

At the Imperial Court of the Russian Czars in the past and lavish days this was a renowned chicken dish. It is still considered one of the peaks of high cuisine. Cotelettes Kiev are cutlets made by flattening breasts of chicken and inserting in the center of each a thumb of chilled butter. This is securely encased inside the meat, which is then rolled in beaten eggs and fine bread crumbs, and cooked in deep fat or oil.

If the butter roll is completely tucked in and the cooking is properly done, a little pool of golden richness will remain inside to squirt out deliciously as you cut into the cotelette.

YOU WILL NEED:

fresh or frozen chicken breasts	bread crumbs
	pepper
butter	vegetable shortening or
eggs	salad oil

To serve six you will need 3 whole breasts of chicken or 6 fresh or quick-frozen halves. If you use frozen breasts, allow them to thaw thoroughly. If you are using whole breasts, cut them in two down the center. Remove the breastbone and pound each of the six halves with a wooden mallet until very flat and thin. Cut off any little bits of gristle or straggly ends. Count on one half breast to make each cotelette.

Cut one-quarter pound stick of butter into six pieces and form into six small rolls about the size of your thumb. Chill the butter rolls for a few minutes in the freezing compartment of the refrigerator. Place each one of the little rolls in the center of the breast. Fold both sides towards the center and then roll the chicken meat around the butter, making a completely closed envelope or package.

Beat 2 eggs slightly. Roll the cotelettes in the beaten eggs and then in 1 cup of very fine toasted bread crumbs. Heat vegetable shortening or salad oil to 350° F. There should be enough oil to cover the cotelettes completely. Fry until golden brown, about 8 to 10 minutes.

Or, if you wish, you may merely brown the chicken in the hot oil first for 2 or 3 minutes and finish in a hot oven, 450° F., for about 8 minutes.

AT SERVING TIME:
Insert a small piece of bone or a small wooden skewer as a handle and decorate with a paper frill. Cotelettes Kiev are traditionally garnished with slices of lemon or orange and bouquets of water cress or parsley, and served with currant jelly.

Twentieth-Century Cotelettes Kiev
DEEP FAT FRYER

You can buy Cotelettes Kiev made from the breasts of Rock Cornish game hen, already cooked, ready to thaw and reheat either in deep fat or in a hot oven. The ready-to-heat variety generally comes in a package containing two cutlets, complete with a gold paper frill to be fastened on each of the little bones.

Specifically designed for restaurants and hotels, but sometimes available on request through your grocer or direct from the farm, are cotelettes which have not been previously cooked at all but are ready for thawing. They are packed twelve to a box, and should be treated exactly like the homemade variety.

If your own dealer looks blank and bewildered at your request for Cornish Cotelettes Kiev, you might write to Mr. Jacques Makowsky, Idlewild Farms, Pomfret, Connecticut.

YOU WILL NEED:
quick-frozen Cotelettes
  Kiev
fat for deep frying

lemon or orange slices
parsley or water cress for
  garnish

Remove the foil wrappings from the cotelettes and allow them to thaw thoroughly in the refrigerator or at room temperature, but do not allow them to become warm. If you are using the ready-cooked cotelettes, you may either heat them in a very hot oven (450° F. to 475° F.; if the oven is too cool the butter will leak out) 8 to 10 minutes, or fry them in deep fat at 350° F. about the same length of time.

Like all deep-fried foods the cotelettes should be drained on paper towels. To keep them warm, place the cotelettes on a heated platter on an electric hot tray, uncovered or *very lightly* covered, so that they will retain their crispness.

Peking Duck   ROTISSERIE

YOU WILL NEED:

duckling   onion
Hueng New Fun spices   honey

Trim any excess fat from a 4- to 5-pound ready-to-cook Long Island duckling. Rub inside and out with Hueng New Fun spices. (See recipe page 193.) Rub also inside and out with an onion cut in half, and if you like, leave the onion inside the duck. Close the cavity with skewers and twine and center it on a spit.

Cook about 2 hours. Brush with ¼ cup honey and cook for another 15 minutes at high heat or until the skin is very crisp.

AT SERVING TIME:

Place on a serving platter and with a sharp carving knife cut dark meat off the bone. Carve crisp skin into pieces about 1 inch wide and 2 inches long. Arrange attractively on a small heated platter and garnish with 3-inch lengths of spring onions and perhaps a dozen onions.

Meats

Use of Meat Tenderizers

Meat tenderizers make news not only to the budgetwise but also to the epicure, because they make it possible to prepare more parts of the finest beef by quick cooking methods. For example, prime beef comprises only about eleven per cent of the beef available and a good proportion of the steaks, the roast and the fillet go to top restaurants. Nevertheless, the rump and the round, the shoulder and the chuck have the same flavor, and when properly tenderized, they provide delicious broiled and roasted meat.

It is important to use the right amount of tenderizer, to apply it properly and to let it stand the right length of time at the right temperature.

As a general rule use the same amount of tenderizer as you would use table salt, about one-half to three-fourths teaspoon per pound of meat. When you use tenderizer do not use salt.

For meats up to one inch thick, pierce with a sharp fork, sprinkle with tenderizer on all sides, allow to stand 30 to 40 minutes at room temperature or overnight or longer in the refrigerator. You have to be careful only when you use room temperatures for the action is very slow in the refrigerator and it stops completely in the freezer.

For thicker meats, roasts of all types, pierce in the same way. Sprinkle with tenderizer in the same way and allow to stand for one hour at room temperature or overnight in the refrigerator or put it in the freezer if you like.

The meat tenderizers have other virtues also. They cut shrinkage and reduce cooking time by about twenty-five per cent.

To Broil Frozen Meats

Test tastes have shown that frozen meats cooked without pre-thawing have more flavor and are juicier. Also there is good evidence that more of the nutritive values are retained. This is particularly true of beef.

Once again you may use your regular method merely increasing the cooking time: (In cooking frozen meats there is only one way to judge when they are cooked—use a thermometer.)

130° F.	Beef very rare
140° F.	Beef rare
160° F.	Beef well done
165° F.	Lamb (continental style)
170° F.	Veal
180° F.	Lamb well done
190° F.	Pork
200° F.	Poultry

We all know that there is no quicker way to ruin a thermometer than to expose it to direct heat. So you simply use your meat thermometer as you would use a clinical thermometer. Wait until the end of the usual cooking period. Insert the thermometer into a small incision. Be sure it gets into the center and then "take the temperature" allowing the thermometer to stay in place for just about a minute or two. Remove the thermometer and continue cooking.

General Directions for Steak

Most steak lovers like thick steaks. For broiling, steaks should be cut at least 1½ inches thick and preferably 2 to 2½ inches thick. Do not look for a steak that has only a very little fat on it, for fat is necessary for good quality. Allow your butcher to trim away all the excess fat however and score the edges deeply so that the steak will lie nice and flat.

Preheat the broiler. Grease the rack very well with oil or suet. Place the steak on the rack and put the rack at least 3 inches away from the heat. For a steak that is 2 inches thick, cook about 3 minutes on the first side, turn and cook about 6 minutes on the second side. Turn again and finish for another 3 or 4 minutes. This meat will be very rare indeed. It may be too rare to suit you. To test for doneness without a thermometer, make a small cut with a sharp knife near the bone and judge for yourself.

AT SERVING TIME:
Sprinkle both sides with salt and freshly ground black pepper. Add a good size pat of butter, if desired. Place on a sizzling hot platter on the hot tray. Cut in diagonal slices and place on toasty hot plates or on warmed or lightly toasted, buttered French or rye bread.

To Broil a Steak

This is a subject as wide as the world or at least as broad as America. Everybody has their own idea about what to broil and how to broil. So we will confine ourselves here to the most general directions.

If you have time, you may massage your steak on all sides including the fat with dry mustard and olive oil. The mustard does not give a mustardy taste but lends a delightful savor and a crispness. The olive oil does fine things too. Generally I do not salt or pepper the steak before it goes to the broiler but prefer to season each side after it is done.

A great many people like to rub their steaks with a cut clove of garlic or sprinkle it with garlic salt. I happen to think that garlic interferes with the taste of beef, but this is personal.

The best of steaks are well aged, well marbled or flecked with fat. The fat should be firm and flaky, cream colored or whitish rather than yellow. Good fresh beef, which is what many people prefer, is bright red in color. Well aged beef, the choice of connoisseurs, has the look of a glass of fine old Burgundy. The preferred steaks for broiling include the porterhouse, sirloin, rib steaks, especially those cut from the first three ribs, shell steaks, T-bone steaks and the filet mignon. The fillet is the tenderest part of the tenderloin of beef. It is in fact so tender that for some people it seems to lack character. If you're buying fillets for several people, it is often wiser to buy it in a whole piece and then cut into individual steaks anywhere from 1 to 1½ inches thick.

Less expensive cuts of meat are often tenderized and broiled exactly like other steaks.

Broiled Chuck or Round Steak   BROILER

Survey after survey shows that steak is America's favorite meat. Yet the finest steaks are so expensive that they cannot be served as often as most of us would like. With the use of modern meat tenderizers you can broil the less expensive cuts of beef.

The meat should be cut about 2 to 3 inches thick from top or bottom round, sirloin tip, heel of round, boneless blade or arm chuck or rump. It should weigh approximately 3 to 3½ pounds boneless, or approximately 3½ to 4 pounds with the bone in. This amount will make sufficient servings for 4 to 6 persons.

YOU WILL NEED:

chuck, round, rump, boneless blade or sirloin tip steak	meat tenderizer, seasoned or unseasoned

Before cooking, slash the fat edges of the meat. Sprinkle all surfaces with meat tenderizer. You may use either the seasoned or the unseasoned tenderizer. Either take the place of salt. The seasoned tenderizer also carries the flavor of garlic and has some paprika and herbs. Pierce all sides of the meat deeply at about 1-inch intervals with a sharp, sturdy fork. Allow the meat to stand at room temperature about 1 hour uncovered or in the refrigerator covered loosely overnight.

Broil 4 to 6 inches from the source of heat. Cook 13 minutes per side for rare, or 15 minutes per side for medium.

AT SERVING TIME:
Cut in thin diagonal slices across the grain at approximately a 30-degree angle. Three or more slices will make a generous portion.

Steak Maxim   SKILLET

When the Vaudables, Louis and Maggie, owners of Maxim's in Paris, came to dinner at our place in New York, Louis insisted that he would cook the steak. This steak was a very thick, well-aged sirloin. He insisted upon a frying pan rather than the broiler and on salt before cooking. "It is not true," he said, "that salt draws out the juices, as you Americans say. On the contrary it makes the meat crisp."

YOU WILL NEED:

steak	butter
cracked peppercorns (see page 194)	Armagnac or American whiskey

To serve 6 or 8, you should have a sirloin steak at least 2 inches thick, weighing about 6 pounds. Cut off most of the fat, massage steak with a little softened butter on both sides. Press coarsely cracked black peppercorns into the meat, patting it so that it sticks. If possible allow to stand at room temperature for an hour, so that the flavor permeates.

Preheat automatic skillet to 380° F. When the red light goes off, rub skillet lightly with a bit of the steak fat, salt the meat lightly and sear first on one side, then on the other. Turn the meat and hold it so that the fat is brown too. Turn heat down to 325° F. and cook 25 minutes altogether, about 15 minutes on one side, 10 on the other. If you are not ready to eat at this point, simply turn the heat down to 180° F. All of this is done uncovered. A cover would make it steamy.

AT SERVING TIME:
Remove steak to a heated platter, scrape all the little brown bits off the bottom of the skillet. Strain fat or not, as you please. (Louis Vaudable did, we don't—we like bits in our sauce). Return juices to the skillet and add an equal quantity Armagnac (or you could use American whiskey), a small piece of butter. Heat at 275° until butter browns slightly. This is your sauce. Carve steak in thin strips and pour sauce over each portion.

VARIATION: *STEAK FLAMBE*   Proceed as above but omit the peppercorns and bring the steak and the skillet to the table. Set the thermostat at 200° F. Pour on ½ cup Armagnac or bourbon. When the red light goes off, set the liquor ablaze with a match and allow the fire to blaze for a minute or two. Cover the pan for a moment in order to put out the blaze and then proceed to carve as above. Generally you will not feel the need of having extra butter.

Family Steak au Poivre   SKILLET

This is an economical version of Steak Maxim (page 137).
    Today it is possible, through the use of a powdered meat tenderizer, to achieve an extraordinarily fine steak *au poivre* using chuck steak or round steak. The meat should be cut about 2 to 3 inches thick from the top or bottom round. Or you could use the less expensive tip of the sirloin. Or ask for the heel of the round or boneless blade or arm chuck (some call it shoulder chuck) or a rump steak. Such a steak should weigh approximately 3 to 3½ pounds if it is boneless meat—about ½ pound more if there is a bone in it, and this should be enough to serve 4 to 6 persons.
    Before cooking, slash the edge of the fat, sprinkle all surfaces with meat tenderizer using about as much tenderizer as you

would salt. But do not add salt. Pierce all sides deeply at about 1-inch intervals with a sharp kitchen fork so that the tenderizer will penetrate. Allow meat to stand uncovered at room temperature about an hour. Or cover loosely and allow to stand in the refrigerator about 8 hours.

After tenderizing the meat may be cooked like any other steak.

YOU WILL NEED:

2- to 3-inch steak	butter
coarsely crushed black peppercorns	Armagnac, cognac or whiskey

You may use the cracked black pepper that comes already to use in jars but never use powdered black pepper. It will be very bitter. Or you can crack your own peppercorns in the blender (see page 194). Do not use the powdery bits. Strain them out. Unless the steak is very much marbled, massage it with soft butter or olive oil. Then press in the coarsely crushed black pepper covering all the surfaces. You will need at least 2 or 3 tablespoons pepper, maybe more. Heat electric skillet to 380°. Add 1 tablespoon butter. Sear steak quickly, first on one side, then on the other, and then sear the fat side too by holding it against the hot surface. Turn thermostat to 325° and allow to cook uncovered 20 to 25 minutes. No further turning is necessary.

AT SERVING TIME:

Remove steak to heated platter and keep warm on hot tray. Scrape any bits off the bottom of the pan and put with the juices in a strainer. Then return to the skillet, add a couple of tablespoons of butter and 3 or 4 tablespoons of Armagnac, cognac or bourbon whiskey. Heat together and serve this sauce over the steak. Cut in thin diagonal slices about ½ inch thick across the grain at about 33° angle. You will need at least 3 or 4 slices per portion.

VARIATION: *STEAK AU POIVRE FLAMBE* Instead of adding the brandy or whiskey to the sauce you may warm ½ cup of whatever spirit you choose, to about 100° F.—not anywhere close to boiling. This can be done very easily on the hot tray in a small silver or copper cup or pan. Set a match to the warm liquor and pour flaming over the meat.

Steak Diane   SKILLET

At the Quo Vadis Restaurant in New York and many other places of astronomical prices and gastronomical fame, Steak Diane is a specialty. Use very thinly sliced sirloin steak. A dramatic dish to prepare at the table! This recipe serves four.

YOU WILL NEED:

very thinly sliced sirloin	
steak	mustard
butter	freshly ground pepper
onion	Worcestershire sauce
parsley	cognac

Have on hand 2 pounds of sirloin steak cut only about ¼ to ½ inch thick. Preheat electric skillet to 380° F. or even 400° F., and when the light goes off, place in the pan 1 tablespoon butter and brown the steaks one at a time very quickly. Transfer to a hot platter on a hot tray. Place in the skillet 2 more tablespoons butter, add ¼ cup onion finely chopped. Cook only about a minute until the onion becomes slightly tender. Add ¼ cup finely chopped parsley, 1 teaspoon prepared mustard, ½ teaspoon freshly ground black pepper, 1 tablespoon Worcestershire sauce. Stir and allow to heat. Return the steaks to the pan, dipping each in the sauce, being sure that each one is well-coated with sauce.

Slightly warm ¼ cup cognac in a silver or copper saucepan or ramekin. Set fire to the cognac with a match and pour the spirit over the steaks in the skillet.

AT SERVING TIME:

The whole operation actually occurs at serving time, but at the very moment of serving the steaks should be aflame.

VARIATION: *ECONOMICAL STEAK DIANE*   Use chuck or round steak instead of sirloin. Sprinkle with meat tenderizer, using ½ teaspoon to a pound of meat. Allow to stand at room temperature about 30 minutes. Proceed as above.

California Sukiyaki   SKILLET

The tenderizer keeps the meat wonderfully juicy and prevents shrivelling.

YOU WILL NEED:

boneless top or bottom round	mushrooms
meat tenderizer	yam noodles
beef suet or peanut oil	pimiento
bamboo shoots	sugar
green pepper	beef bouillon
green onions	sake or dry wine
celery	soy sauce

Sprinkle 2 pounds boneless top or bottom round that have been cut in thin slices about ⅛ inch thick with meat tenderizer. Use it as you would salt. Do not add salt. Work tenderizer in deeply by piercing the meat through with a sharp kitchen fork. Let stand at room temperature 30 minutes or cover loosely and refrigerate overnight.

Set electric skillet at high, about 400° F. Heat ⅛ pound suet or 1½ tablespoons peanut oil. Brown meat quickly about 1 minute on each side. Do not overcook.

Reduce heat to medium, about 350° F. Push meat to center of skillet. In a circle around meat arrange 2 cups thinly sliced bamboo shoots, 1 large green pepper seeded and cut in strips, 1 large bunch green onions cut in 2-inch lengths, 6 stalks celery cut in ½ inch diagonal slices, ½ pound fresh mushrooms sliced, 1

8-ounce can yam noodles, 1 4-ounce pimiento sliced. Sprinkle with 2 tablespoons sugar. Add 1 cup beef bouillon, 3 tablespoons sake or dry white wine and ¾ cup soy sauce. Simmer about 5 minutes.

AT SERVING TIME:
Ladle from skillet. Serve with rice.

Teriyaki-Steak Sticks   BROILER

This delicious Oriental dish is often made with the costliest cuts of tenderloin. But this recipe uses round steak with delicious results because meat tenderizer insures the tenderness, juiciness and full flavor of the menu.

YOU WILL NEED:
   top or bottom round   meat tenderizer

   For teriyaki sauce: honey
   (makes about 3 cups)   garlic cloves
   soy sauce   ginger root (optional)
   sweet sake or sweet
     Italian vermouth

Slice beef across the grain in ¼-inch slices. Each strip will be 2 inches wide and 4 to 5 inches long, depending on individual steak. Sprinkle both sides of each strip evenly with meat tenderizer as you would salt; do not salt. Work tenderizer in by piercing strips clear through with a sharp fork.

To make teriyaki sauce, combine 1 cup soy sauce, ¾ cup water, ½ cup sweet sake or sweet Italian vermouth, ¾ cup honey, 4 large garlic cloves crushed, and if you have it 1 one-inch fresh ginger root grated or slivered.

Place steak strips in a deep bowl. Cover completely with sauce. Refrigerate until needed (may be prepared in advance and refrigerated overnight).

AT SERVING TIME:

Remove steak sticks from sauce. Lace steaks on metal or bamboo skewers, broil for a total of about 3 minutes, turning once. The beef should be rare. This makes about 24 sticks.

(Pour any remaining teriyaki sauce into a jar with a tight-fitting lid and refrigerate for later use. You will find this sauce equally delicious for other beef dishes, as a glaze for roast or barbecued lamb, for broiled or roast chicken, and for sea food. Fresh ingredients may be added to increase the quantity.)

Flaming London Broil   SKILLET

Traditionally a London Broil, that famous and exciting English recipe, is made from flank steak, which used to be inexpensive. Now that so many people have learned about London Broil, the price of flank steak has sky-rocketed, so we use round steak instead, and a meat tenderizer. This again is a dish that can be prepared with drama at the table.

YOU WILL NEED:

round steak cut 1 inch thick
meat tenderizer
canned sliced broiled-in-butter mushrooms
rich beef stock or condensed consommé undiluted
cognac or bourbon whiskey

To serve four, use about 2 pounds of round steak which should be cut about 1 inch thick. Sprinkle both sides of the steak evenly with meat tenderizer, seasoned or unseasoned as you prefer. Use the tenderizer as you would salt. Do not add salt. Work the tenderizer deeply into the meat with a sharp kitchen fork to insure penetration and seal in the juices. Let stand at room temperature 1 hour, uncovered, or cover loosely and refrigerate overnight.

Preheat electric skillet to about 380° F. and pan broil the meat about 5 minutes on each side. Remove the steak to a sizzling hot platter or your electric hot tray. Add to the drippings in the skillet 1 3-ounce can of sliced broiled-in-butter mushrooms with its own liquid and 1 cup very rich beef stock or condensed undiluted consommé. Stir and heat.

AT SERVING TIME:

Put the steaks back into the skillet or pour the sauce over the steaks on the hot platter, whichever you prefer. Slightly warm ½ cup cognac or bourbon whiskey in a tiny saucepan or ramekin. Set a match to the spirit and pour flaming over the meat. Immediately slice the steak diagonally in very thin slices across the grain.

Syrian Stuffed Grape Leaves   SKILLET

This is a very special recipe of a very special friend, Ruth Rigler, who has adapted it from the recipe of one of her forebears. It has been in use in her family for many generations. And right now, on the buffet supper tables of California hostesses, it is having an exciting renaissance. It is particularly well adapted to present-day living because it can be cooked two or three days ahead of time and refrigerated until needed, or it can be put into the freezer where it will retain its full glory for 1 to 3 months.

YOU WILL NEED:

large onion	meat tenderizer
salad oil	(optional)
ground beef, chuck or	preserved grape leaves
round	tomato purée
eggs	tomato paste
slice of bread	lemon
pine nuts	ginger
seedless white raisins	allspice
garlic	sugar

Mince or grate 1 large onion and in an electric skillet, at 370° F., heat 2 tablespoons salad oil and brown the onion.

Combine 2 pounds chopped beef, chuck or round, with 2 eggs, 1 slice of white bread moistened, ½ cup pine nuts, ½ cup water, 1 clove garlic put through the press and ½ teaspoon meat tenderizer. The use of the tenderizer is optional, of course. For some strange reason which I cannot explain, it does seem to keep the meat juicy and reduces shrinkage.

Wash 1 pound of preserved grape leaves to remove the salt or use wilted leaves from your own vines. You have only to dip them into hot water.

Wrap about 1 rounded teaspoon of meat mixture in each grape leaf, roll up securely, place on top of browned onions in the skillet. Add 2 cups tomato purée, 1 6-ounce can tomato paste and the same amount of water, 3 tablespoons lemon juice, ¼ teaspoon ginger, ¼ teaspoon allspice, 2 tablespoons sugar and 1 cup seedless white raisins.

Cover tightly and simmer at 190° F., about 1 hour.

AT SERVING TIME:
Serve warm with rice or pilaf as part of a main course, or serve chilled as an appetizer. Makes 6 servings as a main course. About twice as many for an appetizer.

Russian Bitki   GRIDDLE

This is a classic and quite superior way to use chopped beef.

YOU WILL NEED:

milk	salt
egg	pepper
onion	hamburger meat
white or rye bread	butter

Place in the blender ½ cup milk, 1 egg, 1 small onion cut in pieces, 1 slice white or rye bread broken into pieces, ½ teaspoon salt, ¼ teaspoon pepper. Blend until smooth. Add to mixture one pound chopped round steak or other good hamburger meat and form into 6 patties. Set griddle to 375° F. When light goes off, melt 2 tablespoons butter and brown Bitki on both sides.

AT SERVING TIME:
Serve with potatoes or rice or on hamburger rolls with Russian Scallions (page 182).

Broiled Hamburgers

Even better than charcoal, in the opinion of many experts, is the open electric broiler. The burgers are arranged on a mesh or grid so that fat drains away and the meat does not stew or sauté. Hamburgers should be broiled at least 3 inches below the surface of heat. Slow cooking keeps them juicy.

Frozen Hamburgers on the Griddle   GRIDDLE

Several brands of quick-frozen hamburgers and cheeseburgers are available conveniently packaged. Most of them are exceedingly thin patties and are best cooked on a hot griddle (380° to 400° F.) *for a few seconds.* The problem here is to avoid overcooking and to serve immediately.

As for good thick home-size patties, these you probably have to form yourself and then freeze. Make 3 or 4 patties out of a pound of the best chopped beef, using 20% fat. Place 2 or 3 sheets of waxed paper between patties so they won't stick together.

Cook on a heated griddle or at medium heat, about 350° F. It is best to turn only once during the broiling. Season each side after cooking and before turning.

Beef Stroganoff   SLICER

YOU WILL NEED:

fillet of beef	mushrooms
onion	nutmeg
butter	sour cream

Fillet should be cut in ½-inch slices. Pound 2 pounds of fillet with wooden mallet or potato masher to make very thin and cut in neat finger-shaped pieces. Melt 2 tablespoons butter, add ½ tablespoon minced onion and cook and stir until onion is yellow. Add beef. Cook quickly about 5 minutes, turning the pieces to brown on all sides; set aside. Slice just the caps from ½ pound mushrooms and sauté in remaining butter. Season with salt and a few grains of nutmeg and add to beef.

AT SERVING TIME:

Add ½ pint sour cream, heat and season delicately to taste. Serves 6. Steamed wild rice is excellent as a border of this dish.

Roast Beef au Poivre   ROTISSERIE

There is a strange superstition encouraged, we must admit, by the manufacturers' booklets that roasts must be boned for the rotisserie. This is not true. They must not be too big, not too long, nor too heavy for the motor to turn and they must be properly balanced on the spit. A three- or even a four-rib roast can be beautifully cooked in the rotisserie. It is best, however, that the short ribs at the end be removed (use them to make braised short ribs of beef).

YOU WILL NEED:

3 or 4 rib roast	cracked peppercorns
butter or olive oil	Kitchen Bouquet
(optional)	(optional)

Massage meat with butter or olive oil, press freshly ground black peppercorns into all the surfaces. Allow to stand at room temperature one hour if possible. Place on skewer so that the skewer runs parallel with the bones. For rare (which is the only way roasts should be) cook about 12 minutes to a pound. For a very dark crisp rich brown crust, brush meat before cooking with Kitchen Bouquet. Allow roast to stand. Remove from spit and allow to stand in the rotisserie, set at 200° F. for ½ hour. This makes it easier to carve.

AT SERVING TIME:

Slice meat as thin as possible down to the bone. The bones too may be served like spare ribs, a wonderful tidbit. Serve with pan gravy flavored with Armagnac brandy or bourbon whiskey. Yorkshire pudding is the perfect accompaniment. (See page 243.)

Stews from Frozen Meat

Your pressure cooker is a great boon when you are making stews, goulash or braised dishes from frozen meats. It's fast and sure. Brown meat in the oven or on top of the stove. Place in the pressure cooker along with seasonings and other ingredients called for in your recipe. Then adjust the cover and heat until the steam begins to rise—a thin, steady line. At this point you may be sure that your meat is completely thawed through. There's no guesswork here.

Proceed to finish the job according to the manufacturer's directions. Cooking time varies from dish to dish, from one pressure cooker to another. As a general rule, however, we feel that most recipes we've tried require too much cooking and result in stringy meat. Better bring the pressure down immediately by setting the cooker in cold water instead of allowing the pressure to go down naturally. Then if more cooking is necessary, it can be done at 200° F.

The World's Easiest Stew PRESSURE COOKER

In the freezer and on the shelf the ingredients for making this stew can be kept always on hand. This has been a life-saver to us, when we go to the country on winter weekends.

YOU WILL NEED:

beef stew meat, frozen   dehydrated onion soup
or fresh

Heat your pressure cooker to 300° F. When the light goes off, add 1 tablespoon shortening and brown 2 packages or 2 pounds of beef cut into cubes for stew. The meat need not be thawed. The browning will take longer if meat is frozen, of course, but what you desire will be swiftly accomplished. Keep turning and moving the meat around so that all the surfaces are exposed to the heat.

When meat is brown add the contents of 1 package of dehydrated onion soup mix. This supplies not only the necessary onions but all the seasoning necessary. Now add 1 to 2 cups of water, depending upon the size of the pan. Cover and cook under pressure according to manufacturer's directions 15 minutes. Bring pressure down immediately by letting cold water run down the side. Remove top and replace so that a little air gets into the stew. Set thermostat to simmer, about 190° F. and allow to cook at least half an hour longer or if possible allow to stand for as many hours as practical. The meat will not dry out, the liquid will not boil away and the stew will take on the most melting quality.

AT SERVING TIME:

Serve with boiled potatoes, rice, corn meal mush, barley or any desired starchy vegetable. This makes 4 to 6 servings.

VARIATION: *BEEF STEW WITH CARROTS* After removing stew from pressure cooker add 1 cup carrots cut into ½-inch chunks, and cook until carrots are tender or as much longer as you like. Quartered potatoes may be added to the stew along with the carrots, or better still, cook them separately.

Boiled Beef   PRESSURE COOKER

Either the front or straight cut of brisket is suitable for boiled beef, though some experts favor the fattier front portion as being more flavorful. The leaner straight cut, which yields more edible meat per pound, is the more expensive.

But important as the cut is proper cooking. The name "boiled beef" is misleading because the meat should never be "boiled." But strangely enough it can be done in a pressure cooker. It demands gentle simmering.

Viennese Boiled Beef   PRESSURE COOKER

Duels, they say, have been fought over the proper cut, the proper method, for preparing this aristocratic version of boiled beef. The baked onion, we are told, is the key to perfection. The recipe makes 8 servings.

YOU WILL NEED:

beef brisket	allspice
feet, neck, backs, wings	celery
of a chicken	parsley
carrots	bayleaf
onions	peppercorns

Put into the pressure cooker 4 cups cold water, 3 carrots cut in large pieces, 2 peeled halved onions, 6 stalks celery sliced horizontally, 1 tablespoon salt, 4 sprigs parsley, 1 bayleaf, 6 whole peppercorns, 4 whole allspice, 2 pounds chicken parts— the feet, necks, backs, wings. Cook under pressure 30 minutes.

Meanwhile bake a large unpeeled onion 30 minutes.

Strain the chicken vegetable stock over 4 pounds of brisket of beef, add the baked onion, peel and all. Cook under pressure 15 minutes. If not quite tender enough, simmer covered at about 200° F. till tender but not cooked to pieces.

AT SERVING TIME:
Serve with coarse salt, gherkins and boiled potatoes.

Beef Stew   PRESSURE COOKER

Long slow cooking develops the fine flavor of a perfect beef stew. Particularly a good company or busy-day dish, since it can be prepared in advance—either in the morning or the day before— since reheating improves it. When making this stew you should count on a quarter to half pound of lean meat per person.

YOU WILL NEED:
chuck, round or rump	Worcestershire sauce,
flour	thyme, chopped parsley
onion	(optional)

At the butcher shop, have all gristle and most of the fat cut off meat (chuck, round, rump) but save the fat and use some of it to brown the meat. Also you can cook a piece of the cracked bone with the meat for good flavor, removing it before serving.

Have 4 pounds of meat cut in 1½-inch cubes. Sprinkle with salt and pepper and roll in flour. Melt some of the fat from the meat in a pressure cooker and brown meat cubes till they take on a rich dark color. For added flavor, cook a slice or two of onion with the meat. Cover with boiling water and cook 20 minutes at 15 lbs. pressure. The amount of water to use depends on the amount of gravy you want. For two pounds of meat, the usual amount is 1 quart. If the gravy is not as thick as you like it, mix 2 tablespoons flour (for about 2 cups of gravy) with ¼ cup

water until it is smooth (or shake it in a swirl mixer), stir it into
stew, bring to boil and cook 3 minutes.

Season to taste with salt and pepper and add your choice of
seasonings: thyme, Worcestershire, chopped parsley.

AT SERVING TIME:
A good combination is rice, noodles or dumplings.

VARIATION: After cooking stew 15 minutes, add for each serving
2 small whole carrots or 1 large carrot, sliced or cubed, and 3 tiny
onions. Add 2 small whole potatoes. Add also peas, whole green
beans or mushrooms. Bring up pressure again and cook 5 minutes.

VARIATION: Tomato sauce or red wine may be substituted for
half of the hot water. These, too, should be heated.

Hungarian Beef Goulash   PRESSURE COOKER

This recipe with some slight personal variations of my own was
invented by Ann Williams Heller. It is the prize-winning recipe
which changed my whole attitude toward the pressure cooker.

YOU WILL NEED:

beef for stew	caraway seeds
lard or fat	marjoram
flour	bayleaves
condensed onion soup	parsley sprigs
sweet Hungarian paprika	capers
vinegar	sherry (optional)

In a paper bag with ½ cup flour shake 2 pounds stewing beef
which has been cut into cubes 1 or 1½ inches. The meat should
be evenly covered with flour. Brown the meat well in 1 tablespoon
lard or cooking fat, turning occasionally. You can do this in the
pressure cooker at about 380°. Add 1 can condensed onion soup
or 1 package dehydrated onion soup and 2 cups water, 1 table-

spoon Hungarian paprika, 1 tablespoon vinegar, 1 tablespoon caraway seeds, 1 teaspoon marjoram, 1 teaspoon capers, 2 bay-leaves, 2 sprigs parsley, ¼ cup dry sherry wine if you want it. Cook under 15-pound pressure 15 minutes for 1-inch cubes or 20 minutes for 1½-inch cubes. Bring down pressure immediately and allow to simmer very gently at 180 to 200° until meltingly tender or as long as you please.

AT SERVING TIME:
Serve with broad noodles or boiled potatoes. This recipe serves six.

Swiss Steak   PRESSURE COOKER

Have beef, rump, round or chuck cut about 1 inch thick at your butcher's and you will have the makings of a delightful Swiss steak.

YOU WILL NEED:

beef (rump, round or chuck)
flour
tomatoes, stewed or canned

green peppers, onions or mushrooms (optional)

Season the beef (rump, round or chuck) with salt and pepper and sprinkle with flour, using about 3 tablespoons to each pound of meat. In pressure cooker, which has been greased thoroughly with suet or other fat, brown the meat well on both sides. Add stewed or canned tomatoes (1 cup for each pound of meat). Cook under pressure 15 minutes. Bring down pressure. Thicken gravy if necessary.

This recipe can be delightfully varied by adding minced green peppers, sliced onions or mushrooms.

AT SERVING TIME:
Serve with the fluffiest of boiled or mashed potatoes.

Hashburgers de Luxe   GRIDDLE

A change from hamburgers.

YOU WILL NEED:

corned beef hash   hamburger buns

Open a can of corned beef hash at both ends and push out the meat in a single roll. Cut into 4 thick slices. Brown on both sides. Serve each hashburger on a toasted, halved hamburger bun.

AT SERVING TIME:

Surround with heated canned French fried onions. Serve with a snappy relish.

Corned Beef and Cabbage

PRESSURE COOKER

Some corned beef requires soaking, some doesn't. Ask the man who sells it to you. If it needs soaking, an hour or maybe a little more should be sufficient. The corned beef that comes packed in a plastic bag with a liquid surrounding it is usually ready-to-cook without soaking. If you want to slice the beef for sandwiches, you can tie it with string to keep it in shape.

YOU WILL NEED:

corned beef brisket   carrots
bay leaf   celery flakes or stalk
peppercorns   of celery
onions   cabbage
cloves

To make 6 or 8 servings, use about 4 pounds of corned beef brisket. Place the meat in the pressure cooker, add 2 cups cold water, ½ bay leaf, 4 peppercorns, 1 small onion cut in pieces, 3 whole cloves, 1 carrot cut in slices, 1 teaspoon of celery flakes or a small stalk of celery cut into pieces. Adjust cover. Set thermostat to 400° until steam comes up steadily. Cook at 15 pounds pressure for 1 hour. Reduce pressure immediately by letting cold water run down the side. When pressure is completely down, remove cover, add 6 small onions, 6 small carrots cut crosswise in half, 1 small head of cabbage cut into 6 or 8 wedges. Cook uncovered 10 to 15 minutes longer, until cabbage is tender.

AT SERVING TIME:
Serve the beef on a platter surrounded by vegetables. A little melted butter with or without chopped parsley may be poured over the vegetables. Have on hand a pot of sharp mustard and/or horseradish sauce.

Kentucky Burgoo ROASTER OVEN

Food for a throng—about fifty servings.

YOU WILL NEED:

pork shank	whole corn, fresh or
veal shank	canned
beef shank	red pepper
breast of lamb	okra, frozen or fresh
hen	lima beans
potatoes	celery
onions	Tabasco
carrots	A-1 Sauce
green peppers	Worcestershire sauce
cabbage	cayenne
canned tomato sauce	parsley

Put 2 pounds pork shank, 2 pounds veal shank, 2 pounds beef shank, 2 pounds breast of lamb and 1 4-pound hen into 8 quarts of cold water in electric roaster oven, setting temperature at

350° F. and bring slowly to a boil. Turn down temperature to simmer, and simmer until meat is tender. Pare 6 Irish potatoes and 6 onions and dice, also 6 carrots cut in thick slices, 2 green peppers diced, 2 cups shredded cabbage, 4 cans tomato sauce, 2 cups whole corn, fresh or canned, 2 pods red pepper, 2 cups okra sliced, frozen or fresh, 2 cups lima beans, 1 cup diced celery. Allow to simmer at 275° F. until thickened but still a little soupy. Season with Tabasco, A-1 Sauce, Worcestershire sauce, salt and cayenne. Stir frequently.

AT SERVING TIME:
Add chopped parsley just before serving and dish up into bowls.

Veal Kidneys Flambé   SKILLET

Excellent with rice or hominy grits or cornmeal mush.

YOU WILL NEED:

veal kidneys	brandy
mushrooms	cream
shallots	dry mustard
butter	

In the kitchen beforehand remove fat and membrane from 3 veal kidneys and cut in slices crosswise. Put ½ cup sliced fresh mushrooms and 1 tablespoon chopped shallots in a bowl.

AT SERVING TIME:
At the table melt 3 tablespoons butter in electric skillet set at about 350°. Sauté kidneys, mushrooms and shallots for 5 or 6 minutes, or until kidneys no longer look red. Add ⅓ cup brandy and ignite. When the fire burns out add ¾ cup cream, ½ teaspoon dry mustard, salt and pepper. Mix well and serve as soon as dish is thoroughly hot.

A *Glorious Meat Loaf*   PORTABLE OVEN

YOU WILL NEED:

fresh pork	milk
beef	eggs
bread crumbs	slices of bacon (optional)
onion	

Grind 2 pounds of fresh pork and 2 pounds beef fine. Add 1 cup bread crumbs, 1 small onion, chopped, 1 cup milk, 1 tablespoon salt, ⅛ teaspoon pepper, 3 eggs slightly beaten. Shape into a loaf, put in loaf pan, and if desired, place strips of bacon along the top of the meat loaf. Bake 1½ hours at 400° F. Baste every 10 minutes with 2 tablespoons liquid, using hot water until enough juices have accumulated in the pan.

AT SERVING TIME:

Serve with gravy enriched with plenty of chopped and sautéed or drained, canned, browned-in-butter mushrooms.

Spring Lamb on a Spit   ROTISSERIE

If you have an enormous rotisserie you could use a whole baby lamb, if you could get a small enough lamb. But a leg of lamb, a baron, a rack or even a series of chops could be roasted in this fashion.

YOU WILL NEED:

lamb	olive oil
lemon	orégano, rosemary, thyme
garlic	(optional)

Rub the meat all over with the cut lemon and rub the peel side over the meat too. Cut cloves of garlic and rub those into the meat and then massage with olive oil. Sprinkle with salt, pepper and herbs, using orégano, rosemary or thyme or a mixture of all three. If you are roasting a leg of lamb, ignore the usual directions and do not have the bone removed. Simply put the spit parallel with the bone and make sure that the meat is nicely balanced. Cook about 15 minutes to the pound or until the meat thermometer registers about 160° for rare or pink, and 180° F. for well done. Baste every now and then with a sauce made by adding about ¼ cup of lemon juice to the drippings in the pan. If you need a little extra liquid for basting, add some olive oil too.

In Tuscany they use a long thick branch of orégano or rosemary to do the basting.

AT SERVING TIME:
Circle the lamb with a garland of parsley or watercress. And if it is spring, or you feel like spring, stud the garland with tiny flowers.

Baron of Lamb   ROTISSERIE

The saddle and the two legs of a very young lamb may be called the baron—a cut highly prized in the lush era when Ward McAllister was choosing the Four Hundred and Newport was in full flower.

In France they will tell you that the best barons come from the lambs of Pauillac, but we think that those of Bucks County, Pennsylvania, are pretty fine too. Even a small baron should provide about 16 portions.

YOU WILL NEED:
baron of lamb	herbs to your liking
lemon	salt and pepper

Rub meat well with lemon, salt and pepper and herbs. Although many a great baron has been roasted in an oven, grilling on a spit seems to produce a finer, juicier meat and a crisper, more interesting skin. When placing the lamb on the rotisserie make certain that it is perfectly balanced upon the spit and securely fastened with prongs so that it does not flop around. Cook and baste like any other cut.

AT SERVING TIME:
Classic accompaniments to the baron are pyramids of cauliflowerettes or bundles of broccoli, lightly cooked, well drained and masked with Hollandaise or Bearnaise sauce. Watercress is perfect and a risotto au gras is often served (see page 186).

Grilled Rack of Lamb   ROTISSERIE

The next time you are about to order lamb chops for four or six, why not have instead an impressive rack of lamb, the same chops but all in one piece, not separated. Here again the butcher should remove the chine (chef's word for backbone) and cut the mat away from the bones as in the crown. Protect the bones from burning by wrapping them in aluminum foil and roast in the oven at 325° F. or grill on a spit. It is a fallacy to believe that meats need to be boned in order to go on the spit. After all, in the rotisserie you cook a chicken or turkey complete with bones.

Be sure that the meat is properly balanced on the spit so that it cooks evenly on all sides.

YOU WILL NEED:
rack of lamb	lemon juice
garlic clove or half a	dry white wine, very dry
lemon	sherry or Solera
olive oil	

Season the rack by rubbing it well with a cut clove of garlic or half a lemon and baste occasionally with the drippings to which you should add a couple of tablespoons of olive oil, a tablespoon of lemon juice and a half cup of dry white wine, very dry sherry or Solera.

Roast in roaster oven at 325° F. or on a spit in the rotisserie.

AT SERVING TIME:
Classic accompaniments for a rack of lamb are Dauphine potatoes and buttered carrots, heavily parsleyed. An excellent way to come by Dauphine potatoes: Use frozen potato puffs, heat according to package directions and sprinkle lightly with nutmeg.

Rack of Lamb   PORTABLE OVEN

A rack of lamb is nothing more than a series of lamb chops that have not been cut apart. Provide 2 chops per person.

YOU WILL NEED:
lamb   shallots
parsley   bread crumbs
butter

Roast rack of lamb ½ hour at 180° F. Prepare paste of ¼ cup chopped parsley, ¼ cup butter, 3 chopped shallots, and ¼ cup fine bread crumbs. Put a layer of paste on top of the lamb and brown under a broiler.

AT SERVING TIME:
Serve with broiled tomatoes, string beans, and rissole potatoes.

Broiled English Cutlets   BROILER

Often you will hear these referred to as English lamb chops. They are made by cutting across the entire width of an unsplit loin. This cut is usually about 2 inches thick. The rib bones are removed and a lamb kidney inserted between the two chops, and held in place by wrapping the thin flank ends of the chop around the kidney and fastening with a metal skewer to form a compact round shape.

YOU WILL NEED:
English lamb chops
lamb kidneys
skewers

Kitchen Bouquet (optional)

Broil like any other lamb chop, and if you like a caramelized charcoal flavor without using charcoal, brush the chops, fore, aft and around, with Kitchen Bouquet. For medium to well done chops, cook 10 to 20 minutes on each side.

AT SERVING TIME:
Serve with rice pilaf or baked potato.

Noisettes of Lamb   SKILLET

Literally translated the noisette means the nut, the kernel, the heart, the very best part. In a lamb the noisette is comparable to the filet mignon in beef.

YOU WILL NEED:
noisettes of lamb
butter
toasted rounds of bread
(optional)

mushroom caps
(optional)

Usually this boned lamb fillet is removed in one strip and sliced 1½ to 2 inches thick. Noisettes may be sautéed quickly in butter, pan broiled or grilled. Since they have very little fat, sautéeing is perhaps the best method. Sautée at 350° F. in butter and place on rounds of bread which have been toasted and buttered, or better still, browned on both sides in foaming butter.

AT SERVING TIME:

Top with large grilled or sautéed mushroom caps. Serve with Duchesse potatoes formed into cups and filled with new peas cooked Parisian style with a leaf of lettuce and tiny white onions or shallots.

Lamb Cutlets in Jackets   SLICER

Another version of the ubiquitous chop in a different guise, often served in Paris.

YOU WILL NEED:

lamb cutlets or chops	egg
butter	canned consommé
mushrooms	meatless spaghetti sauce
pie pastry	red wine or brandy (op-
cooked ham sliced wisp-	tional)
thin on the slicer	

Sauté 6 lamb cutlets or lamb chops in butter on both sides until they are cooked but not brown or crisp. Let them cool. Drain a 6-ounce tin of chopped broiled mushrooms and heat in butter. Set these aside too. Make up a package of pie pastry according to directions. Use slicer to cut 12 very, very thin slices of ham.

Cut circles of pie pastry large enough to enclose each chop comfortably. Place in the center of each circle a teaspoon of mushrooms, then a paper-thin round of cooked ham, then the lamb chop, another slice of ham on top. Cover the whole thing with dough, allowing the bone to stick out. Press edges together by wetting them with a little water, place on baking sheet, brush the tops with slightly beaten egg and bake at 425° F. for 20 minutes. One package of mix makes jackets for six chops.

AT SERVING TIME:
Serve with a light tomato sauce made by using equal parts of undiluted canned consommé and a meatless spaghetti sauce. A spoonful of red wine or brandy picks up the flavor miraculously.

Lamb Shish Kabob   BROILER

YOU WILL NEED:

leg of lamb or shoulder of lamb
meat tenderizer (optional)
tomatoes

mushroom caps
green peppers
sliced bacon

For marinade:
red wine
onions
bayleaf
garlic
parsley
olive oil

For sauce:
caraway seeds
butter
cayenne pepper
brandy
onion
parsley
sour cream

Have 4 pounds leg of lamb or boneless shoulder of lamb cut into 1½-inch cubes. Sprinkle with meat tenderizer as you would salt; do not add salt. Work in deeply by piercing all over with sharp kitchen fork.

For marinade: Combine 2 cups red wine, ½ teaspoon freshly ground pepper, 2 medium-sized onions grated, 1 bayleaf crumbled, 1 small clove garlic minced or pressed, 1 tablespoon chopped parsley and 6 tablespoons olive oil. Pour marinade over lamb cubes. Stir so that each lamb cube is well coated with marinade. Marinate in the refrigerator overnight.

When ready to cook, remove meat cubes from marinade and place on skewers alternately with tomatoes, mushroom caps, peppers and bacon . . . using 3 firm tomatoes quartered, 6 mushroom caps, 3 small green peppers seeded and quartered and 4 slices bacon cut in thirds.

In a saucepan combine 1 teaspoon caraway seeds, ½ cup butter, dash salt, dash freshly ground pepper, dash cayenne pepper, ½ cup brandy, 2 tablespoons finely chopped onion and 2 tablespoons chopped parsley. Cook for about 5 minutes, stirring constantly. Remove from heat. Add marinade to sauce; then whip in 1 cup sour cream. Roll filled skewers thoroughly in sauce. Broil skewers 15 to 20 minutes, brushing frequently with sauce. They are done when the meat is richly browned on the edges.

AT SERVING TIME:
Pour the sauce over the shish kabob. This recipe makes 6 servings.

Lamb on Skewers, Grecian Style   ROTISSERIE

Many long centuries ago when brave Achilles turned the spit and Petrocles roasted onions in the fire, meat was cut into collops and speared upon skewers or sometimes swords. So the bivouac fires of warriors in the field gave rise to the shish kebab of the Near East, the shaslik of Russia and the Greek souvlakia, the simplest and most ingeniously flavored of them all.

The Greeks use no vinegar or wine for they believe that these acids alter the true lamb taste. Sometimes lemon juice is sprinkled over the meat at the table.

YOU WILL NEED:

lamb leg or shoulder	tomatoes
onion	bayleaves
olive oil	orégano
parsley	lemon juice (optional)
salt and pepper	

To serve 4 to 6, cut 2 pounds of meat from leg or shoulder of lamb into pieces the size of a large walnut. Place in a bowl half of a small onion chopped fine, 1 tablespoon olive oil, 2 tablespoons chopped parsley, 2 teaspoons salt, ½ teaspoon pepper; mix thoroughly. Dip meat into this mixture and roll around until well covered. Cut 2 solid tomatoes into quarters and the quarters into halves, place 5 to 6 pieces of meat on each skewer, alternating with tomatoes and bayleaves. Tomatoes should be pierced through the skin side so that they will not fall off. Broil about 10 minutes, turning often, and sprinkle with chopped orégano.

The bayleaves will probably begin to glow around the edges, imparting a glorious flavor to the meat far more delicate than you get when you marinate the meat for several hours with the bayleaves as the Russians do.

AT SERVING TIME:
Souvlakia is generally served with a tossed salad, rice pilaf and yogurt often flavored with fresh chopped mint or dill.

Lamb Dolmades PRESSURE COOKER

The origin of this recipe is Greek, but many variations are to be found in the foods of Turkey and Syria. In fact, as far back as Biblical times, people probably used grape leaves (or a loose leaf variety of cabbage known at that time) in cooking their leftover bits of meat and grain. You can use cabbage leaves, too, in place of the grape leaves.

YOU WILL NEED:
ground lamb
onions
cooked rice
dried mint or parsley
rosemary

grape leaves, canned
or fresh
tomatoes, sliced
consommé or bouillon

Mix lightly 1 pound ground lamb, 1 cup cooked rice, 2 medium-sized onions finely chopped, 1 tablespoon dried mint or parsley,

¼ teaspoon rosemary, 1 teaspoon salt, ½ teaspoon pepper. Place a little of the meat mixture on each leaf, fold in the sides of each leaf and roll. Arrange rolls in a buttered 10- or 11-inch frying pan or pressure cooker. Top with tomato slices, add water and about half of 1 can (10½ ounce) consommé or bouillon. Cover and cook at 325° F. for about 45 minutes (or 15 minutes in pressure cooker). Add the other half can consommé, a little at a time, every 15 minutes; or cook without extra consommé 15 minutes in the pressure cooker. Makes 5 to 6 servings.

AT SERVING TIME:
Serve on platter and garnish with sliced lemon cut into fancy shapes.

Crown Roast of Pork   ROASTER OVEN

One of the most impressive and I might as well say it—most expensive roasts you can serve is a crown roast of pork. Crown roast has been almost forgotten in our chain-store age, and in a small town you may have some difficulty finding a butcher who can trim one for you. In that case, you can do it yourself.

YOU WILL NEED:
crown roast of pork   chestnut stuffing
  (2 loins of pork from   honey
  rib end)   Kitchen Bouquet

To make a crown roast of pork yourself, simply order two loins of pork from the rib end, equal in height and size. Have the backbone removed. You should have at least 12 chops in a crown. Provide 2 ribs for each person. Tie the loins together and secure with skewers. With poultry scissors cut the skin around the bone into neat scallops. Protect the ends of the bones from burning by twisting a bit of aluminum foil on each one.

    Mound chestnut stuffing into the hollow center of the crown. Roast like any other pork in a shallow open roasting pan in a slow oven, 300° to 325° F., 30 to 35 minutes per pound or until the meat thermometer registers 185° F., which is well done. Line roaster oven with foil. Set crown on foil.

To give your crown a beautiful ruddy glaze, brush, one half hour before it is finished, with ½ cup honey combined with 1 tablespoon Kitchen Bouquet.

AT SERVING TIME:
Remove aluminum foil from bones and replace foil with paper frills, which may be bought at fancy food department. Or you can make them yourself with strips of gold or silver foil snipped at the edges.

Glaze for Roast Pork   BLENDER

Gives a beautifully rich red glow to pork and an exquisite flavor.

YOU WILL NEED:
   green ginger or garlic   honey
   soy sauce

Place a few slices of green ginger or a couple of cloves of garlic with a half cup of soy sauce, half cup of honey and half cup of hot water into the blender for a few seconds. Use the sauce to baste roasting pork or chops.

Line your roasting pan with aluminum foil for this sauce can be very difficult to remove from the pan after the pork has been cooked.

Szekely Gulasch   PRESSURE COOKER

This is a Hungarian specialty which has been enthusiastically adopted in Viennese gastronomic circles. Generally the sour cream is stirred into the gulasch before serving, but here we suggest passing the sour cream separately, so that the dish can be kept in the refrigerator or the freezer, and reheated at will, without danger of curdling. Makes 6 servings.

YOU WILL NEED:

onions	sauerkraut
lard or other fat	sour cream
paprika	caraway seeds
pork	chopped chives

Slice 2 large onions and sauté in 2 tablespoons hot lard or other fat until soft and golden. Sprinkle with two tablespoons sweet Hungarian paprika and 1 tablespoon salt. Add 2 pounds pork shoulder meat, cut into inch squares. Brown with onions for a few minutes. Add 1 large (27-ounce can) sauerkraut and 2 cups hot water. Cook under pressure 15 minutes. If not quite tender, allow to cook at 200°. Keep warm at 180°.

AT SERVING TIME:

Stir in 1 cup sour cream or present a bowl of sour cream turned pink by adding 1 teaspoon paprika. Pass also caraway seeds and chopped chives, so that those who want them may sprinkle them over their gulasch. Fluffy boiled potatoes, dill pickles and sour rye bread are traditional accompaniments.

VARIATION: *GULASCH OF SPARERIBS*   Spareribs cut into serving pieces may be used instead of cubed pork. You will need about 3 pounds for six generous servings.

Whole Ham Baked in Foil   PORTABLE OVEN

In most present-day households, the complications, equipment and space required for preparing a whole ham are formidable. Buying it is one answer but often you cannot buy an old-fashioned ham ready-cooked. This method is so easy that anybody anywhere can do it. And you don't need that big wash boiler any more. Heavy duty aluminum freezer foil is the secret.

YOU WILL NEED:

country ham   fine bread crumbs or
bourbon (optional)   coarse water-ground
dark brown sugar   corn meal

Scrub the ham and soak in water overnight, or longer if very salty. Place a large piece of aluminum foil in a large pan. Place the ham on the foil and pour over it 2½ cups of water, ½ cup bourbon, 2 cups brown sugar. Wrap ham in foil. Place in a very slow oven, 250° to 275° F. Forget it for five or six hours. When it feels tender to the fork, when the bones protrude a little and the rind lifts off easily, your ham is done. Unless you want to use it immediately, the ham is generally left to cool in its wrappings. Then the rind is removed.

Sprinkle ham with fine bread crumbs or coarse water-ground corn meal, mixed half and half with old-fashioned dark brown sugar, patting the mixture well over the top. Brown at 375° to 400° F. until the sugar is bubbly and a crust forms. If you want to anoint the meat with a most exquisite aromatic flavor, baste from time to time with a little bourbon.

AT SERVING TIME:

Such a ham should never be served hot, nor should it be stone cold, but "at proper room temperature, like a great Burgundy wine." The slices should be always paper thin. Serve with hot baking powder biscuits or beaten biscuits.

Decorating Hams

Of all viands the ham is probably the most decorated, but generally with an astounding lack of imagination. Pineapple slices and maraschino cherries deserve a long rest. Instead you might try fresh or canned sliced peaches, or apricot halves or sweet pickles, or watermelon rind cut into designs, or lemon or orange slices or tangerine sections, or canned mandarin oranges from Japan held in place with toothpicks. A cold ham may be covered with an aspic flavored with white wine or champagne, or sherry or port or Madeira or bourbon, if you like.

Baked Virginia Ham   ROASTER OVEN

The traditional and preferred method of dealing with an aged, old-style Virginia ham breaks down into four steps: soak, scrub, simmer, bake.

Cover the ham with cold water and let it stand overnight. Hams that are more than 18 months old will require at least 24 hours of soaking, or if very hard and salty, maybe even more. Forty to 48 hours are not at all unusual.

Scrub with a vegetable brush to remove all traces of mold, for even a bit of it may ruin the flavor of the whole ham. Use plenty of lukewarm water.

Simmer at 300°; don't ever boil. Place the ham skin-down in a deep pan on a rack. Cover with water. Many people cook their hams with claret, burgundy, sauterne, and sometimes even champagne is added. Occasionally someone will sacrifice a bottle of bourbon. Bring the liquid to the boiling point and then immediately cut back the heat so that it is barely simmering. Do not boil, for even a few minutes of boiling will make the ham tough and thready.

Cooking time varies, depending upon the age and character of the ham. A 1-year-old ham will probably require 15 to 20 minutes per pound. An older ham might take 30 minutes. There is only one way to tell when the ham is cooked enough. The flat bone at the butt end will separate from the meat. When this happens, turn off the heat and let the ham cool in its own liquid for several hours or even overnight.

When the ham is cool and drained, loosen the skin at the butt end and peel it off carefully to avoid tearing the fat. Test the thickness of the fat at the edges and trim off any fat that seems to you excessive.

In baking, place the ham fat side up on a rack in a baking pan or broiler pan. Cover the fat side with brown sugar and stick with cloves or, even more interestingly, with cassia buds, placing them about an inch apart. Bake in a roaster oven 400° F. for about 15 minutes.

Blue Grass Ham   ROASTER OVEN

YOU WILL NEED:

country ham

vinegar

cloves

brown sugar

egg yolks

bread crumbs or cracker
  crumbs

wine, ginger ale or beer
  (optional)

Scrub ham thoroughly. Then cover with cold water, soak overnight in the roaster. Pour off this water. Cover again with fresh water—add ½ cup vinegar and about 8 to 10 cloves. Simmer about 20 minutes per pound at 250° F. Let cool in water. Remove skin—score. Make paste of brown sugar, a little powdered cloves and 2 egg yolks. Rub on top of ham. Sprinkle with grated bread crumbs or fine cracker crumbs and pepper.

Return to roaster and bake slowly at 325° F. for 1 hour. You may baste with wine, ginger ale or beer if you wish, but it is not necessary.

AT SERVING TIME:

Bring to the table neither hot nor cold but just warm. Slice wafer thin. Serve with hot baking powder biscuits or beaten biscuits or spoon bread.

Quick Ham Croustades   BROILER

A delicious dish which could be put together from materials kept on hand.

YOU WILL NEED:

brioche or clover-leaf buns	mushrooms
butter	milk
deviled ham	lemon juice
cream of mushroom soup	lemon rind
	nutmeg

Cut tops from 6 brioche or clover-leaf buns. Hollow out and brush with melted butter. Toast lightly under the broiler.

Simmer together small (4-ounce) can deviled ham, 1 can condensed cream of mushroom soup, 1 6-ounce can whole mushrooms with liquid, ¼ cup milk, 1 tablespoon lemon juice, ½ teaspoon grated lemon rind, few grains pepper and nutmeg.

AT SERVING TIME:

Keep toasted rolls and sauced mushrooms hot on electric tray. Fill 6 rolls; replace tops.

Jellied Ham Loaf   BLENDER

YOU WILL NEED:

cooked ham	celery
gelatine	onion
lemon	tomato juice
pepper	

Dice 1 pound cooked ham sliced ¼ inch thick and grind by blending ½ cup at a time on high speed for 5 seconds. Empty into a mixing bowl. Into container of blender put 1 envelope gelatine and ½ cup very hot water. Cover and blend on high speed for 40 seconds only. Add juice of ½ lemon, ¼ teaspoon pepper, 1 cup coarsely cut celery (2 large stalks), ½ green pepper, seeded and sliced, and 1 thinly sliced medium onion. Cover and blend for 4 seconds only. Pour mixture over ham. Add 1 cup tomato juice and mix thoroughly. Pour into a 4-cup loaf pan and refrigerate for several hours or overnight.

AT SERVING TIME:
Unmold on a bed of romaine leaves and garnish with sliced tomatoes.

VARIATION: Pour into ring mold and chill until set. Unmold on bed of romaine leaves and fill center with tiny canned peas (petit pois) and mayonnaise.

Jellied Ham Mousse

ICE CRUSHER
AND BLENDER

For a buffet supper nothing could be more dramatic than this ham mousse piled into a hollowed cabbage, with the leaves spread out all around. Prettiest of all would be the dark green curly Savoy cabbage, which you can often find in the supermarkets or in the Italian shops. In the fall red cabbage is not too difficult to get. Incredibly beautiful with the pink mousse! Use the inside of the cabbage to make cole slaw.

YOU WILL NEED:

gelatine	eggs
onion	Worcestershire sauce
celery	crushed ice
cooked ham	cream
prepared mustard	

Put ½ cup hot water into the blender with 2 envelopes un-flavored gelatine. Cover and blend 40 seconds. Add a quarter of a small onion cut in pieces, 1 stalk celery and leaves broken up, 1 cup cubed cooked ham, 2 egg yolks or 1 whole egg. Cover and blend 5 seconds. Add 1 teaspoon Worcestershire sauce, 1 teaspoon prepared mustard. Blend 5 minutes longer. With motor on remove cover; add 1 cup finely crushed ice, 1 cup cream. Continue to blend for 40 seconds or until mousse begins to thicken. Serve immediately or mold.

AT SERVING TIME:
Garnish with pimiento stuffed olives, hard-cooked eggs and watercress.

Mousse of Ham and Chicken Livers
BLENDER

To serve on lettuce as an appetizer with crackers or as an hors d'oeuvre or as an accompaniment to a salad.

YOU WILL NEED:
cooked ham	black truffles or mush-
chicken or duck livers	rooms
whipped butter	whipped cream

This involves no cooking except sautéeing a few chicken livers. Or you can buy some chopped liver at a delicatessen.

Blend 2 pounds of diced cooked ham, a cupful or two at a time, in the blender. Sauté a pound of chicken or duck livers in a little butter until they are lightly done (3 to 6 minutes). Cool, then blend these also—about a cup at a time.

Mix the ground ham and the chopped livers, stir in ½ pound whipped butter. Add some not too finely chopped tinned black truffles. Quantity determined by your extravagance. Or you can use some peeled, chopped raw or canned mushrooms instead. Add salt and pepper. Fold in 2 cups of firm whipped cream. Pour into a mold and set in refrigerator.

AT SERVING TIME:
Serve in the mold, garnish with chopped parsley, or unmold it
and decorate with slices of black truffles. Serves twelve.

Barbecued Canadian Bacon   ROTISSERIE

A delightful adjunct to a breakfast or supper party is Canadian
bacon grilled on a spit. Canned Canadian bacon may be used.

YOU WILL NEED:
slab of Canadian bacon   barbecue sauce (optional)

Place on the skewer a 4-pound piece of Canadian bacon and cook
with the setting at 350° F. for 1 to 1½ hours. You may baste, if
you like, with any favorite barbecue sauce.

AT SERVING TIME:
Remove from skewer and cut into slices ¼-inch thick. This
is a fine dish for a large party. A 4-pound piece should serve 10
to 12 people.

Vegetables

Artichokes

Artichokes are one vegetable that take most kindly to pressure cooking. Choose smooth dark green, tightly closed heads that are not too big. Wash them carefully. Cut the stem close to the leaves. If the tops are dry and prickly, cut them down with scissors or a long sharp knife on a carving board. Actually, if the artichokes are fresh and not too mature, there is no reason why you should have to do anything more than wash and remove part of the stems.

With pressure cooking, tieing is unnecessary. The artichokes will keep their shape.

YOU WILL NEED:
    artichokes   butter
    lemon juice or vinegar

Place artichokes in the pressure cooker along with 1 cup water, 2 tablespoons lemon juice or vinegar, ½ teaspoon salt. Cook 10 minutes at 15 pounds pressure. Reduce pressure immediately. Test the artichokes for doneness by pulling off a leaf and seeing if it is tender. Count on one medium-sized artichoke for each serving.

AT SERVING TIME:
Serve hot with melted butter, flavored if you like with lemon juice and parsley or with Hollandaise sauce, Bearnaise sauce or Sauce Vinagrette.

VARIATION: *ITALIAN ARTICHOKES* Instead of lemon juice in the above recipe, use 2 tablespoons olive oil in the water, 1 clove garlic, a sprig of parsley, and serve the liquid from the pressure cooker as a sauce, removing garlic and parsley.

Asparagus Duet Amandine BLENDER

Most practical and sophisticated is this combination entree. The less tender pieces of asparagus are used to make a soufflé, which is served as a kind of counterpoint with the tender tips.

YOU WILL NEED:

asparagus	egg whites
milk	Gruyère cheese
butter	onion salt
flour	white and cayenne pepper
egg yolks	

For Sauce Amandine:

lemon juice	almonds

Cut up the bottoms of the stalks, discarding only the woody pieces. Cook until tender in boiling, salted water. You should have about 2 cups. Put into blender along with 1 cup milk, 3 tablespoons butter, 4 tablespoons flour, 5 egg yolks, 2 ounces Gruyère cheese, ½ teaspoon onion salt, ½ teaspoon salt, ¼ teaspoon white pepper, a few grains of cayenne pepper. Cover. Blend about 15 minutes. Pour into saucepan. Bring to boil over moderate heat stirring constantly. Gently fold hot vegetable mixture into 5 egg whites (stiffly beaten with a rotary beater). Bake in an ungreased soufflé dish or casserole, filling it about ⅞ full, at 375° F., 40 minutes or until set. Serve at once.

AT SERVING TIME:

Pass lightly cooked asparagus tips along with the soufflé. And in a separate bowl—Amandine Sauce—made in seconds nowadays by browning ever so slightly in 4 tablespoons butter, 4 tablespoons canned slivered almonds. Add 1 tablespoon lemon juice. This recipe makes 6 main course servings.

Baked Sliced Beets   SLICER

An extraordinarily good vegetable dish to serve for a company meal. Makes 8 servings.

YOU WILL NEED:

beets	butter
sugar	lemon juice
nutmeg	onion

Slice 16 medium-sized beets. Grease a 7-inch baking dish. Place the beets in layers. Season them with 2 tablespoons sugar, ¾ teaspoon salt, ¼ teaspoon nutmeg. Dot them with 3 tablespoons butter and add 1 tablespoon lemon juice, ⅓ cup water and 1 grated or sliced onion. Cover the dish closely and bake the beets in a hot oven 400° F. for 30 minutes or until they are tender. Stir them twice.

AT SERVING TIME:
Sprinkle with chopped parsley, chives or chervil.

Cole Slaw   SLICER

Served in a large hollow cabbage, cole slaw can make a most dramatic adjunct to the buffet table. In the garden or at the roadside stand, find a large red cabbage, complete with leaves, or a Savoy type bright green cabbage or a common or garden variety cabbage with leaves. Lay it face down into a sink of cold water and swish it around to remove the sand. If it seems a little limp, allow it to remain in the water for an hour.

YOU WILL NEED:
red cabbage, Savoy or garden variety with leaves

old-fashioned cooked salad dressing (see page 201) or equal parts mayonnaise and sour cream

To make the shell, cut around the top of the cabbage with a sharp, sturdy knife, leaving a rim about ¾-inch thick. Then cut the center part into quarters, loosen at the bottom and remove the quartered cabbage, then cut out the core. Place each quarter on the platform and slice in very thin strips. Mix with special old-fashioned cooked salad dressing (see page 201) or equal parts mayonnaise and sour cream.

AT SERVING TIME:
Place slaw in the cabbage shell, sprinkle with fresh chopped parsley, chives, or dill, celery or caraway seeds may be used. Since there is some waste involved in making the shell, you should choose a rather large head of cabbage to make 6 or 8 servings.

Fresh flowers make a charming garnish for a cabbage shell—pink roses, for instance, or pink zinnias tucked in among the purply leaves, or bright yellow or red garden flowers for a green or green and white cabbage.

Carrots Vichy   SLICER

This is a vegetable dish that you will serve at your proudest little dinners. Don't be surprised if your guests ask for 2 or 3 helpings.

YOU WILL NEED:
carrots   butter
nutmeg

Slice 6 good-sized carrots or 12 small carrots lengthwise. Pour water into skillet or saucepan ¼ inch deep. Add carrots, ½ teaspoon salt, ¼ teaspoon pepper, ¼ teaspoon nutmeg and 3 table-spoons butter. Cover tightly and heat at 350° F. until the water boils, then turn down the heat to 250° F. and cook 10 minutes.

AT SERVING TIME:
Sprinkle chopped parsley over the carrots. Serves 6.

Cauliflower with Sauce Aurore   BLENDER

YOU WILL NEED:
cauliflower, cooked

For Sauce Aurore:
mayonnaise
fresh tomato pulp

Arrange on a big dish either one enormous or several small heads of cold, cooked cauliflower, very firm and whole. Mask with Sauce Aurore.

For Sauce Aurore: To 2 cups homemade mayonnaise add about ½-cup fresh tomato pulp, just enough to tint it and give it a rather tart flavor. Chill.

AT SERVING TIME:
Give the masked cauliflowers a discreet dusting with paprika and see that they are very cold. They will look handsome and do service as a vegetable as well as a salad.

Grilled Vegetables   BROILER

Excellent for broiling are halved or thickly sliced tomatoes, sliced eggplant with or without the peel, thickly sliced potatoes and wedges or thick slices of zucchini or carrots.

YOU WILL NEED:
fresh or parboiled
vegetables

salad oil or butter

Brush the vegetables with salad oil or melted butter and salt and pepper. Broil until tender and lightly brown.

AT SERVING TIME:
Serve piping hot and if desired, sprinkle with appropriate herbs. Try finely chopped basil or orégano on the tomatoes, parsley or chives on the potatoes, chopped mint on the carrots.

Escarole with Pine Nuts   SKILLET

Something different in the way of a vegetable is not too easy to come by. This one has great distinction—a classical Italian background.

YOU WILL NEED:

escarole	capers
olive oil	raisins
garlic	Italian black olives
pine nuts	

To serve six, use 6 bunches of escarole, about 2 pounds, and cut in pieces about 2 inches long, using both the outside and inside leaves.

Measure 4 tablespoons olive oil into the skillet. Heat to 350°. Add 1 large clove of garlic which has been put through the press, ⅓ cup pine nuts, ¼ cup capers, ⅓ cup raisins, about a dozen Italian black olives which have been pitted. Cook 2 minutes. Add the escarole which has been cut up in 2 inch pieces, washed and well drained. Turn thermostat to 275° and cook covered about 15 minutes or until just tender. Keep warm at 180°. Add 1 teaspoon salt and ½ teaspoon black pepper, or more if needed.

AT SERVING TIME:
Chopped black olives and extra capers are often passed along with this vegetable.

VARIATION: *SPINACH WITH PINE NUTS*   Instead of escarole in the above recipe, you may substitute frozen leaf spinach.
Use 2 (12-ounce) packages to serve six. Cook spinach according to
package directions. Drain carefully and proceed as above.

Russian Scallions   SLICER

This is the perfect accompaniment to serve with a broiled lamb
chop, or try it with Russian Bitki. On the slicer you can do a
whole bunch of scallions at one time.

YOU WILL NEED:
    green onions and tops   sugar
    vinegar

Cut the onions into half-inch pieces. Mix 1 cup apple cider
vinegar with 1 teaspoon sugar, ¼ teaspoon salt, and ¼ teaspoon
pepper.

AT SERVING TIME:
Pour vinegar dressing on onions. Generous servings for 6 to 8.

Pommes de Terre Soufflés   SLICER

Pommes soufflés are the most glorified of fried potatoes, all puffed
up, nothing but air in the center like crisp gilded little pillows.
The most glamorous of cocktail accompaniments and perfect to
serve with a filet mignon, broiled chicken, or as an adjunct to
fried fish.

YOU WILL NEED:
    potatoes   corn or peanut oil

Pare and cut 8 baking potatoes into ⅛-inch slices on your slicer. Soak in ice water 5 to 30 minutes. Remove from water, dry thoroughly. Heat corn or peanut oil to 225° F. Drop the potato slices a few at a time. Cook until blistered and just beginning to show a fine line of gold around edge. Remove from fat. Drain.

Raise temperature of oil to 425° F. Replace potato slices. They will begin to puff immediately—or not at all. Keep turning them so that they brown evenly. Don't be upset if every slice doesn't puff. If three-fourths or even half of them do, that's good. (Unpuffed slices make good eating too.) Drain on brown paper or paper towels.

AT SERVING TIME:

Serve immediately or return for a few seconds to the frying kettle 425° to 450° to heat and crisp. Sprinkle with salt.

Pommes de Terre au Gruyère   SLICER

This is another molded baked sliced potato dish which is usually inverted on a heated plate and served hot cut into wedges.

YOU WILL NEED:

potatoes   butter
Swiss cheese

Peel and slice thinly 6 medium potatoes and arrange them in a buttered baking dish. Cover each layer of potatoes with thin slices of Swiss cheese and season with salt and pepper. Sprinkle the whole with 3 tablespoons of melted butter, cover the dish and bake in a hot oven (400° F.) for about 40 minutes until the potatoes are cooked through.

AT SERVING TIME:

Invert the baking dish on a heated serving platter and serve hot. Serves 6.

Scalloped Potatoes   SLICER

YOU WILL NEED:
potatoes   milk
butter

With your slicer, slice 4 potatoes in ¼ inch slices. Put layer of potatoes in buttered baking dish, sprinkle with salt and pepper and dot over with 1½ teaspoons of butter; repeat. Add milk until it may be seen through top layer. Bake 1¼ hours in moderate oven (350° F.) or until potato is soft.

AT SERVING TIME:
Serve hot. Serves 4 to 6.

VARIATION: An interesting variation of scalloped potatoes also uses the slicer. Slice an onion in thin slices and place with potatoes in layers in the baking dish.

Pommes de Terre Anna   SLICER

This is a classic and very beautiful potato dish. When sufficiently cooked until the bottom and the top are crisp and brown, the whole thing can be turned out on a plate like a huge flower with gold brown petals.

YOU WILL NEED:
potatoes   butter

Peel and trim 6 uniform potatoes to form cylinders of equal size and shape. Slice the cylinders into thin rounds. Butter a small round baking dish and line it with slices of potato in circles that overlap first in one direction and then in the other, to make an attractive pattern. Spread each layer with softened butter, using ½ cup in all, and sprinkle each layer with salt and pepper.

Bake in a hot oven (400° F.) for about 40 minutes until the potatoes are cooked through. Drain off the excess butter and invert the dish on a serving platter to unmold it. Serves 6.

AT SERVING TIME:
Cut into 6 or 8 pie-shaped wedges and serve.

Rotisserie Potatoes ROTISSERIE

Small whole potatoes, peeled or unpeeled, or larger potatoes cut in halves or quarters are delicious when parboiled for five to ten minutes, drained, and placed in the dripping pan to catch the juices. Cook under the meat at least 1 hour. Turn once during the cooking period. The longer the cooking time the browner and crustier the potatoes will get. One large or two small potatoes will be necessary for each serving.

VARIATION: Sweet potatoes, either parboiled or canned, may be used; but in that case the cooking time must be shortened by half.

Potato Pancakes BLENDER

Deliciously hearty for late breakfast or to serve as an accompaniment to meats.

YOU WILL NEED:

eggs	parsley clusters
onion	potatoes
salt	flour

Place 2 eggs, 1 sliced onion, 1 teaspoon salt, ¼ cup parsley clusters and 1 cup diced raw potatoes into blender. Turn on high, remove cover and add ¼ cup flour and 1 more cup diced raw potatoes. Do not overblend. Pour onto hot greased griddle and cook until brown on both sides. Makes 8 small cakes.

AT SERVING TIME:
Serve hot with bacon or ham and warm applesauce or as an accompaniment to pot roast or sauerbraten.

French Fried Sweet Potatoes

DEEP FAT FRYER

YOU WILL NEED:
sweet potatoes

Cook medium-size sweet potatoes in boiling, salted water 5 minutes. Drain, peel and cut lengthwise into ½-inch sticks about 3 inches long. Fry 2 or 3 minutes at 385° F. Drain on paper towels, sprinkle liberally with salt—preferably coarse salt crystals. Do not fill the fry basket over half full.

AT SERVING TIME:
Delicious with chicken, ham or pork.

Risotto au Gras

SAUCEPAN

Delightful to serve with lamb chops or a baron of lamb.

YOU WILL NEED:
rice
butter

consommé or chicken broth

Lightly brown 1 cup of rice in 3 tablespoons butter. Add 2 cups hot rich consommé or chicken broth. Undiluted condensed consommé or broth may be used. Cover and cook over low heat about 225° twenty minutes.

AT SERVING TIME:
Fluff with a fork.

Spinach Soufflé PORTABLE OVEN

At the Four Seasons Restaurant in New York they serve an extraordinarily fresh-tasting and delicious spinach soufflé. Here is a quick adaptation which tastes remarkably similar and it is made from quick-frozen chopped spinach and cream of chicken soup.

YOU WILL NEED:
quick-frozen chopped spinach
cream of chicken soup
eggs, separated
onion
nutmeg (optional)

Cook for only 1 minute a package of chopped quick-frozen spinach. Drain and place in the blender with 1 can condensed cream of chicken soup, 5 egg yolks and ¼ of a very small onion cut into a couple of pieces. Blend 1 minute. Fold in lightly 5 stiffly beaten egg whites. Pour into a buttered straight-sided soufflé dish about 8 inches in diameter. The dish should be filled about ⅞ full so that the soufflé will rise well above the dish. Bake at 400° F. about 30 minutes or, if you prefer a firmer soufflé, set in a pan of hot water and bake at 325° F. about 45 minutes.

AT SERVING TIME:
Serve immediately and pass around sour cream, which can be used as a garnishing sauce. This amount should serve 6 persons as a vegetable course. If you serve it as a main luncheon dish, it will be sufficient for 4 persons.

Spinach with Sesame Dressing   BLENDER

If possible, use fresh spinach. Quick-frozen spinach may be used but the dish is not as authentic or dramatic.

YOU WILL NEED:
spinach with roots   soy sauce
sesame seeds

Boil 1 pound spinach (washed with roots intact) in very little water for 3 minutes, keeping roots together.

Heat 3 tablespoons black or white sesame seeds in a skillet at 375° until they begin to brown and pop. Grind in your blender. Add 2 tablespoons soy sauce and blend 30 seconds.

Press excess water out of cooked spinach.

AT SERVING TIME:
Top cooked spinach with sesame dressing and serve in small individual bowls. Makes 5 or 6 servings.

Chrysanthemum Turnips   SLICER

Beauty borrowed from the Japanese.

YOU WILL NEED:
small turnips or white   sugar
radishes   pale dry sherry
vinegar   sweet red pepper

Peel 6 small turnips or large round white radishes and cut them halfway through lengthwise and crosswise. Sprinkle with salt, and when they become soft, soak in a mixture of 4 tablespoons vinegar, 1 tablespoon sugar and 2 tablespoons pale dry sherry for about an hour.

AT SERVING TIME:

Chop up one sweet red pepper, place two or three pieces in the center of the turnip and you have an edible and charming decoration for your fish dish.

Soufflé de Tomates à la Napolitaine

PORTABLE OVEN

A Neapolitan-style tomato soufflé, according to Escoffier, calls for a reduced tomato purée, a very stiff béchamel sauce, a "litter of freshly cooked macaroni" and grated Parmesan cheese. And we find all these necessaries in a tin of cooked macaroni in cream sauce with cheese and a can of condensed tomato soup. To approximate the classic seasoning, however, you must add to the condensed soup a bit of bayleaf, a small sprig of thyme, a couple of chicken bouillon cubes.

YOU WILL NEED:

macaroni in cream sauce with cheese	eggs
	thyme
condensed tomato soup	bayleaf
Parmesan cheese	chicken bouillon cubes

Place the heated canned macaroni in the bottom of the casserole, sprinkle with grated Parmesan cheese.

Blend ¼ cup grated cheese and 3 or 4 very well-beaten egg yolks into a can of condensed tomato soup. Add a bit of bayleaf, a small sprig of thyme and 2 chicken bouillon cubes. Then fold in 4 slightly beaten egg whites and place on top of macaroni. Bake about 30 minutes in a hot oven 400° F.

AT SERVING TIME:

Serve at once. An excellent lunch or supper entree for 4.

BLANCHING VEGETABLES IN
ELECTRIC UTENSILS

Your electric pressure cooker, with a fry basket or large strainer, sans pressure, of course, or your electric deep fat fryer, Dutch oven, or automatic saucepan can all be used to blanch vegetables and get them ready for freezing.

And your freezer becomes infinitely more useful to you in epicurean flights when you freeze the not-so-easy-to-get ingredients of extra-special dishes. Like artichokes, for example, and bean sprouts, Chinese cabbage, eggplant, ginger root, grape leaves, lotus or lily roots, mushrooms, Chinese peas, chestnuts and water chestnuts.

The technique of blanching is very simple. Put them into a big strainer or fry basket. Give them a quick dip into boiling water, just long enough to stop the action of certain enzymes, not long enough to cook the food. This process has the rather fancy name of blanching.

Generally you use enough boiling water to cover the vegetables completely. Set thermostat at high, about 400° so that the water returns quickly to the boil. When water is briskly boiling, immerse vegetables. Start counting the time when the water returns to a boil. This should not take more than 2 minutes. If it takes longer, use a smaller amount of vegetables.

Artichokes   Pull off the coarse outer leaves and coarse part of stem. Wash thoroughly in running water. Add ½ cup lemon juice to 2 quarts boiling water. Place artichokes in wire basket, blanch about 8 minutes or cook until tender. Cook quickly. Drain and pack. If desired, artichokes may be blanched and then stuffed with a regular poultry dressing before freezing.

Bamboo Shoots   Extra portions of canned bamboo shoots may be put into a plastic bag covered with liquid from the can or water and lemon juice. Use 1 tablespoon lemon juice to a cup of water.

Bean Sprouts   You can make your own bean sprouts or buy them in Chinatown. Always latch onto two or three times as many as you can use immediately. Blanch about a cupful at a time for only about 20 seconds after the water returns to boiling. Chill at once. Drain and pack in plastic bags.

Celery Root   Cut out stem and wash. Cook until 50 per cent done either in the usual way or under pressure about 2 minutes. Peel and slice or cut into dice. Pack in plastic bags.

Chestnuts   Cover with water, bring to a boil. Cook under pressure five minutes. Shell or not, as you prefer, and pack in plastic bags.

Chinese Cabbage   Throw away the outside leaves and cut stem. Split through the center of the stalk and cut into 2-inch pieces. Blanch 1 minute, cool quickly, drain and pack.

Chives and Other Herbs   Chives, basil, and other herbs can be available all year. Some people chop them before freezing, but I simply pack them into the smallest size plastic containers available and chip off as needed. Parsley retains its color and so for a little while will chives. Others like basil become as black as truffles or mushrooms, but they do retain their most excellent flavor —a lot more flavor than dried herbs. It is not necessary to blanch them.

Frozen herbs should be used within six weeks.

Eggplant   You can have eggplant all the year. Peel or not, as you please. Slice or cut into dice. Blanch 4 minutes. After removing from the kettle, immerse the eggplant in a bowl containing a quart of cold water and ½ cup lemon juice. Cool quickly in the refrigerator or in the freezer. Drain, pack and tag.

Fennel   Both the savory leaves and the celery-like stalk of fennel may be frozen. The feathery green leaves are treated like any other herb. The stalk should be cut into pieces about an inch long. Blanch 3 minutes. Cool quickly, drain and pack.

Ginger Root   Fresh ginger root gives to many dishes a flavor which cannot be approximated in any other way. Powdered ginger is completely different. Fresh ginger root is generally available only in Chinese or Puerto Rican markets and it does not keep well either on the shelf or in the refrigerator. However, it will freeze. It does not require blanching. Simply place each root separately in a tiny plastic bag. Grate or slice off what you need without thawing.

Grape Leaves   Any grape arbor and any type of grape, white or red grapes, wine or table grapes, can provide you with enough grape leaves to last a year. Simply pick the young tender leaves that have not been chewed by insects, wash well. Cut off hard stems and blanch about a dozen at a time for just about 1 minute. Drain and pack just enough in each bag to supply you with leaves for your favorite recipe.

Lotus or Lily Root   Check on which types can be used for food. When you divide your lilies in the garden, you want to put some of the roots in the freezer to use in your cooking. Peel, wash and dice or slice ¼-inch thick. Blanch 1 minute, cool quickly, drain and pack. Use either in Chinese dishes or in chicken à la king or other creamed dishes to give a delightfully crisp texture contrast.

Chinese Snow Peas   Select the flat tender pods. Remove the ends and any strings. Blanch only about 2 cupfuls at a time and only about 20 seconds so that they will remain crisp. They need the least possible cooking. Cool quickly, drain and pack.

Water Chestnuts   Dried water chestnuts may be bought at the Chinese or Japanese shops. They should be soaked in water to cover several hours or overnight. These require no blanching. Simply peel and cut into pieces or freeze whole. Leftover canned water chestnuts may be covered with liquid from the can or lemon juice flavored water and frozen in plastic bags. Use 1 tablespoon lemon juice to each cup cold water.

Sauces and Seasonings

Exotic Salt   BLENDER

To serve with raw vegetables, which the French call *crudités*, or with boiled beef, nothing takes the place of the coarse gray salt that comes in big crystals. Paris gourmets like Alice Toklas say that sea salt has more flavor than plain salt. All over the world you can buy different types of salt crystals. In Honolulu, for instance, there is a pink salt. You don't need a salt mill; just put the crystals into the blender. Flick it on and off.

AT SERVING TIME:
Present in a tiny receptacle with a bone or ivory spoon, not metal, since it turns green.

Heung New Fun Spices   BLENDER

This particular combination of spices is traditional for Peking duck. It also goes beautifully with pork—chops or loin pork.

In China, Heung New Fun spices can be purchased already mixed and sometimes you can find it in Chinatown. However, our Americanized version approximates the flavor delightfully.

YOU WILL NEED:
cinnamon   anise seed
cloves   fennel seed
black peppercorns

193

Place in the blender 2 3-inch sticks of cinnamon broken into small pieces, 2 tablespoons whole cloves, 2 teaspoons whole black peppercorns, ½ teaspoon anise seed, ½ teaspoon fennel seed. Blend until finely powdered.

AT SERVING TIME:
Use immediately or keep closely covered in a jar with a tight-fitting lid.

VARIATION: If you have no whole spices, you can use the powdered or ground spices in the same proportion, but the flavor is not quite so pungent.

Cracked Black Pepper   BLENDER

Right now freshly cracked black pepper seems to be even more stylish than the all too ubiquitous pepper mill. You can, of course, buy cracked Java pepper, and very good it is when the jar has just been opened. However, it is so simple to do in your blender. White or black peppercorns may be used. The black is more flavorsome. So push away that linen towel and rolling pin or milk bottle and mallet and turn to the blender when you are about to fix a steak or a rib roast au poivre.

YOU WILL NEED:
peppercorns

Blend peppercorns only about half a second for a small amount or until they are just fine enough to suit your purpose. If you are using them to rub into a steak or a roast, sieve out the finer particles for they will make the meat bitter. For table use this need not be done.

AT SERVING TIME:
Place in a small covered receptacle.

New England Butter Sauce   SAUCEPAN

The required adjunct to steamed lobster or clams.

YOU WILL NEED:
butter   curry powder or celery
lemon juice   seed
Tabasco or cayenne
  pepper

To serve four, melt ½ pound stick butter in saucepan, setting
temperature at 200° F. (simmer). Do not allow it to boil. Add
2 teaspoons lemon juice, ½ teaspoon freshly ground black
pepper, 2 or 3 drops Tabasco or a few grains of cayenne pepper
and ½ teaspoon curry powder or celery seed. Allow to stand in
electric saucepan at about 150° for at least half an hour to blend
and mellow.

AT SERVING TIME:
Pour into individual cups or ramekins.

Sauce Aurore   MIXER

A marvelous accompaniment to fish or cooked vegetables, hot
or cold.

YOU WILL NEED:
mayonnaise   cream
Hollandaise sauce

Fold 3 tablespoons mayonnaise and ½ cup whipped cream into
¾ cup Hollandaise sauce. Store in refrigerator.

AT SERVING TIME:
Pass in a chilled bowl.

Sauce Bearnaise   BLENDER

This classic sauce is actually a Hollandaise flavored with tarragon.

YOU WILL NEED:
> white wine   shallots or onion
> tarragon vinegar   black pepper
> tarragon, fresh or dried   Hollandaise sauce

In a skillet combine 2 tablespoons white wine, 1 tablespoon tarragon vinegar, 2 teaspoons chopped fresh tarragon or 1 teaspoon dried tarragon, 2 teaspoons chopped shallots or onion and ¼ teaspoon freshly ground black pepper. Bring liquid to a boil and cook rapidly until almost all liquid disappears. Pour remaining mixture into Hollandaise sauce, cover and blend on high speed for 4 seconds.

AT SERVING TIME:
Serve with broiled steak or chops.

Hollandaise Sauce   BLENDER

There need never be another curdled Hollandaise! With the magic of a blender a perfect Hollandaise equal to that served in the best French restaurants can be made in less than a minute. The recipe is foolproof. All you do is blend hot melted butter into egg yolks and the sauce is ready to serve.

YOU WILL NEED:
> butter   lemon juice
> egg yolks   cayenne

In a small saucepan heat ½ cup (1 stick) butter to bubbling, but do not let it brown. Into container of the blender put 3 egg yolks, 2 tablespoons lemon juice, ¼ teaspoon salt and a pinch of cayenne. Cover container and turn motor on high. Immediately remove cover and quickly pour in the hot butter in a steady stream. When all the butter is added turn off motor. Makes ¾ cup—enough for 4 servings. For larger quantity, use 4 egg yolks, 1 cup butter.

AT SERVING TIME:
Serve immediately or keep warm at 180° F. by setting the container into a saucepan containing 2 inches hot, not boiling water. Serve with cooked broccoli, asparagus, cauliflower or with poached fish or poached eggs.

Barbecue Sauce   BLENDER

Of the hundreds of barbecue sauces that we have tasted, this one seems to have the most distinguished character.

YOU WILL NEED:

onion	salad oil
garlic	dry mustard
chili sauce	Tabasco
dry orégano	Worcestershire sauce
tarragon	sugar
lemon juice	red wine (optional)

Quarter 1 medium onion and place it in the blender. Add 1 clove garlic, 1 12-ounce bottle of chili sauce, 1 teaspoon dry orégano, 1 teaspoon tarragon, the juice of 1 lemon, ¼ cup salad oil, 1 teaspoon salt, 1 teaspoon dry mustard, 3 dashes Tabasco, 1 tablespoon Worcestershire sauce, 2 to 4 tablespoons sugar, ¼ cup red wine or water. Cover and blend for 10 seconds.

AT SERVING TIME:
Use cold for basting roasts or chops. Or simmer 30 minutes and serve hot.

All-Purpose Barbecue Sauce   SAUCEPAN

Very quick, very easy and exceptionally tasty.

YOU WILL NEED:

butter or salad oil	celery salt
tomato catsup	brown sugar
vinegar or lemon juice	bouillon cubes
onion salt	Tabasco

Combine in saucepan ¼ cup melted better or salad oil with 4 tablespoons tomato catsup, ¼ cup vinegar or lemon juice, 1 teaspoon onion salt, 1 teaspoon celery salt, 4 tablespoons brown sugar, 2 bouillon cubes, 2 cups hot water, 3 or 4 drops of Tabasco. Bring to a boil. Simmer 5 minutes at 200° F. Makes about 3 cups.

Ham Gravy—Red or Red-Eye Gravy

SKILLET

Though milk gravy brings a blur of gentle memories to Midwesterners, it is the red or red-eye gravy that calls forth greatest enthusiasm from anyone with roots in the South. Red gravy can be made only by frying, which actually means pan broiling, raw smoked ham.

YOU WILL NEED:

raw smoked ham	sugar (optional)
coffee (optional)	mustard (optional)
red pepper or Tabasco	paprika (optional)

First rub skillet with a good piece of amber-hued ham fat, and when the pan is fairly hot, add ham slices cut about ¼-inch thick. Keep turning the ham frequently as the slices cook to keep them flat. Remove the ham from the skillet and keep it warm. Add about a cup of water or coffee to the drippings in the pan or enough to loosen the brown particles that are there.

Stir and cook until most of the water evaporates. Some people add milk or cream—another version of milk gravy. Season to taste with a touch of red pepper or Tabasco, a mite of sugar, maybe, and the same of mustard, and you may add, if you wish, a speck of paprika.

AT SERVING TIME:
Serve promptly with ham, for if the ham is allowed to stand too long, it will harden and be tough as leather.

Chinese Duck Sauce BLENDER

Not only with duck but with Chinese egg rolls, barbecued spare ribs, roast pork or ham, almost any kind of curry or a rice pilaf, there is no relish more delightful than the so-called duck sauce which can be procured in tins from the Orient and bought in Chinese shops or sometimes in fancy food stores. But what a joy it is to be able to evolve it yourself in just about 15 seconds in your blender and from easy-to-get ingredients!

YOU WILL NEED:
plum or peach jam or preserves	cider vinegar
Kitchen Bouquet or soy sauce	allspice
	dry mustard

Place in the electric blender 1 cup of any kind of plum or peach jam or preserves. Add 1 teaspoon Kitchen Bouquet or soy sauce to give the authentically rich brown look. Add ¼ cup cider vinegar, ¼ teaspoon ground allspice, 1 teaspoon dry mustard. Cover and blend until very smooth. This will take about 15 seconds.

AT SERVING TIME:
Bring to the table in an oriental-looking bowl or jar, or if you want to be more Chinese, serve individual dabs in tiny saucers as

in a Chinese restaurant. Usually with Chinese egg roll a dab
of hot mustard is presented at the same time. This recipe makes
about 1½ cups sauce.

Dashi Sauce   HOT TRAY

A requisite for tempura.

YOU WILL NEED:
soy sauce   ginger root or horseradish
sugar   monosodium glutamate
sherry

Combine ½ cup soy sauce, ½ cup water, 2 teaspoons sugar, 2
teaspoons sherry, ¼ teaspoon fresh crushed ginger root or horseradish, 1 teaspoon monosodium glutamate. Bring to a boil and
keep hot on your electric hot tray until used. Makes 1 cup of
sauce.

Sauce Mayonnaise   BLENDER

Mayonnaise and a variety of delectable mayonnaise sauces for
sea food or salad greens can be made in your blender in a matter
of seconds. This new faster technique makes the recipe foolproof.

YOU WILL NEED:
eggs   salad oil
dry mustard   Tabasco
vinegar or lemon juice

Place 2 eggs into the blender along with ½ teaspoon dry
mustard, ½ teaspoon salt, ⅛ teaspoon pepper, 4 tablespoons
vinegar or lemon juice, ½ cup salad oil and a couple of drops

of Tabasco. Cover container and turn motor on high. Immediately remove cover and quickly add 1½ cups oil in a steady stream. When all the oil is added, turn off motor. This makes about 2½ cups mayonnaise.

AT SERVING TIME:
Pass in a chilled bowl.

Frozen Mousse of Horseradish, Epicure
MIXER

Novel and delectable, marvelous with smoked or chilled fish, cold roast beef or tongue.

YOU WILL NEED:
heavy cream	dry mustard
Worcestershire sauce	grated horseradish
Tabasco	white vinegar

Beat ½ cup heavy cream until stiff. Season with a dash of Worcestershire sauce, a few drops of Tabasco, ½ teaspoon of dry mustard, 4 tablespoons grated horseradish, 4 teaspoons white vinegar. Half freeze in the refrigerator tray about 45 minutes.

AT SERVING TIME:
Serve from a bowl set in crushed ice.

Old-Fashioned Cooked Salad Dressing
BLENDER

This is the kind of dressing that brings sighs of nostalgic delight. Although it belongs to good old-fashioned, farm-style cooking, it was, in the old days, inclined to curdle and needed considerable babying. Vinegar had to be added very, very slowly, drop by drop, or else disaster lay in wait. Now the blender and automatic sauce-pan make it failproof.

YOU WILL NEED:

eggs	dry mustard
butter	sugar
milk	cayenne pepper or
flour	Tabasco
salt	cider vinegar

Into the blender place 2 whole eggs, 2 tablespoons butter, 1½ cups milk, 4 tablespoons flour, ½ tablespoon salt, 1 tablespoon dry mustard, 2 tablespoons sugar, a few grains of cayenne pepper or 2 or 3 drops of Tabasco. Blend 40 seconds. While blender is still going, pour into the center ½ cup cider vinegar; blend 10 seconds longer. Pour into automatic saucepan or skillet, set at simmer point (200° F.). Cook and stir until mixture begins to thicken. If dressing seems a little pale, stir in a few drops of yellow vegetable coloring.

AT SERVING TIME:

Use warm on cole slaw or to make hot potato salad cool. Serve immediately. Or allow to mellow in the refrigerator several hours or even overnight. This recipe makes a little more than a pint of dressing—enough for a good big head of cabbage—8 to 10 servings.

Mayonnaise Chaud-Froid   BLENDER

The flavor of the chaud-froid is extremely delicate and its good-ness depends on the quality of the mayonnaise.

YOU WILL NEED:

gelatine	mayonnaise

To make a thin, smooth, professional glaze, soften 1 envelope of unflavored gelatine in 2 tablespoons cold water. Add 1½ cups hot water—enough to dissolve the gelatine. Stir well until it has cooled to lukewarm. Then mix into it 2 cups of mayonnaise.

Coat cooked fish or fowl at once before the mayonnaise has become jellied. Just spread it on thinly, using a spoon as though it were a trowel and smooth as you go.

AT SERVING TIME:
Decorate with black olives or truffles or circles of carrot. Be discreet about how much to decorate.

Gregorian Relish   BLENDER

In this century-old dish, folk wisdom has evolved a modern nutritionist's dream. A fast-day food with fine flavor, it is so full of food values and vitamins that orthodox Armenians during the 40 days of Lent literally live on it along with stout, honest, wholegrain bread. It's a fine adjunct to fish or meats, delectably serviceable as a dressing for greens or slaw, or it may be used as a cocktail dunk.

YOU WILL NEED:

olive or sesame seed oil	Worcestershire sauce
green peppers	Tabasco
tomatoes	mint leaves
onions	ketchup or chili sauce
tomato or sweet pickle juice	walnuts

Brush with olive or sesame seed oil and broil 2 halved green peppers, 2 tomatoes, 2 onions. Cut into pieces.

Place vegetables in your blender with ½ cup tomato or sweet pickle juice. Add 1 teaspoon Worcestershire sauce, 1½ teaspoons salt, ¼ teaspoon pepper, 3 dashes Tabasco, 1 teaspoon mint leaves. Blend 5 seconds. Combine in bowl with 1 cup ketchup or chili sauce. Relish keeps for a long time in the refrigerator but should be well covered to avoid darkening. Fresh nuts should be scattered over the top for crisp texture contrast.

AT SERVING TIME:
Cover top with coarsely chopped walnuts. Makes about one quart.

Cranberry and Kumquat Relish   BLENDER

There's nothing quite so cool, so fresh and so refreshing to the palate as the tart tingle of the cranberry especially when it is untouched by heat. Raw cranberry relishes have achieved wide popularity during the last few years. And now that we have discovered how easily fresh cranberries can be stored year round in the home freezer, this delight is no longer confined to a brief cranberry season. Even the botheration of the grinding can be dispensed with. In seconds (only 20) you can make this delicious relish in your blender.

YOU WILL NEED:
kumquats, orange or tangerine
sugar

quick-frozen orange or tangerine concentrate
cranberries

Cut 4 kumquats or 1 medium-sized unpeeled orange or large tangerine into small pieces, removing any seeds. Place in blender container along with ½ cup sugar, a 4-ounce can of thawed undiluted quick-frozen orange or tangerine concentrate (such flavor, such grandeur—the zest of a heap of fruit concentrated into a few tablespoons). Blend until peel is coarsely cut, just about 10 seconds. Now put in 2 cups raw or quick-frozen cranberries. Blend just until whole cranberries disappear, about 10 seconds longer. Chill thoroughly before serving.

AT SERVING TIME:

Garnish with whole cranberries. Relish gets better and better as it stands, and keeps admirably in your refrigerator for several weeks. It freezes, of course!

Sauce à la Ritz   BLENDER

This is somewhat similar to a mayonnaise but with the distinctly Provençal flavor of tomatoes and garlic.

YOU WILL NEED:

egg	tomato
dry mustard	chili sauce
lemon juice	garlic
salad oil	parsley clusters

In the container of the blender put 1 large egg, ½ teaspoon dry mustard, ½ teaspoon salt, 2 tablespoons lemon juice and ¼ cup salad oil. Cover container and turn motor on high. Immediately remove cover and quickly add ¾ cup oil in a steady stream. Turn off motor. Add 1 fresh tomato peeled and quartered, 1 tablespoon chili sauce, 1 clove garlic and 2 tablespoons parsley clusters and stir with rubber spatula to combine. Cover and blend on high speed for 6 seconds.

AT SERVING TIME:

Serve instead of regular mayonnaise.

Clarified Butter   SKILLET

As a general rule, pancakes are cooked at about 370° F., although one of the world's acknowledged pancake experts, Lester Highet, owner of the Pancake House of Portland, Oregon, has his griddles set at 380° F. This higher temperature does give a crisper product, but there is the danger of burning the butter, a danger which he obviates by returning to a method devised in India, where traditionally the cooks clarify the butter of buffalo milk in order to make "ghee," called for in almost all recipes.

Clarifying butter is no particular chore. Simply melt it slowly, skim off the froth or pass through a fine cheesecloth. Freed of its milk solids, butter does not burn so readily. Clarified butter is a wonder-thing to have on hand, not only for pancake-making but also for pastries. Vegetable shortening and salad oils may be used but do not impart the same flavor.

Homemade Whipped Butter   BEATER

For spreading bread with butter to serve as the English do at tea time, or for making all sorts of sandwiches or just to set on the table in an attractive bowl or to serve on pancakes, whipped butter is incomparable.

In certain markets in larger towns and cities whipped butter is always available, but plain stick butter is much easier to come by.

On the following page you will find directions for transforming heavy cream into whipped butter. This one does it in reverse, by adding a small amount of cream or top milk to plain butter.

YOU WILL NEED:

butter   whipping cream or rich
                                               milk

Let a half pound of butter stand at room temperature until it becomes malleable. Break into pieces and place in the beater along with ½ cup cream or top milk. Beat at low speed until all the liquid has been absorbed. Sweet or salted butter may be used.

AT SERVING TIME:

Place in an attractive bowl or crock. Serve at "cool room" temperature. When too cold, whipped butter loses its character.

VARIATION: *LINGONBERRY BUTTER*   At the famous Pancake House in Portland, Oregon, they serve along with their incredible Swedish and German pancakes a whipped butter made by beating together equal quantities of whipped butter and lingonberry preserves, which you can get in any fine food shop. The lingonberry is a very small Swedish berry akin to our cranberry. In Germany it is called preiselbeeren. The lingonberries may be added to the softened stick butter and the cream all at the same time.

VARIATION: *WHIPPED HONEY BUTTER*   Use honey instead of lingonberry preserves, but only half as much, *i.e.* ¼ pound butter, 4 tablespoons cream, 4 tablespoons honey. This makes 1 cup of whipped honey butter. Delicious on pancakes, waffles, French toast or regular toast.

Sweet Whipped Butter   BLENDER

Sweet whipped unsalted butter—the gourmet's delight—can be yours any time.

YOU WILL NEED:
   heavy whipping cream
   (40% butter fat)

Break surface of cream in blender and blend. After the cream turns to butter, take out of blender and place in a bowl of cold water. This is done to remove the milk from the butter so that it will not sour.

AT SERVING TIME:
Serve at room temperature.

Instant Vanilla Custard Sauce   BLENDER

Three full cups of custard sauce may be made this way instantaneously.

YOU WILL NEED:
milk   pure vanilla extract or
instant vanilla pudding   vanilla bean

Place in the blender 3 cups milk, 1 package instant vanilla pudding, ½ teaspoon pure vanilla extract or a 2-inch piece of vanilla bean. Blend about 40 seconds.

AT SERVING TIME:
Pass in a pitcher or a sauce boat with snow pudding or with gelatin desserts. Also good on fruit or cake.

VARIATION: *INSTANT BUTTERSCOTCH SAUCE* Use a package of butterscotch instant pudding. Flavor with rum or rum extract instead of vanilla.

INSTANT CHOCOLATE SAUCE Use a package of instant chocolate pudding mix and if you like a mocha flavor, add 1 teaspoon instant coffee or a couple of drops of Angostura bitters.

Uncooked Hot Fudge Sauce   BLENDER

If you like a bittersweet chocolate flavor you will not add the sugar.

YOU WILL NEED:
chocolate pieces   coffee
superfine sugar

Place 1 package (6 ounces) chocolate pieces into blender. Cover and blend for 6 seconds. Scrape chocolate away from the sides of container with a knife. Add 2 tablespoons superfine sugar and ½ cup steaming hot coffee. Cover and blend for 10 seconds longer.

AT SERVING TIME:
This goes on any sort of cake as well as ice cream or puddings.

Creamy Sauce   MIXER

YOU WILL NEED:
    egg   vanilla
    butter   whipped cream
    confectioner's sugar

Beat 1 egg until foamy. Blend in ⅓ cup melted butter, 1½ cups sifted confectioner's sugar and 1 teaspoon vanilla. Fold in 1 cup whipped cream whipped stiff.

AT SERVING TIME:
Wonderful with any kind of pudding.

Fruit Sauce   BLENDER

YOU WILL NEED:
    fresh or frozen berries or   lemon juice
        fruit   sugar (optional)

Put 2 cups sliced fresh fruit or berries or 1 12-ounce package of frozen fruit or berries which have been defrosted, plus 1 tablespoon lemon juice and sugar to taste into blender. Cover and blend until smooth.

AT SERVING TIME:
Serve over cake, ice cream, sherberts or with fritters.

Vanilla Sugar　　BLENDER

A great number of the best and most famous of European desserts depend for their exquisite and subtle flavor upon the addition of vanilla sugar.

The old way to make it is very simple but it takes two weeks. You simply split a vanilla bean down the center and bury it in a couple of pounds of sugar. Eventually the sugar is permeated with the glorious flavor and scent of vanilla.

Now with a blender two weeks is condensed into 5 seconds!

YOU WILL NEED:
　vanilla bean　　　　　　　　　sugar

Quarter a vanilla bean. Place in blender with 1 cup sugar, blend about 5 seconds or until the vanilla bean disappears into flecks. Remove from blender and mix with 2 cups sugar.

AT SERVING TIME:
Use immediately or keep in a covered jar to lend distinction to all sorts of puddings, cakes, fruits, omelets, desserts of all kinds or what you will.

VARIATIONS: *LEMON SUGAR* Use 4 tablespoons grated lemon rind instead of vanilla. Delicious in tea or coffee.

ANISE-FLAVORED SUGAR Add 1 tablespoon anise seed and a couple of drops of red coloring if desired.

ORANGE SUGAR Use 5 tablespoons grated orange rind and add a drop of orange coloring if desired.

Eggs and Cheese

Poached Eggs

More people are frightened of poaching eggs than any other process of cooking. As a result, innumerable gadgets have been invented requiring usually the most careful greasing of dinky poachers, the use of strange hoops of metal and no mean knowledge of sleight-of-hand to extricate them from the shapes into which they have been tortured.

All sorts of additives have been suggested, turning the poaching water into something not unlike a pickling liquor—lemon juice, vinegar, salt. All calculated to keep the whites firm. Generally these things make the whites not only firm but tough and rubbery.

An electric skillet makes a wonderful egg poacher for anywhere from one to six or even eight eggs, depending on its size. The secret of this absolutely failproof method is a little neglect. We happened upon it by accident. While I was poaching eggs one busy day the phone rang. The eggs were in the water. Hastily I covered the eggs, turned the thermostat off and talked on the telephone for at least ten minutes. The poor eggs, I thought, ruined no doubt. But no, they were perfect.

YOU WILL NEED:

eggs   hot water

Notice that we do not add salt, pepper, seasonings, lemon juice or vinegar. Use hot water from the tap if you wish to save time. Water should stand at least 1½ inches deep in the pan. Set thermostat at 350°. When light goes off, place eggs one at a time in the water. Push whites together with spatula so that eggs have a pretty shape. Cover. Turn thermostat off. Forget for at least five minutes or until you want to serve them.

AT SERVING TIME:

Remove with a slotted spoon and serve on toast, fried tomato slices or English muffins (halved and toasted) or whatever you like. Sprinkle with salt, pepper and maybe a sprinkle of chives or a drop of Tabasco.

VARIATION: *EGGS BENEDICTINE* (or some call them Benedict) For each serving prepare one or two rounds of toasted and buttered white bread or English muffins. Top with a thin slice of cooked ham which may be warmed in butter, if you insist. It is the classic way but actually unnecessary. Place poached eggs on top of ham and mask with Hollandaise sauce which you can buy in a jar or make in your blender with perfect ease and complete confidence (see page 196).

Eggs Mollet   EGG COOKER

Almost everyone interested in fine cooking has some one specialty which through the years continues to elude. Alice Toklas, for instance, one of the world's most epicurean gastronomes, is afraid to attempt an angel cake even with a mix. Another friend almost as skillful is completely baffled by Eggs Mollet. These are similar to poached eggs but they are cooked in the shell and the shell is removed. A great variety of French creations—some warm, some cold, depend upon eggs in this form.

With a wild hallelujah my friend broke the news to me recently that Eggs Mollet are as nothing when you have an electric egg cooker.

In this cooker you simply add water up to a certain point. One ring is marked "very soft," the next section is marked "medium and poaching" and the next is for hard cooked. To make Eggs Mollet you use the amount of water required for poaching but you cook the eggs in the shell. As soon as the water has cooked away the switch gives a loud sigh and turns itself off. At this point you remove the eggs immediately, run cold water over them and shell them. If you want to keep them warm, place in bowl or pan of lukewarm water and keep them on an electric hot tray.

If the eggs are cooked even a few seconds too long or if you do not remove the shell quickly, the shells will cling to the whites and you cannot possibly get a smooth, unmarred egg.

French Omelet   SKILLET
(*made with or without an omelet pan*)

To make a generous single serving,

YOU WILL NEED:

   eggs   butter
   herbs, ham or mushrooms
     (optional)

Place in blender 2 eggs, 2 tablespoons warm water, ½ teaspoon salt, ¼ teaspoon pepper. Flick on and off until eggs are barely mixed. This can, of course, be done with a fork but the blender saves work. Also you may add any sort of herbs or ham or mushrooms.

AT SERVING TIME:

Heat griddle or skillet to 400° F. When light goes off, add 1 tablespoon butter and push butter around so it melts without too much browning. Empty eggs into pan and immediately begin pushing the omelet together so that it forms an oval. The moment it is gathered together or starts to set, flop it over and place immediately on an unheated plate. The whole process takes less than a minute. Use a non-flexible spatula. It is much easier than it sounds.

VARIATION: *OMELET FINES HERBES*   Add a sprig of parsley, a couple of blades of chives and a bit of chervil or tarragon or basil.

VARIATION: *OMELET FINES HERBES FROM DRIED HERBS*   Add ½ teaspoon dried parsley and chives to the warm water and allow to stand for a few minutes in the blender. Then add eggs. Blend and proceed. If stronger herbs are used, use ¼ teaspoon to two eggs.

Omelets using 4 or 6 eggs may be made in this fashion. But don't attempt larger quantities. Better make several smaller ones.

Special Scrambled Eggs   SKILLET

So you know how to make scrambled eggs? A lot of other people think they know how, too, but try this way. It *is* special. Serves 4 to 6.

YOU WILL NEED:
butter   cream
eggs

Melt ¼ cup butter in electric skillet at 350° F. Beat together only enough to mix 8 eggs, ¼ cup cream, ½ teaspoon salt, ¼ teaspoon pepper. When butter sizzles pour in the eggs all at once. Turn heat to 150° F. As soon as the eggs set at the bottom, draw your spoon across in long strokes, using as many strokes as are needed to turn over all the eggs. Don't beat or stir.

AT SERVING TIME:
Serve as soon as set and while eggs still look shiny not dry.

New York Style Egg Sandwich   SKILLET

The original recipe, we are told, dates back to Peacock Alley days. It's an open-faced scrambled egg sandwich, but with high style.

YOU WILL NEED:

cooked or canned ham	mushrooms
butter	eggs
onion	sliced white bread

Cut into thin strips 1½ cups cooked or canned ham (about 12 ounces.) Heat in 2 tablespoons butter along with ½ small onion chopped at 360° F. After two minutes add 10 to 12 mushrooms sliced thin. Cook about two minutes longer. Meanwhile, scramble 8 eggs by your favorite method.

Sauté six slices bread in frying pan in butter at 360° and keep warm on electric hot tray while you prepare the eggs.

AT SERVING TIME:

Pile scrambled eggs on sautéed bread and top with meat and mushroom mixture. Serves six.

Cheese Soufflé   BLENDER

Bread is used here instead of the usual white sauce. The cheese is merely diced, not grated, and if you have a portable electric beater, you can beat the egg whites in a 2-quart straight-sided soufflé dish and merely pour on the cheese mixture.

YOU WILL NEED:

milk	nutmeg
butter	Cheddar cheese
white bread	eggs
mustard	

Heat 1 cup milk and 3 tablespoons butter until butter is melted. Put 1 slice thinly sliced white bread into blender with ½ teaspoon mustard, ½ teaspoon salt and ¼ teaspoon nutmeg. Cover and blend for 5 seconds. Remove cover and gradually add hot milk mixture. With motor on add 1 cup firmly packed, diced Cheddar cheese and blend for 10 seconds. Add 5 egg yolks, cover and blend for 12 seconds. Beat 5 egg whites with an electric beater until stiff but not dry. Gradually pour cheese mixture over egg whites, folding the cheese into the egg whites with a rubber spatula until lightly blended. Bake in an ungreased 2-quart soufflé dish in 375° F. oven 30 to 35 minutes.

AT SERVING TIME:
Serve immediately.

Cottage Cheese Mold   BLENDER

YOU WILL NEED:

gelatine
cottage cheese
horseradish
heavy cream

cucumber
green pepper
green onions

Put 1 envelope gelatine, ½ teaspoon salt and ½ cup very hot water in the blender. Cover and blend on high speed for 40 seconds. Add 2 cups cottage cheese and 1 tablespoon horseradish. Cover and turn motor on high. Remove cover and, with motor on, gradually pour in the heavy cream. Turn off motor and pour the mixture over 2 cups diced cucumbers, ½ cup diced green pepper and ¼ cup sliced green onions and chill until firm.

AT SERVING TIME:
Unmold on salad greens and serve with French dressing or mayonnaise.

Timbales

With the blender and the pressure cooker, suddenly it becomes easy and convenient to achieve some of the elegant and formerly elaborate dishes of the turn of the century. These include a variety of timbales, a kind of steamed soufflés that are delightful to serve for luncheons, for suppers or buffets. Like custards, they were traditionally baked in molds, set inside of pans of hot water. But now once again, like custards, these cook in three minutes in the pressure cooker, and the texture when done under pressure is even more smooth and delicate.

Chicken Timbales   PRESSURE COOKER

YOU WILL NEED:

milk	parsley
butter	cooked chicken
bread crumbs	Tabasco
eggs	sauce poulette (page 128)

Place in the blender ⅔ cup milk, 2 tablespoons butter, ¼ cup bread crumbs, 2 eggs, 2 sprigs parsley, 1 cup cooked chicken cut in pieces. Blend about 10 seconds or until smooth and well mixed. Season to taste with salt, pepper and a drop or two of Tabasco.

Butter 6 custard cups or small molds and fill two-thirds full. Cover each mold with wax paper or aluminum foil and tie or press down firmly.

Place ½ cup water in the pressure cooker. Put custard cups on a rack and cook at 15 pounds for 3 minutes. Reduce pressure immediately by letting cold water run down the side. Remove the cover, allow the timbales to rest undisturbed about six minutes.

AT SERVING TIME:
Unmold and serve with sauce poulette (see page 128).

VARIATION: *HAM TIMBALES* Use cooked ham instead of chicken and cut down on the salt. Leftover veal, pork or turkey may be used to make timbales. Instead of a sauce you could use leftover gravy.

Spinach Timbales   PRESSURE COOKER

These are among the most popular.

YOU WILL NEED:

milk	lemon juice or vinegar
eggs	onion
butter	toast
spinach	tomato slices

Into the blender, pour 1 cup milk, 2 eggs, 2 tablespoons butter, 2 cups cooked or frozen spinach thawed, ½ teaspoon salt, ⅛ teaspoon pepper, 2 slices onion, 1 tablespoon lemon juice or vinegar. Blend about 10 seconds.

Pour into six buttered custard cups, filling them two-thirds full. Set cups or molds on rack. Cover with wax paper or aluminum foil tied or pressed down to keep it in place. Place ½ cup water in pressure cooker. Cook under 15 pounds pressure 3 minutes. Reduce pressure immediately letting cold water run down the side. Allow to rest 3 or 4 minutes.

AT SERVING TIME:

Provide 1 round of toasted buttered bread and 1 large slice tomato for each serving. Place the tomato on the buttered toast, top with the spinach timbale. Serve with Sauce Mornay or melted cheese. Sprinkle with salted pistachio nuts or toasted slivered almonds.

VARIATION: *BROCCOLI TIMBALES* Simply substitute broccoli for spinach and flavor with a clove of garlic instead of onion, and add a bit of anchovy paste, if desired.

Timbale Shells   DEEP FAT FRYER

The same batter as rosettes (see page 242). The same method, but differently shaped irons will enable you to make delicious, crispy and delicate timbale shells to fill with creamed crabmeat, Newburg mixtures, or, for a ladies' luncheon, tiny green peas.

One thing to remember—timbale shells should be filled at the last moment or they become soaked and soggy.

Breads and Cereals

Onion Rolls

PORTABLE OVEN

YOU WILL NEED:

salad oil

onion

brown 'n' serve rolls

sesame seeds

Blend salad oil with small chopped onion and pour into a cup. Now dip the top of each brown 'n' serve roll into the salad oil mixture and place a thin, thin slice of onion on top. Also sprinkle the top of the rolls with sesame seeds. Bake in your portable oven 6 to 8 minutes at 450° F., 8 to 10 minutes at 425° F., or at 400° F. for 10 to 12 minutes.

AT SERVING TIME:

Serve piping hot with soup, salad, or cheese.

Garlic Bread

BLENDER

YOU WILL NEED:

French, Italian or

Viennese bread

butter

garlic

Cut one loaf of French, Italian or Viennese bread on the bias at 1-inch intervals. Slice down to bottom crust but do not slice through. Blend ½ cup (1 stick) melted butter and 1 or 2 finely minced cloves garlic. Using a pastry brush or a spoon, coat the cut surfaces. Wrap in aluminum foil and bake in a hot oven (400° F.) 10 minutes. Serve hot.

VARIATION: *BROWN 'N' SERVE LOAVES OF FRENCH BREAD OR ROLLS* need not be baked before the garlic-butter treatment. Simply add 10 minutes to the baking time. If frozen they should be thawed before you attempt to slice them.

Deviled Bread   PORTABLE OVEN

This bread can be made ahead, reheated in foil.

YOU WILL NEED:
butter	French loaf
garlic	cheese or onion
canned ham, bacon	(optional)
spread or other meat	

Combine ¼ lb. softened butter with 1 clove garlic put through press, 1 small can deviled ham, bacon spread or any other favorite meat spread. Cut French bread diagonally. Spread seasoned butter generously between slices. Wrap in foil and bake in moderate oven 375° F. 15 minutes. If loaf has been frozen, use a hot oven 450° F. or increase the time. Thin slices of cheese or onion may be inserted.

AT SERVING TIME:
Serve as a hearty accompaniment to a soup or salad.

SKILLET BECOMES OVEN

Your electric skillet may be used instead of a table oven. Simply preheat the skillet with the cover on it to the desired temperature. This can be done in a very short time because you have such a small area to heat. You may use a small rack in the bottom of the pan in order to avoid hot spots over the heating elements. Or if you wish, you can line the bottom of the skillet with two thicknesses of aluminum foil. Potatoes may be baked, brown 'n' serve rolls can be heated and you can do an excellent job of making custard.

Brown 'n' Serve Rolls   SKILLET

If you want to get a good brown on your brown 'n' serve rolls be sure to brush them very well with melted butter. Preheat skillet and cover to 450° F. Keep the steam vent open so that the heat is dry.

NEW BATTER METHOD
FOR BREAD-MAKING

The batter method is the newest and quickest method for those concerned with saving time and labor. This is the blitz-plan to develop yeast concoctions as fast as possible, particularly casserole breads and sweet rolls. Kneading and shaping are neither necessary nor possible. The bread mixture is limited to a single rising in the bowl or right in the baking pan. Then it is ready for the oven.

Cottage Bread   MIXER

Old-time favorite. Deliciously moist. Somewhat coarser than many of the modern breads.

YOU WILL NEED:
active dry yeast   shortening
sugar   flour

Measure into mixing bowl 2¾ cups warm water (not hot— 110° to 115° F.), add, stirring to dissolve, 2 packages active dry yeast. Stir in 3 tablespoons sugar, 1 tablespoon salt, 2 tablespoons soft shortening, 3½ cups sifted flour. Beat 2 minutes until smooth. Mix in 3 cups flour thoroughly. Cover, let rise in warm place (85° F.) until double (30 minutes). Beat batter down for ½ minute. Pour into well buttered 4 small loaf pans or baking dishes. Let rise 20 to 30 minutes. Brush with melted shortening. Bake until brown at 375° F. approximately 40 to 45 minutes.

Bacon Bread Baked in a Casserole

PORTABLE OVEN

This amount of batter may be baked in two small well-buttered or well oiled casseroles holding about 1½ pints each or in 4 onion soup ramekins which hold about a cupful each.

YOU WILL NEED:

milk	all-purpose flour
salt	whole wheat flour
brown sugar	coriander seeds
bacon drippings	bacon
egg	white pepper
yeast	

Blend 1 cup hot milk with 2½ teaspoons salt, 2 tablespoons brown sugar, 2 tablespoons bacon drippings and 1 egg. Cool to luke-warm.

Meanwhile measure in a warm mixing bowl, 1 cup lukewarm water, add 1 tablespoon brown sugar. Crumble 2 cakes or packages of yeast into the warm water. Stir gently. Allow to stand about 5 minutes, until it looks bubbly. Then add the milk and egg mixture from the blender.

Now add 3½ cups sifted all-purpose flour, 1 cup sifted whole wheat flour, ⅓ teaspoon ground coriander seeds. Beat with electric beater 3 minutes. Cover. Allow to rise in a warm place 82° to 85° F. until twice its size. This will take about 40 minutes. Stir in 2 slices bacon that has been cooked crisp and crumbled. Sprinkle lightly with white pepper. Beat with electric beater 2 minutes longer.

Bake in well-buttered casseroles or baking dishes in an oven preheated to 400° F. about 40 minutes.

AT SERVING TIME:

Turn out of the casseroles or serve in the baking dishes. This bread is best when slightly warm. It may be sliced in the usual way or in very small pie-shaped wedges. Especially good with sweet butter and whipped cream cheese.

Mixer Buns   MIXER

Light and good . . . and easy to make!

YOU WILL NEED:

active dry yeast	eggs
sugar	flour
vegetable shortening	

Measure 1¼ cups warm water (110°–115° F.) into mixing bowl; add, stirring to dissolve, 2 packages active dry yeast. Add ¼ cup sugar, 1 teaspoon salt, ½ cup soft shortening, 2 eggs, 2 cups sifted flour. Combine with the mixer on low speed. Beat 2 minutes on medium speed, guiding batter into beaters with rubber scraper. Add 1¼ cups sifted flour. Beat with rubber scraper until smooth. Spoon into greased muffin cups a scant half full. Let rise in warm place (85° F.) until batter reaches top of muffin cups (30 to 40 minutes). Bake at 375° F. 18 to 20 minutes or until golden brown.

AT SERVING TIME:

Serve warm. Makes about 2½ dozen buns.

Sally Lunn   MIXER

This delightful cake-like bread is said to have come to America
from Bath, England, home of Sally Lunn. The distinctive feature
is the shape—it is baked in a tube pan or an angel cake pan.
The texture is fluffy, porous and spongelike.

YOU WILL NEED:

yeast, active dry	eggs
milk	butter
sugar	flour

Measure ½ cup warm water (110° to 115° F.) into a mixing bowl.
Add, stirring to dissolve, 2 packages active dry yeast. Stir in
1½ cups lukewarm milk, 2 tablespoons sugar, 1½ teaspoons salt,
2 eggs, ¼ cup softened butter, 5½ cups sifted flour. Beat until
smooth 2 minutes in an electric beater. Cover and let rise until
very light about 1 hour. Beat down and pour into greased 10-inch
tube pan. Let rise to within 1 inch of top of pan 45 minutes. Bake
at 350° F. 45 or 50 minutes or until golden brown.

AT SERVING TIME:

Serve hot in wedges with butter, or serve when a day old toasted
and buttered.

Brioche from a Hot Roll Mix   MIXER

This recipe cuts out half a dozen operations, rises in a third the
time, makes a brioche as French as Paris. It will make 12
brioches.

YOU WILL NEED:

hot roll mix	lemon rind or powdered
egg yolks	cardamon
sugar	butter

Place in a large bowl 1 envelope of yeast from 1 package of hot roll mix and dissolve in 4 ounces very warm water; add ⅓ package of the dry mix along with 3 egg yolks (4 ounces) slightly beaten, ⅛ cup sugar, 1 teaspoon grated lemon rind or ¼ teaspoon powdered cardamon. Beat the mixture 3 minutes at high speed with an electric beater. Add the rest of the package dry mix and mix well. Turn into lightly buttered bowl, cover with a damp towel and let stand in a warm place until double in bulk. Now chill or not, as you please, 3 hours or overnight. Let rise again until double in bulk.

Now you divide dough and reserve a quarter of it for the traditional little caps to go on top of the brioche. Butter your hands generously and form 12 balls the size of golf balls; form the rest into 12 balls the size of marbles. Grease 12 iron gem pans or fluted brioche molds with butter. Place a large ball in each pan and top with a small ball. Allow to rise again until double in size. Brush with this butter and egg glaze: 2 tablespoons melted and cooled butter mixed with 1 well-beaten egg yolk. Brioches are baked in an oven slightly less hot than ordinary rolls, 375° F. for about 20 minutes. Turn out and cool on racks.

AT SERVING TIME:
The French never serve brioche warm but we do. They are excellent split crosswise toasted under the broiler and buttered. Or buttered first and toasted.

Homemade Bread from a Mix
PORTABLE OVEN

If you want to build up your courage to attempt baking bread, it's a very wise idea to start with a hot roll mix. You will find in the package all the necessary directions, making it next to impossible to fail. We have discovered a new but actually very old way to give the loaves a highly professional glaze.

YOU WILL NEED:

hot roll mix

water or milk

egg white or melted
butter

Follow directions in the package. When the dough is well risen, punch it down. Turn it out on a floured board and work the dough by folding and turning, rolling and kneading. Unlike pastry, yeast dough takes kindly to handling. According to the directions in some packages, hot roll mixes do not require kneading but you will get a more close-textured, finer-grained loaf if you do knead 3 to 5 minutes. After you have shaped the loaves and placed them in greased bread pans (we like to make 2 small loaves from a package of mix rather than 1 large one) brush lightly with melted butter. Cover with a paper towel. Set in a warm place not above 95° F. until doubled in size. Bake in a preheated oven 400° to 425° F. 45 to 55 minutes.

If you like a soft and tender crust, brush the tops of the loaves with melted butter 10 minutes before the baking is complete. For a crusty bread brush the loaves with slightly beaten egg white instead of butter.

Whole Wheat Batter Bread   MIXER

Moist and delicious, open-textured. Requires no kneading. Just pour the batter into the pan.

YOU WILL NEED:

active dry yeast

whole wheat flour

flour

soft shortening

honey or brown sugar

Put 2½ cups warm water (110°–115° F.) into a mixing bowl. Add, stirring to dissolve, 2 packages active dry yeast. Mix on a paper 2 cups unsifted whole wheat flour, 4 cups sifted flour, 4 teaspoons salt. Add half flour mixture and ¼ cup soft shortening, ¼ cup honey or brown sugar. Beat on medium speed 2 minutes, guiding batter into beaters with rubber scraper. Add remaining flour mixture and blend in with rubber scraper or spoon until smooth (1–1½ minutes). Scrape down batter from sides of bowl. Cover with waxed paper and let rise in warm place (85° F.) until double, about 30 minutes. Stir down batter by beating about 25 strokes. Divide batter into 2 greased 9 × 5 × 3-inch loaf pans. Let rise until edges of batter reach top of pans, about 40 minutes. Bake until brown at 375° F. about 40 to 50 minutes.

OLD-FASHIONED BREADS

For the inspiration and the basic techniques of these wondrous old-time European breads, all my grateful thanks go to Frances Kalnay, author, artist, producer, world traveler and a gourmet who practises in at least seven languages and a dozen cultures. Over the years I have been able in some cases to simplify the techniques but never has anything been changed when it would interfere with the original flavor and texture.

Old-Fashioned Whole Wheat Bread
BLENDER AND PORTABLE OVEN

This is one of the most delicious breads imaginable. It is difficult to say just what gives it its extraordinary flavor. Maybe it is the combination of honey and molasses, orange juice and a touch of cumin seed. Frances Kalnay, who first introduced me to this recipe, also uses in it some grated St. John's bread, which is the fruit of the locust tree, and it is sold in Greek, Syrian or Turkish markets. Often you can find it in Jewish neighborhoods too.

YOU WILL NEED:

milk	yeast
salt	all-purpose flour
golden molasses	whole wheat flour
honey	soya flour
butter	cumin seed
orange juice	St. John's bread (optional)
egg yolk	egg white
brown sugar	butter

Place in the blender 1 cup hot milk, 1½ teaspoons salt, 3 table-spoons golden molasses, 3 tablespoons honey, 4 tablespoons butter and 1 egg yolk. Blend a few seconds and cool until lukewarm. Then add 2 tablespoons orange juice.

Measure into a warm mixing bowl 1¼ cups lukewarm water, ½ teaspoon brown sugar, crumble or sprinkle into the water 2 cakes or packages of yeast. Stir. Allow to stand about 5 minutes or until it looks bubbly. Combine with milk mixture.

Sift into the batter 1½ cups all-purpose flour, 2 cups whole wheat flour, beat with an electric beater one minute. Then add another cup of sifted all-purpose flour and 2 more cups whole wheat flour. Beat 2 minutes longer. Add 2 tablespoons soya flour, ⅓ teaspoon ground cumin seed and 1 tablespoon grated St. John's bread, if you have it. Beat 1 more minute. Turn onto a floured board, knead until dough is smooth and no longer sticks, using as little flour as possible. Place in a lightly buttered warm bowl, brush top with butter. Cover and let rise till doubled about 1 hour. Stir for a couple of seconds. Knead lightly one minute. Allow to rise again for about ½ hour. Shape into 4 small loaves. Cover and let rise 15 minutes.

Set loaves on a buttered baking sheet at least 3 inches apart, cut a line or two on the surface with a sharp knife. Brush with egg white slightly beaten with 4 tablespoons water. Bake in a pre-heated oven at 400° F. 15 minutes. Reduce temperature to 375° and continue baking 20 to 30 minutes longer or until the crust is really firm to touch and gives forth a hollowed sound when lightly thumped on the bottom crust.

AT SERVING TIME:

Absolutely unbelievable when served warm with butter. Or allow to cool and slice quite thin, spread with softened butter and pass with English-style tea and milk in the late afternoon.

The Grant Loaf   PORTABLE OVEN

Not so long ago I went to England specifically to learn about spirits—not the ethereal but the drinking type. Naturally I sought out the Grants, whose Stand-fast Scotch is one of the "greats." I discovered that the name of Grant is famous also in another field. Mrs. William—Doris—Grant has invented a loaf of unkneaded bread that has swept across the British Isles. Mrs. Grant insists that the flour must be stone ground, the salt should be sea salt and the sugar should be Barbados muscovado cane, all of which can be found at health stores. But regular brown sugar, honey or molasses can be substituted.

Like many other perfectionists, she also insists upon fresh, compressed yeast rather than dry yeast. It is true that compressed yeast cake does seem to give a better flavor. Still, if it is too difficult to find, a package of dry yeast will do.

YOU WILL NEED:

whole wheat flour, prefer-   Barbados muscovado
   ably stone ground   sugar or brown sugar,
compressed yeast cake   honey or molasses

Mix 1 tablespoon salt with 3 pounds stone-ground whole wheat flour. In very cold weather, Mrs. Grant suggests that the flour should be warmed slightly, just enough to take the chill off. Mix 1 ounce fresh yeast and 1 tablespoon Barbados muscovado sugar, brown sugar, honey or molasses in a small bowl with ½ cup lukewarm water. Blood heat is the English term, i.e., 98° F. Leave for 10 minutes or until it becomes frothy. Pour the yeasty liquid into the flour, adding 3½ cups lukewarm water. Beat

2 minutes at low speed. Divide the dough into 3 quart-size bread tins which have been warmed or greased. Or you may use 6 pint-size bread tins to make small loaves. Place the tins in a warm place, about 80° F. Cover with a cloth and leave for about 20 minutes to rise about one third or until dough is within an inch of top of the pan. Bake in a moderately hot oven 400° F. for about 35 to 40 minutes.

AT SERVING TIME:
Serve this bread warm from the oven with whipped butter. There is no greater delight. To keep the bread in the freezer it is best to slice and place in plastic bags. In this way the whole loaf need not be defrosted. Frozen slices may be popped immediately into the toaster or they may be thawed quickly at room temperature.

Anadama Bread   PORTABLE OVEN

The name comes from a New England fisherman whose lazy wife always served him corn meal mush and molasses. One day, tired of the same corn meal mush for dinner, he mixed it with flour and yeast and baked it as bread, saying: "Anna damn her." At least, that's the story! This makes 1 regular or 2 small loaves.

YOU WILL NEED:
yellow corn meal   shortening or butter
molasses   active dry yeast

Bring 1½ cups water, 1 teaspoon salt to boil in saucepan. Then stir in ⅓ cup yellow corn meal. Return to boiling point, stirring constantly. Pour into a large mixing bowl. Stir in ⅓ cup molasses and 1½ tablespoons shortening. Cool to lukewarm. Dissolve 1 package active dry yeast in ¼ cup warm water (not hot—110 to 115° F.). Add to lukewarm corn meal mixture. Mix well. Then mix in 2 cups sifted flour. Add enough more flour to handle easily (2 to 2½ sifted cups); mix with hand (dough will be sticky). Turn onto lightly floured board. Knead and let rise in warm place (85° F.) until double (about 1½ hours). Press 2 fingers into dough. It will leave indention when dough is doubled. Punch down. To shape, place dough in greased loaf pan and pat into a loaf shape. Let rise until almost double (about 1 hour). Brush top with melted butter. Sprinkle with a little corn meal and salt. Bake at 375° F. for 40 to 45 minutes.

AT SERVING TIME:
Best when served warm with sweet, whipped butter. If you wish to freeze, slice first thinly and place in plastic bags. If whole loaves are frozen and then thawed, bread has a tendency to crumble.

Sour-Dough Starters for Rye Bread

STARTER No. 1:

YOU WILL NEED:
yeast cake   light rye flour

Dissolve ½ yeast cake in 1 cup lukewarm water. Gradually add 1½ cups sifted light rye flour. Stir into paste. Cover and store overnight in a warm place 80° to 85° F.

STARTER No. 2:

yeast cake   light rye flour

Dissolve ½ yeast cake in 1 cup lukewarm water. Gradually add 1½ cups sifted light rye flour. Stir into paste. Cover and store overnight in a warm place (80° to 85° F.). In the morning add ½ cup lukewarm water and sift in ¾ cup of rye flour and mix.

Repeat once more after 5 hours. In the evening the sour dough is ready. Total time 24 hours.

STARTER No. 3:

leftover dough   medium rye flour
buttermilk

Add to 1 cup of leftover dough 1 cup of lukewarm water, 4 tablespoons buttermilk and ½ cup medium rye flour. Mix thoroughly, pour into a lightly buttered bowl, cover and let ferment in a warm place overnight.

Sour Rye Ponies   PORTABLE OVEN
(Straight dough method, with "starter")

This is the new look for home-baked light sour rye; small form, rust color crust and a semi-blond, light crumb. Be sure to try some with homemade "starter."

YOU WILL NEED:
honey   malt extract
yeast   unsulphured molasses
wheat flour   caraway seeds
graham flour   corn meal
butter

Measure into mixing bowl ⅔ cup lukewarm water. Dissolve into 2 teaspoons honey. Crumble in 1 cake or 1 package yeast. Stir. When fully active (5 minutes), add 3 cups sifted wheat flour, 4 tablespoons medium coarse graham flour, 2½ teaspoons salt. Beat for 3 minutes, adding a little lukewarm water if needed. Cream in a cup 1 tablespoon butter, and add 1 tablespoon malt extract, 1½ tablespoons unsulphured molasses, 1 tablespoon crushed caraway seeds.

Work in 1 cup sour dough from rye (see sour dough starters, page 232). Combine with batter, then beat 3 minutes. The dough at this point is sticky and should be quite stiff. Turn onto lightly floured board and knead until dough is elastic and smooth. Place in greased bowl, brush surface with butter, cover and permit it to rise in a warm place until double its bulk. This will take about 1 hour. Punch down. Reverse position of dough in the bowl and let it rise again, covered. Limit this second rising to 25 to 30 minutes. Divide into 2 small loaves (each about 4½" in diameter) and 12 small rolls (each 1½" wide). For double or even triple recipe the amount of yeast will suffice.

Let the breads rest about 15 minutes while the oven is being preheated. Puncture each loaf at three places with a fork. This allows the carbon dioxide gas to escape during baking and prevents the loaves from cracking. Arrange breads to be baked on baking sheets, slightly buttered and sprinkled with a tablespoonful of corn meal.

Place a pan of hot water in the oven for steam. Start baking at 425° F. and after loaves have risen (about 15 minutes) and begin to brown, lower heat to 375° F. At the same time remove water. In another 10 minutes the rolls should be ready. The loaves will take about 15 to 20 minutes longer to bake. Tap the bread. If it sounds hollow, it is completely baked.

Sour Dough Pumpernickel   MIXER

STARTER:

YOU WILL NEED:

yeast cake	onion
medium dark rye flour	

Dissolve 1 yeast cake or package in 1 cup of lukewarm water in a mixing bowl. Mix in enough medium dark rye flour to make a soft paste. Wrap a small, peeled onion in cheesecloth and let it sink into the paste. Cover. Twice a day add to this ferment ½ cup water and about ¾ cup rye flour. Keep the mixture soft and at room temperature. When urgently needed, the starter may be used on the second day. However, it will have a more mature taste and more kick on the third day. Use it up in mixing your bread dough, but be sure to save some mixed dough for the next batch. Keep such reserve well wrapped in the refrigerator.

DOUGH:

YOU WILL NEED:

yeast	sour dough
brown sugar	all-purpose flour
molasses	powdered milk
butter	medium rye flour and rye
grated stale pumpernickel	meal
or mashed potatoes	corn meal
caraway seeds	

Measure into warm mixing bowl ⅓ cup lukewarm water and dissolve it in 1 package yeast. In 4 to 5 minutes, when bubbly, add 1 cup lukewarm water, 1 tablespoon brown sugar, 2 tablespoons dark molasses, 1 tablespoon butter, ½ cup grated stale pumpernickel bread (or ½ cup mashed potatoes, optional), 1 tablespoon caraway seeds, 1 tablespoon salt, 1 cup sour dough. Mix thoroughly. Then sift and blend 2 cups all-purpose flour, 2 tablespoons powdered milk (nonfat milk solids). The mixture should be soft. Beat it vigorously for 3 minutes. After a few minutes rest, gradually add 1 cup sifted medium rye flour and about ½ cup rye meal.

The dough must be still soft enough to beat it for 2 to 3 minutes, then turn onto floured board and knead energetically until the dough is no longer sticky but smooth, elastic and fairly stiff. Place in the usual manner in bowl and let rise in a warm spot until double. This shouldn't take more than 90 minutes. Rye flours cannot stand overfermentation and when forced to stretch too far may result in flat bread. Punch down. Play with the dough on the board for one minute, then to bowl for a second rising lasting about 20 minutes. Punch down. Divide into 4 loaves. Shape on board sprinkled with yellow corn meal. Place on buttered baking dish and with a sharp knife make a couple of slashes in the dough or puncture with fork. Preheat the oven to 400° F. Place a shallow pan of hot water in the oven to provide steam. Bake 15 minutes, then reduce heat to 375° F. Total baking time about 40 to 50 minutes. For a softer crust brush with melted butter after baking.

VARIATIONS IN PUMPERNICKEL

Pumpernickel is a misunderstood bread. People generally think that it is made from very fancy flours and other mostly top secret ingredients. Not so!

In its purest form, pumpernickel has only these five ingredients: water, rye meal, yeast, salt and shortening. The latter is optional. The coarse meal or dark rye flour will produce a natural dark shade in the crumb. Most commercially baked breads of this type are of lighter flours and then colored for effect with chicory, dark molasses, caramel or Kitchen Bouquet. You are probably familiar with two types of pumpernickel: the sweet and the sour. The first has no unusual flavoring agent; the latter, however, must be made with sour dough.

Corn Cakes or Corn Oysters   GRIDDLE

Although they sound and are so simple to make, these corn cakes, or call them corn fritters if you like, have made the reputation of more than one hostess. They are worlds apart from the usual flour and baking powder type of fritter. Ideally, there is in them no flour at all but if they are made from fresh corn that is inclined to be a little watery, anywhere from a teaspoonful of flour may be added. Essentially they are like tiny puffy omelets. This recipe as given here will serve 4 persons generously. In our household we count on 1 egg and ½ cup of corn for each person.

YOU WILL NEED:
eggs	butter
corn (canned kernels,	flour (optional)
fresh corn straight from	
the cob or frozen)	

To 4 slightly beaten egg yolks add 2 cups corn, ½ teaspoon salt. Fold in the whites of the 4 eggs which have been beaten until stiff but not dry. Set the griddle at 370°. Melt 2 tablespoons butter on griddle and drop the batter by tablespoonfuls. Bake on one side until the corn cake looks dry and is pocked with little holes. Turn and brown on the other side.

AT SERVING TIME:
Serve hot off the griddle with honey or maple syrup. Crisp bacon, frizzled ham or sausages make an ideal combination.

Skillet Spoon Bread   SKILLET

Delicious with ham or fried chicken!

YOU WILL NEED:
corn meal	milk
baking soda	buttermilk
eggs	butter

Sift ⅓ cup corn meal with ½ teaspoon baking soda, add ½ teaspoon salt. Put 3 eggs into the blender with 1 cup milk, 1 cup buttermilk. Combine egg and milk mixture with corn meal mixture and stir. Don't blend. Stir just enough to mix.

Preheat electric skillet with cover on to 460° F. Add ¼ cup

butter and when melted, pour in batter and cook with skillet covered for 25 to 30 minutes, or until brown and puffy.

AT SERVING TIME:
Serve immediately from skillet or it will flatten. Add a dab of butter to each serving if you like.

Superior Corn Bread   BLENDER

YOU WILL NEED:

large egg	butter
corn meal	baking powder
flour	salt
sour cream	

Place in blender one egg, ¾ cup corn meal, ¼ cup flour, 1 cup sour cream, 3 tablespoons melted butter, 1 teaspoon baking powder, ½ teaspoon salt. Blend 2 minutes. Set oven at 400° F. Butter generously an 8×8-inch baking pan. Pour mixture into pan. Bake 20 minutes or until brown.

If you use an iron pan or skillet it should be preheated and then brushed well with butter, lard or vegetable shortening.

AT SERVING TIME:
Cut into squares and serve hot.

Virginia Spoon Bread   BEATER

According to an old story, spoon bread was "invented" by a talented Negro cook at the home of George Washington on an occasion when important guests arrived for luncheon and there was nothing much on hand except some corn meal mush left from breakfast time.

From family to family, from county to county in Virginia, as well as from state to state all through the South, spoon bread recipes vary greatly. Sometimes white, sometimes yellow corn meal is used; sometimes a combination of hominy grits and corn meal. Though in some traditional Williamsburg recipes the eggs are not separated, the essential quality and technique are those of a soufflé.

YOU WILL NEED:

water-ground white corn meal	eggs
	baking powder
butter	milk

Stir 1 cup of white water-ground corn meal into 1 pint of boiling water with ½ teaspoon salt. Stir 1 minute, remove from fire and add 2 tablespoons butter. Beat well, add the yolks of 3 large or 4 small eggs and ½ teaspoon baking powder, if desired. Then beat in 1 cup cold milk. Beat again. Fold in the stiffly beaten whites of the eggs and pour into a hot buttered baking dish, preferably one with straight sides. Bake 25 minutes in a hot oven 400° F.

AT SERVING TIME:
Serve immediately directly from the baking dish with butter or gravy. This recipe serves 6.

Egg Yolk Glaze for Breads

Mix with fork 1 egg yolk and 2 tablespoons cold water. Brush over breads just before baking for shiny golden brown finish.

Egg White Glaze

Mix one unbeaten egg white and 2 tablespoons water. Brush over breads just before baking for shiny, light finish.

POINTERS ON POPOVERS

Here are a few pointers. If you want popovers to "hold over," bake at 500° F. for 15 minutes and then turn oven to 250° F. until done.

How do you know when a popover is "done"? They will have popped way above the pan. They should be crisp, brown and glossy on the outside and soft but not soggy on the inside. The toothpick is still a good tester. If it comes out dry the popover is cooked enough. If you like dry centers, punch a little hole in the side about 5 minutes before they are ready to come out of the oven. This will let out the steam, making crisp popovers that are excellent to serve along with creamed dishes or with salad and cheese instead of bread sticks. Popovers make fine "cases," much easier and just as pretty as patty shells.

Popovers take kindly to freezing too. No need to thaw; just place frozen into the oven.

Popovers   BEATER

Even without a mix, popovers are not at all difficult to make and they're so rewarding—if they pop! This recipe is considerably "speeded-up"—it eliminates the sifting of flour, the melting of shortening and it adds for those who want further insurance a bit of baking powder.

YOU WILL NEED:

eggs
milk
salad oil

all-purpose flour
baking powder (optional)

Beat 2 eggs until light. Add 1 cup milk, 1 tablespoon salad oil (not olive oil). Beat together with an electric beater. Add ⅞ cup all-purpose flour. Sifting is not necessary but if you wish to sift the flour, then use 1 cup flour measured after sifting. The reason for the difference is quite obvious for sifting aerates flour, makes it less bulky. With the flour add ¼ teaspoon salt, ¼ teaspoon baking powder, if you have it. Beat until smooth with the egg beater. The mixture should be heavy as whipping cream. If too thick, add a little more milk. Heavy iron muffin pans are generally used for popovers but they are not necessary. You may use aluminum pans if you wish, or ovenproof custard cups. Grease thoroughly bottom and sides. Fill half full with mixture. Have the oven preheated to at least 500° F. When the popovers have popped, that is in about 15 minutes, turn down the oven to 400° F. and continue baking 10 to 15 minutes longer or until done. The crust should sound crackly-crisp when tapped with your fingernail, the inside staying pleasantly moist—almost doughy but not wet. To be really sure you must break one open.

AT SERVING TIME:
Serve hot with plenty of butter, jam, honey or preserves with a luncheon salad or a hearty supper soup. Makes 8 popovers.

Popovers from a Mix   BLENDER

In the old days popovers were beaten until the arm ached and the cook was exhausted. All this has changed. Even more revolutionary are the changes in baking. Once we believed that you must have hissing-hot iron pans which you handled gingerly with tongs and layers of holders, greased over the hot stove, filling the kitchen with fumes of smoky fat. Now you use stone cold metal pans or custard cups—whatever is handy—and bake for 15 minutes instead of the old-fashioned 45, starting the popovers at 500° F., then turning the oven down to 400° F. for another 15 minutes or until done.

YOU WILL NEED:
    packaged popover mix   eggs
    milk

The recipe on the package is fine, but to make things easy, easier, easiest, mix the batter in your electric blender, placing in the glass container first 1 cup milk, then 2 whole eggs. Whir about 10 seconds till pale and foamy. Add mix all at once. Blend 10 seconds longer. Done!

AT SERVING TIME:
Serve hot with whipped butter.

Rosettes   DEEP FAT FRYER

Rosettes have always been considered hazardous, for both irons and fat must attain and keep a temperature of 370° F. (Many standard cookbooks will give you a recipe for the batter.) But the quickest and surest method is to use a package of popover mix.

YOU WILL NEED:
    package of popover mix

Stir up popover mix according to directions. Heat irons to 370° F., wipe off and dip into batter not more than ¾ of the way up. Let excess batter drip off. If there are bubbles, press down with your finger tips. Place irons in fat 370° F. When rosettes take form, shake or gently ease them from irons with a fork. Dry until golden brown. Drain upside down on paper towels. Rosettes may be made days, even weeks ahead and kept tightly covered in a jar or canister until they are to be used.

AT SERVING TIME:
Sprinkle with sugar and serve with tea, hot chocolate or mulled wine.

VARIATION: *ROSETTES POIVRADES* Instead of adding sugar, sprinkle with salt and freshly ground white or black pepper. These are delightful to serve with cocktails, soups or salads.

Yorkshire Pudding   BEATER

The traditional English accompaniment to roast beef.

YOU WILL NEED:
popover batter (page 240)   sausage, bacon or roast
                                beef drippings

Grease 9 × 12-inch pan with drippings from roast beef, sausage or
bacon. Pour popover batter (page 240) ½ inch deep into the pan.
Bake 15 minutes at 500° F.; reduce heat to 400° F. and bake 10 to
15 minutes longer, or until done. (To give a "homemade feeling"
to roast beef from a tin or delicatessen, warm the meat in a well
flavored gravy and serve with Yorkshire pudding. Or bake Yorkshire pudding like popovers in muffin tins.)

AT SERVING TIME:
Bring to the table right in the pan and cut into squares.

Crêpes from Popover Mix   BLENDER

These are known internationally as French pancakes, though in
different forms with different flavorings they are popular all over
the world not only for dessert but also as the basis of exquisite
entrées. The French pancake cannot be made properly from our
popular packaged "pancake mixes," designed to produce griddle
cakes which are puffier and of a different texture and flavor.

YOU WILL NEED:
popover mix   confectioner's sugar
eggs   (optional)
jelly or jam (optional)

To make up very thin and delicious crêpes, blend a package of
popover mix according to package directions but add 3 eggs

instead of 2. If possible, allow the batter to stand in the refrigerator for ½ hour. Cook in a 4- or 5-inch skillet, greasing it with a few drops of salad oil. Add a small quantity of the batter. Tip the skillet so that the bottom is covered. Cook over moderate heat. When brown underneath, turn and brown the other side. Use a few drops of oil for each pancake. Package makes 18 to 20 5-inch pancakes.

AT SERVING TIME:
For dessert, roll crêpes with jelly or jam and sprinkle with confectioner's sugar.

Peter Pan Pancakes   GRIDDLE

At an inn in Carmel, California, set high among live oaks and surrounded by mountainous gardens draped in Spanish moss, we discovered a modified crêpe suzette which blends certain Oriental elements with a continental sauce. This recipe will serve six, two apiece.

YOU WILL NEED:

eggs	lemon
milk	Cointreau
cornstarch	Chartreuse
butter	brandy
powdered sugar	

To make the crêpes, mix the well-beaten yolks of 3 eggs with 1 cup of milk and ¼ cup of cornstarch. This is most easily done in the blender. Add a pinch of salt to 3 egg whites and beat until stiff. Fold the egg whites into the egg yolk mixture and cook on a very lightly buttered electric griddle at 380° F., first on one side until the pancake begins to look a little dry and is covered with pin holes, and then turn and cook on the other side but very briefly.

For the sauce, cream together and cook in a saucepan at 180°
for ½ hour ⅓ cup of butter, 1 cup of powdered sugar, the juice
of 1 lemon, about 3 tablespoons.

AT SERVING TIME:
Roll the crêpes and add 1 tablespoon brandy, 2 tablespoons
Cointreau and 2 tablespoons Chartreuse to sauce and pour
heated sauce over crêpes.

Sour Dough Hot Cakes   GRIDDLE

These sour dough hot cakes are the king of all Sunday breakfasts,
especially when served with plenty of sweet whipped butter and
syrup or wild blackberry jam.

YOU WILL NEED:

eggs	soda
milk	baking powder
sour dough starter (see	flour
pages 232–233)	sugar

Combine 3 well-beaten eggs with 1 cup of milk and 2 cups sour
dough starter. To 1¾ cups sifted all-purpose flour add 1 tablespoon soda, 2 teaspoons baking powder, 1 teaspoon salt and
¼ cup sugar. Combine these mixtures, bake on a greased electric
griddle. These can be made on an ungreased griddle but in that
case ¼ cup melted fat must be added to the batter. To make
thinner cakes add more milk.

The old recipe says "test griddle as usual by flipping a drop of
water in center, and if it bounds off slowly it is the right temperature." We suggest setting your thermostat between 380° and
390° F.

AT SERVING TIME:
Keep hot on an electric hot tray. Do not stack.

Crêpes on the Griddle   GRIDDLE

An automatic griddle or even a skillet can with a slight amount of skill be used to take the place of considerable special equipment. You will find on page 213 a method for making a French omelet which completely dispenses with the need of a special omelet pan. You can also on the griddle or even in the fry pan make the thinnest of French crêpes as for crêpes suzette. For these you must set your thermostat at about 400° F. It may be helpful in a case like this to spray the griddle with a non-caloric shortening and use clarified butter or peanut oil. The high temperature stops the batter almost immediately upon contact. Sometimes you will find that crêpes made on the griddle are not too shapely but actually it doesn't matter too much for they are generally rolled or folded so that the contours do not show.

Blini   BLENDER AND GRIDDLE

A package of buckwheat pancake mix or any other good pancake mix will make delicate and authentic-tasting blini. Perfect to serve with red or black caviar and sour cream for a Sunday luncheon, this recipe makes about three dozen dollar-size blini.

YOU WILL NEED:

buckwheat pancake mix	butter
sour milk or buttermilk	egg yolk, egg white
or yogurt	

Place in the blender or a mixing bowl 1 cup buckwheat pancake mix, 1 cup sour milk, buttermilk or yogurt, 1 tablespoon butter, 1 egg yolk. Blend 30 seconds. Leave uncovered at room temperature until ready to use. Fold in 1 stiffly beaten egg white.

Drop batter by tablespoonfuls onto a well greased griddle preheated to 380°. As soon as the cake begins to look dry and is pocked with tiny air holes, turn with a spatula and cook briefly on the other side. Never turn a blini or pancake more than once or it will lose its delicate tenderness. As pancakes are finished place them on a preheated hot tray. Do not stack. Do not cover.

AT SERVING TIME:
Brush with melted butter and serve on heated plates. Have on hand in little bowls sour cream, chopped onion or chives, caviar, red or black. Each person puts on his blini a dab of caviar and sour cream and/or onion or chives if desired.

Homemade English Muffins   GRIDDLE

English muffins may be made from almost any sort of white bread dough, a hot roll mix, or even ready-to-bake biscuits.

YOU WILL NEED:
white bread dough or hot   flour or corn meal
    roll mix or ready-to-bake
    biscuits

After the dough has risen, place it on a board sprinkled with flour or corn meal. Flatten with a rolling pin or pat until dough is half an inch thick. Cut with a biscuit cutter or floured glass into circles 2 or 3 inches in diameter.

Or you can form the dough into balls about 1½ inches in diameter and pat out into circles ¼ to ½ inch thick.

Or if you use ready-to-bake biscuits, pat them into circles on a floured board.

Preheat the griddle to 370° F. Cook the muffins 10 to 15 minutes, turning several times during the cooking. If the insides seem doughy, split and turn raw side over on griddle for a minute or two.

AT SERVING TIME:
Serve hot off the griddle with butter or allow to cool, pull apart and toast under the broiler. Dough made from 2½ to 3 cups of flour or 1 package of hot roll mix will make a dozen muffins.

Home-Ground Cereal   BLENDER
AND SAUCEPAN

A long time ago at the home of a gourmet friend far up on the plateau in the Valle de Bravo in Mexico, we ate for breakfast a cereal that had been ground that morning in a special mill imported from Minneapolis. For years we yearned for that special mill and that very special cereal. Then one day we got some wheat from the local seed store and ground it in the blender, cooked it in the automatic saucepan. Served with cream and shaved maple sugar from Vermont, it was as good and maybe even a touch more delicate than the remembered breakfast.

Whole Grain Cereals   SAUCEPAN

An epicurean delight is whole grain cereal or old-fashioned steel-cut oats cooked ever so gently in an automatic saucepan at about 200° F., which is equivalent to the double boiler. Practically every cereal has its own cooking time but here is a general rule:

Start the cereal in cold water, if you like, or if you are a traditionalist, use the hot water and cook about 5 minutes at boiling temperature, about 212° F. Then lower the heat to 200° and continue cooking. Fifteen or twenty minutes will be required for finely ground cereal and regular oatmeal. Two or three hours is better for stone-ground corn meal, cracked wheat, hominy or steel-cut oats. The pan should be kept covered during this cooking and the steam vents closed. Under those circumstances the water will not evaporate, the cereal will not stick. The result will be extraordinarily smooth, rich and luscious.

It is perfectly possible and highly desirable to set the cereal cooking many hours before you want to eat it, even the night before, just as our grandmothers did when they had the back of the stove. If time is not a factor you do not even need to bother to reset the thermostat. Simply adjust it to the simmering point, about 200° F. It will overshoot enough to give the desired effect without any more trouble.

Automatic Cereals   SAUCEPAN

The Home Economics Department of a large appliance company reveals that an amazing proportion of their letters include questions about cooking cereals. Actually there has been a revolution in cooking methods. The old recipes require you to boil the water and then very very slowly, so as not to interfere with the boiling, add the cereal. No matter how hard you try it is often impossible to avoid lumps. And so many people—smart or lazy—began stirring a certain amount of cold water into the cereal and adding it to the hot water.

Now we have discovered that the best way of all is to use all the water cold, add the cereal and the salt, set the thermostat on your saucepan at boiling, about 212° F., and boil the usual time required on the package and then allow to stand at simmering temperature, about 200° until ready to serve.

QUICKEST, EASIEST OATMEAL

Among the best of the quick-cooking cereals is oatmeal which has been precooked in steam by the manufacturer and needs only the briefest preparation. You can add the oatmeal to briskly boiling water and cook for 1 minute, but if you want a creamier, smoother, lusciously melting dish of oatmeal, try this method:

Place 2 cups of quick cooking oatmeal, 4 cups cold water and 1 teaspoon salt into the automatic saucepan, set thermostat at about 200° F., cook 1 minute, stirring occasionally. Cover the pan and set the thermostat at warm and allow to stand for a few minutes. This makes 4 servings.

Fritters

French Style Fritters   DEEP FAT FRYER

There are many different kinds of fritter casings for meats, fish, vegetables as well as fruits. Some are thick baking-powder crusts, hiding their morsels in a bready ball. We are concerned here only with the aristocratic Parisian version where the crust is as thin as the calyx of a flower. Many different flavorings and fillings are possible. This batter is made from a packaged popover mix.

YOU WILL NEED:

popover mix	milk or white wine or
eggs	brandy
sugar	fruit
	vegetable oil for frying

Make up a package of popover mix, adding to the mix 2 egg yolks, 1 tablespoon sugar and ½ cup milk or white wine, or ⅜ cup warm water and 2 tablespoons brandy. Combine with a few swift strokes. Don't handle too much at this point. Let stand at room temperature a half hour. Just before making your fritters, fold in stiffly beaten whites of 2 eggs. The mixture should be as thick as whipping cream.

Heat vegetable oil to 370° F. Take up pieces of well-dried, floured or sugared fruit on a fork. Dip into batter. Allow batter to drip through the tines of the fork. Drop a few at a time into hot fat and cook 3 to 5 minutes until golden brown.

One thing to remember: Fruits should be well drained and

250

then dried on a paper towel and dusted with a little flour or confectioner's sugar. Otherwise, during the frying, steam develops and the fritters are not as crisp as they should be.

AT SERVING TIME:
Sprinkle with sugar or sugar and cinnamon. Glaze or not as desired. Serve plain or with a fruit sauce.

Very Special Fritter Batter   BLENDER

This is perfect for bananas, orange sections or pineapple chunks that have been well dried on paper towels. It is a stiff batter so do not attempt to thin it down.

YOU WILL NEED:

egg	double acting baking
milk	powder
flour	sugar
	butter

Place into the blender 1 egg, ⅓ cup milk, 1 teaspoon butter, 1 cup sifted flour, 2 teaspoons double acting baking powder, 1¼ teaspoon salt, ¼ cup sugar. Blend about 15 seconds or until well mixed and smooth. It may be necessary to stir down once or twice with a rubber spatula.

Fritter Batter   BLENDER

This batter makes a very thin delicate coating. You may use it for all kinds of fritters. For the unsweet type omit sugar. If you want a fluffy crust, beat the eggs separately and add the egg whites to the batter at the last minute. Stir very little afterwards.

YOU WILL NEED:

eggs	salad oil
milk	all-purpose flour
sugar (optional)	brandy or lemon juice

Place in the blender 2 eggs, 2 teaspoons sugar, 1 cup milk, 1 teaspoon salad oil, 1 tablespoon brandy or a dash of lemon juice, ¼ teaspoon salt. Blend about 15 seconds. Add 1 cup sifted all-purpose flour and blend only a second or two, or just until mixed.

Creole Rice Calas   DEEP FAT FRYER

"Belles Calas! Tout chaud!" In the French Quarter of New Orleans, even 50 years ago, each morning began with this musical cry. The calas woman made her rounds in time to supply these delicious rice fritters for the morning cup of café au lait. Her dress was guinea blue, her headdress and apron white as clouds. And the capacious towel-covered bowl which she carried on her head was crowded with calas. Light as air, sun-gold and scented with spices that echoed the fragrance of the wisteria and jasmine that bloomed around the jalousies.

Except in a few homes, the calas is almost forgotten. The oldest recipes called for long cooking of rice and an overnight rising with yeast, which was a bother. Then the capricious business of frying! This version is simple and certain to be a success.

YOU WILL NEED:

rice	lemon rind
eggs	baking powder
sugar	flour
nutmeg	

Cook ⅔ cup rice with ½ teaspoon salt until rather soft, or use 2 cups cooked rice. Do not drain rice but let the water be absorbed. Mash lightly with a fork. Add 3 beaten eggs, ½ cup sugar, ¼ teaspoon nutmeg, 1 teaspoon grated lemon rind, 2¼ teaspoons baking powder, 6 tablespoons flour. Stir well. Drop by teaspoonfuls into fat at 365° F. Fry until golden brown. Drain. Sprinkle with confectioner's sugar. Makes about 36.

AT SERVING TIME:
Serve warm with coffee or chocolate for Sunday breakfast or supper or as a dessert at lunchtime.

Banana Fritters   DEEP FAT FRYER

YOU WILL NEED:
bananas   French Style fritter batter
lemon juice   (see page 250)
rum or brandy   whipped cream or fruit
                               sauce

Split bananas in half lengthwise and cut each piece into thirds. Sprinkle with lemon juice and rum or brandy. Cover. Let stand about ½ hour. Drain well. Fry in the usual manner (see French Style Fritters page 250).

AT SERVING TIME:
Serve hot with whipped cream as is done in Julian's Castle in San Francisco, or an orange sauce made by adding ½ cup water or white wine to ½ cup marmalade.

San Francisco Banana Fritters
DEEP FAT FRYER

These may be made either in deep fat or in shallow fat, just about 1½ to 2 inches deep, which means that you can use your deep fat fryer or automatic saucepan or electric skillet.

To deep fry, fill fryer half full of salad oil or melted vegetable shortening.

To shallow fry, place 1½ to 2 inches of oil or shortening in the electric skillet. Set thermostat at 375° and heat until the light goes off.

YOU WILL NEED:
 bananas   fritter batter (see
 flour   page 251)

Peel 3 firm bananas. Cut into 4 diagonal pieces and coat with flour, using about 4 tablespoons flour. Dip into Very Special Fritter Batter making sure each piece is completely coated. With a slotted spoon or a strainer place the pieces into the hot fat and cook 4 to 6 minutes, turning once or twice until golden brown. Drain on paper towels.

AT SERVING TIME:
These fritters may be served hot with ham, roast pork or chicken or they may be served as a dessert with a hot fruit sauce with honey or with maple syrup. Makes 12 fritters and you will want to serve 3 or 4 apiece.

Pineapple Fritters   DEEP FAT FRYER

YOU WILL NEED:
 French style fritter batter   pineapple
  (page 250)   kirsch or rum (optional)

Sprinkle drained, canned or quick-frozen pineapple with kirsch or rum and let stand 30 minutes. Drain again. Dip into fritter batter. Fry as directed in French style fritter batter (page 250). Drain on paper towel. Sprinkle with granulated sugar and place under the broiler just long enough to form a glaze.

AT SERVING TIME:
Serve warm with or without sauce.

VARIATION: *APRICOT OR PEACH FRITTERS*   Fritters of canned halved apricots or quartered canned or fresh peaches are made the same as pineapple fritters. Being sweet, they need a tart accompaniment. A clear lemon sauce is delicious.

VARIATION: *ORANGE FRITTERS*   Use fresh orange sections or thinly sliced oranges with seeds removed. Serve with powdered sugar and pass a bottle of Grand Marnier or Cointreau liqueur.

VARIATION: *APPLE FRITTERS*   Thin slices of raw apple or canned sliced apples for pie can be used. Especially good for apple fritters is a batter lightly flavored with rum. Since apples take so kindly to cinnamon, glaze them by sprinkling with sugar and cinnamon. (See French style fritters, page 250). Serve with a scatter of chopped walnuts.

Tangerine Fritters   DEEP FAT FRYER

The old name for tangerines is mandarin and that is how you ask for them in a can. (The best brands come from Japan, by the way.)

YOU WILL NEED:
French style fritter batter   tangerine or canned man-
    (page 250)   darin orange sections
                                     lime or lemon juice

Break tangerines into sections or drain canned mandarin orange sections. Sprinkle with lime or lemon juice. Let stand about 15 minutes. Drain again and dry on paper towel. Flour lightly and fry as usual. (See French style fritters page 250).

AT SERVING TIME:
Serve warm with or without sauce.

Squash Flower Fritters　　DEEP FAT FRYER

Did you know (it took me years to discover) that you can eat the blossoms and have squash too, if you pick off only the male flowers? The male flowers are not difficult to distinguish. They lack the plump lobe at the base. But don't take all the male flowers, leave a few "roosters" for the flock!

YOU WILL NEED:
squash flowers   fritter batter (page 251)

Dip squash flowers in fritter batter (see page 251). Fry in deep hot salad oil (375° F.). Drain on paper towels or napkins.

AT SERVING TIME:
Pass clear pale honey, preferably sage honey from Vermont.

VARIATION: *FLOWER FRITTERS* Use nasturtiums in the same way as squash blossoms to make fritters; you may also use borage flowers, elderberry blossoms. Acacia flower fritters are revered in Hungary.

Glazed Fritters　　DEEP FAT FRYER

Most professional and beautiful eating are fritters which have been sprinkled after frying with sugar and then placed under the broiler just long enough to melt the sugar into a lovely glisten. Practical idea, for you may then fry the fritters some hours ahead of time. They'll reheat as they glaze.

Crêpes or pancakes, by the way, may be reheated the same way. To keep warm and crisp, place in a single layer on a heated hot tray. Do not cover.

Japanese Tempura   DEEP FAT FRYER

Connoisseurs have called Japanese tempura the most delicious food in the world. Written in picture letters which represent silk gauze, it means "to wear a light stuff of flour, as a woman wears silk gauze, that the desire may be stimulated in the beholder by glimpses of the beauty beneath."

Tempura, which Tokyo claims as its specialty, is made by deep-frying pieces of fish or shrimp covered with a batter. In Osaka and Kyoto, sweet potatoes, string beans, shoestring carrots, thinly sliced lotus root, chrysanthemum leaves, etc., are prepared in the same fashion. Popular, too is a clam tempura in which the clams are minced rather than used whole and added to the batter along with fresh chopped chives or green onion tops and dropped by spoonfuls.

Famous tempura chefs guard the secret of the ingredients and method of combining them for the batter with an intensity that at times seems amusing. Some use eggs while others claim that the best batter is made with only flour and water. Most of the best chefs make their own blends of oils for frying. The oils of sesame, rice, rapeseed, peanut and soy bean are used in Japan, but any of the standard salad oils can be substituted.

Here is a batter recipe from one of the famous chefs in Tokyo:

YOU WILL NEED:
   egg   flour

Beat 1 egg lightly, add ⅔ cup water, then 1 cup flour and ½ teaspoon salt, beating gently but constantly with a fork or a French wire whip. Or put in blender for 5 seconds.

Vegetable Tempura   DEEP FAT FRYER

Unusual and exceptionally delicious are these fritters.

YOU MAY USE:
Eggplant peeled and cut into ¼-inch slices, celery cut into 3-inch strips, sliced onions, carrots, quick-frozen Frenched green beans and cauliflower (thawed), or any other combination of vegetables.

All except the potatoes (which are sliced and fried like potato chips) should be dipped into tempura batter (page 257).

Dip vegetables into batter (page 257) and let drip along the side of the bowl so that any excess drains away. Drop no more than 5 or 6 at a time into deep hot fat, 375° F. Fry 2 or 3 minutes until browned. Drain on paper towels.

AT SERVING TIME:
Serve with special tempura sauce called Dashi (page 200).

Sandwiches

Sunday Morning Sandwiches GRIDDLE

Your breakfast ham and toast make a fine pair grilled together. It's interesting to use two different breads—one slice of white, one of whole wheat.

YOU WILL NEED:
    ham or bacon spread   bread
    butter

For the filling use a breakfast meat—ham or bacon preferred. Butter the top and bottom of the sandwich as well as the inside for extra goodness.

AT SERVING TIME:
Brown sandwiches on each side and serve immediately.

French Toast Sandwiches GRIDDLE

An interesting, easy version of New Orleans' Lost Bread, Bavarian Poor Knights or California's Monte Christo!

YOU WILL NEED:
    white bread   eggs
    ham, tongue spread or   milk
       liver or chicken paté

259

Make sandwiches from thinly sliced white bread, leaving the crusts for extra flavor. For filling, use ham or tongue spread, liver or chicken paté. Dip into milk and egg mixture (2 eggs slightly beaten with 1 cup milk, salt, pepper). They can be baked waffle style or on a sandwich grill, griddle or frying pan. Just brown in butter, first on one side, then on the other. Serves at least 4.

AT SERVING TIME:

Serve with sugar and cinnamon, honey, maple syrup, applesauce, or apple butter.

Baked French Toast Sandwiches

PORTABLE OVEN

Another version—instead of dipping the bread into the milk and eggs you pour it on.

YOU WILL NEED:

white bread	egg
ham, tongue spread or	onion salt
liver or minced	celery salt
chicken paté	dry mustard
milk	

Make sandwiches as described in French Toast Sandwiches (see page 259), or use thinly sliced luncheon meat or chopped beef and some thin slices of sharp cheddar cheese.

Season the milk and egg mixture with ½ teaspoon onion salt, ½ teaspoon celery salt, 1 teaspoon prepared mustard. Pour over sandwiches in a shallow buttered baking dish. Bake in moderate over 350° F.

AT SERVING TIME:

Serve immediately and your sandwiches are puffy almost like a soufflé.

Heroes Trinacria

SKILLET

People from all over New York trek to a little shop on Third Avenue for these. They use veal. We have substituted luncheon meat.

YOU WILL NEED:

olive oil	orégano
onion	marsala or sherry wine
garlic	green peppers
tomatoes	French loaves
basil	luncheon meat

Sauté lightly in 2 tablespoons olive oil 1 onion sliced, 1 clove garlic crushed. Add 1 can luncheon meat and 2 fresh tomatoes cubed, ¼ teaspoon basil, ¼ teaspoon orégano, ¼ cup wine. Simmer gently 5 minutes. Push to one side. Cook until just tender 4 green peppers each cut in 6 strips. Pile on heated brown 'n' serve French loaves cut lengthwise.

This makes 3 hero sandwiches.

AT SERVING TIME:

Slice diagonally in pieces almost an inch thick for more genteel eating.

Riviera Loaf

PORTABLE OVEN

On the Mediterranean coast they serve such whole-loaf, whole meal sandwiches.

YOU WILL NEED:

Italian, French or Vienna bread	cheese
butter	tomatoes
	frankfurters

Use crusty Italian, French or Vienna bread cut crosswise in 2 or 3 thick slices. Butter generously. Top with sliced cheese, fresh tomatoes and frankfurters split lengthwise. Heat in moderate oven at 350° F. for 15 to 20 minutes.

AT SERVING TIME:
Cut into generous pie-shaped wedges and serve steaming hot.

Denver Sandwich　　　　SKILLET

Some call it "Western." Any number of different types of meat may be used. But you should always include some fresh green peppers and some onions.

YOU WILL NEED:
<table>
<tr><td>cooked ham</td><td>onion</td></tr>
<tr><td>green peppers</td><td>eggs</td></tr>
</table>

To make three sandwiches use a cup of cooked ham. Cut it into small cubes. Lightly brown in butter or bacon fat along with 1 onion and green pepper, both chopped. Stir in 4 eggs slightly beaten. Brown lightly on both sides like a pancake.

AT SERVING TIME:
Serve between lightly toasted, well-buttered bread.

Sweet and Sour Pork Sandwiches　　GRIDDLE

Call this a leftover if you must. This open-faced sandwich makes a delightful entree. Baked ham or even canned luncheon meat may be used.

YOU WILL NEED:

gravy	cinnamon
red wine vinegar	cayenne pepper
onion salt	raisins
brown sugar	roast pork (12 slices)
allspice	toasted buns (optional)
bayleaf	

Heat 2 cups gravy, homemade or canned, with 2 tablespoons red wine vinegar, 1 teaspoon onion salt, 2 tablespoons brown sugar, 1 teaspoon allspice, a bayleaf, ½ teaspoon cinnamon, a few grains of cayenne pepper and ¼ cup raisins. Simmer about 5 minutes.

AT SERVING TIME:

Heat slices roast pork 1 or 2 minutes in sauce. Serve on heated or lightly toasted split buns or bread. Makes about 6 servings.

Desserts

Mabel Stegner's Apple Sauce   BLENDER

This is an incredibly easy apple sauce. The unpeeled apples are blended while raw and simply brought to a boil. That's all!

YOU WILL NEED:
tart apples, greenings or   sugar
McIntosh

Put 3½ cups (1 pound) diced unpeeled tart cooking apples in the blender, add 1 cup water and half to three-fourths cup sugar. Run until just blended, about 30 seconds. Pour into a saucepan and bring to a full boil.

AT SERVING TIME:
Serve warm or cool. Makes 2½ cups apple sauce.

Tart Green Apple Sauce   BLENDER AND
SAUCEPAN

YOU WILL NEED:
greening or tart green   sugar
apples   lemon juice, cinnamon

Wash carefully and cut but do not peel greening apples or tart green apples. Remove cores, of course. Add just enough water to cover and cook at 350° F. about 10 to 15 minutes or until tender.

While still warm, place in the blender. Blend until peeling disappears. The peel of the apple adds an incredible amount of extra flavor to homemade apple sauce.

Add sugar to taste—how much depends upon the tartness of the apple. If apple sauce seems flavorless, add a bit of lemon juice, a touch of cinnamon and maybe a touch of salt.

AT SERVING TIME:
This is most delicious when served slightly warm.

Apples Croûtes   PORTABLE OVEN

YOU WILL NEED:
sliced white bread or	currant jelly
English muffins	vanilla or almond extract
butter or margarine	heavy cream or sour cream
canned baked apples	

Butter six slices of white bread (remove crusts or not) or use English muffins, split. Place buttered side down on buttered foil. Butter top side of the slices. Cut down through the center 3 canned baked apples. Set cut side down on the bread. Melt ½ cup currant jelly and add ½ teaspoon vanilla or almond extract. Spoon carefully over the apples. Allow to stand long enough for the jelly to thicken—about half an hour or less in the refrigerator.

AT SERVING TIME:
Serve with plain cream, whipped cream or slightly sweetened sour cream. (Whole baked apples may be used, but they make rather a large dessert—too much for most people.) Serves 6.

VARIATION: *APPLE SAUCE* (see page 264) without the addition of jelly or flavorings may be served in the same manner on the toasted slices of bread or English muffins with plain or whipped cream.

Grilled Fruits   BROILER

Delicious to serve with broiled meats or as a dessert!

YOU WILL NEED:
    fresh or canned fruits   melted butter
    sugar (brown or white) or
      honey

Bananas are probably one of the most popular fruits to grill. Slice them lengthwise and brush on both sides with melted butter. Or use fresh or canned pineapple slices or wedges, halved peaches or apricots, quartered peeled apples or even canned sliced apples, grapefruit sections or sliced oranges. Brush generously with melted butter, sprinkle with sugar (brown or white) or honey. Place under the broiler and cook until well heated and lightly tinted a golden brown.

AT SERVING TIME:
Serve hot.

VARIATION: *GRILLED FRUITS AFIRE*   Broil the fruits as above. At serving time, slightly warm ¼ to ½ cup rum, cognac, bourbon or vodka. Set a match to the warmed spirit and pour blazing over the fruits.

Steaming Puddings in the Pressure Cooker

Pour pudding batter into generously greased molds, filling them a half to two-thirds full. This allows for expansion of batter.

Place on rack above water in pressure cooker. Tie waxed paper loosely over mold to prevent steam which collects on cover dropping on pudding.

Remove cover after prescribed time. Remove waxed paper.

Loosen pudding at one side to let in air. Turn out on a heated serving dish. The flaming pudding of old had heated brandy poured over it. A lighted match touched off the brandy. Nowadays we warm the brandy slightly, set it afire and pour on flaming.

A new nonalcoholic way is to soak lumps of sugar in vanilla, lemon or orange flavoring extract; place around pudding. Touch match to one lump and the pudding is encircled with bright flames.

Miracle-Easy Plum Pudding
PRESSURE COOKER

This recipe makes a large, dark pudding, not overly rich but wonderfully pungent and delicate. It may be stored in its own mold in the pantry. (If you must re-use the mold, wrap the pudding in aluminum foil.) Freeze, if you wish, or sprinkle with a little liquor and store in a covered crock or tin box.

YOU WILL NEED:

devil's food cake mix	sherry, Madeira, brandy,
fruit cake mix	rum, whiskey or grape
egg	juice

Combine 1 package devil's food cake mix with half the amount of water called for on the package. Add 1 package fruit cake mix, 1 egg and 2 tablespoons sherry, Madeira, brandy, rum, whiskey or grape juice. Stir until well blended. Put mixture into a well-buttered 2-pint pudding mold (it should not be more than two-thirds full). Place mold on the rack in the pressure cooker; pour boiling water around the mold (2½ cups for 4-quart cooker, 3 to 4 cups for 6-quart cooker) and steam 30 minutes. Reduce pressure instantly.

AT SERVING TIME:
Serve flamed with a liquor that matches the one used in the pudding. Pass the traditional hard sauce.

Plum Duff   PRESSURE COOKER

Moist, fruity, yet delicate and light. An old English specialty.

YOU WILL NEED:
eggs	cooked prunes
brown sugar	flour
shortening	soda

Beat 2 eggs thoroughly, and blend in 1 cup brown sugar,
½ cup melted shortening, 2 cups well drained, cut-up pitted
cooked prunes. Sift together and stir in 1 cup sifted flour, ½
teaspoon salt, 1 teaspoon soda. Pour into well greased one quart
mold. Pressure cook at 15 pounds for 15 minutes.

AT SERVING TIME:
Serve with creamy sauce (page 209). Serves 8.

Chocolate Soufflé   BLENDER

YOU WILL NEED:
milk	chocolate pieces
butter	eggs

Heat ½ cup milk and 2 tablespoons butter until butter is melted.
Empty 1 6-ounce package of chocolate pieces into container of
your blender. Add hot milk, cover and blend on high speed for
20 seconds. Add 4 egg yolks, cover and blend for 20 seconds
longer. In a 1½-quart soufflé dish, beat 5 egg whites with a
portable electric rotary beater until *very* stiff but not dry. Gradually pour chocolate mixture over egg whites, folding gently with
a rubber spatula until thoroughly blended. Bake in a 375° F. oven
for 30 to 35 minutes. Serves 4.

AT SERVING TIME:
Sprinkle with sugar. Serve at once, with whipped or sour cream.

Ginger Soufflé   BLENDER

YOU WILL NEED:

cream   preserved ginger
butter   ginger syrup
white bread   eggs

Heat 1 cup cream and 3 tablespoons butter until butter is melted.
Break 1 thinly sliced piece of white bread into the blender. Add
hot cream, cover and blend for 20 seconds. Add ⅔ cup preserved
ginger and ½ cup syrup from a jar of ginger, cover and blend for
20 seconds longer. Add egg yolks, cover and blend for 12 seconds.
In a 2-quart soufflé dish beat 5 egg whites with a hand or electric
rotary beater until *very* stiff, but not dry. Gradually pour ginger
mixture over egg whites, folding gently with a rubber spatula
until thoroughly blended. Bake in 375° F. oven for 30 to 35
minutes. Serves 4.

AT SERVING TIME:

Sprinkle with sugar. Serve immediately.

Dinner Table Soufflé   BLENDER, MIXER,
AND ROTISSERIE

Because it requires no basic sauce and no previous preparation,
this soufflé is ideal to prepare right at the dinner table a few
minutes before the guests sit down. Or if you want a longer time
to eat, you can prepare the soufflé after the meal has started.
Practically any type of liqueur or spirit can be used. Generally
this soufflé is served very soft in the center, and so it is cooked
in the French fashion at a fairly high temperature for just about
20 minutes.

Because it contains no thickening this soufflé is extremely delicate and except in the hands of the most experienced cook it might prove troublesome if you tried to cook it in the kitchen and bring it to the table in the usual way. I bake the soufflé in the rotisserie oven right at the table. Great drama for the guests to watch! If the bell rings before you are ready for your dessert, simply turn the oven down to 300° F. Don't touch; don't peek.

YOU WILL NEED:

eggs, separated	coffee-flavored liqueur
sugar	and instant coffee (or
	rum, cognac, or orange
	juice)

Into the glass container of the blender place 4 egg yolks, 4 table-spoons superfine sugar, 2 tablespoons coffee-flavored cordial, and 2 teaspoons instant coffee. Or you may substitute rum, cognac, or orange juice for the cordial and instant coffee. Blend about 20 seconds or until the mixture is thick and pale.

Preheat the oven to 400° F.

Place 5 egg whites in a straight-sided 1½-quart baking dish. (It is the rule in France that you use 1 more white than yolk.) Beat the whites with a portable electric mixer until they are stiff but not dry. Pour the egg yolk mixture onto the whites and fold into the whites with a rubber spatula—or, if you work lightly, you can use a spoon. Bake at 400° F. about 20 minutes.

AT SERVING TIME:

Which is instantaneously, of course, sprinkle with superfine sugar and serve with whipped cream or some of the liqueur or spirit that was used to make it. Serves 4.

For *SOUFFLE FLAMBE*, warm ever-so-slightly about ¼ cup of the liqueur or rum in a small heatproof ramekin or ladle or porringer; set a match to the liqueur and pour, flaming, over the soufflé.

Zabaione BLENDER

This famous Italian dessert is highly controversial as to the spelling, the technique, and the ingredients. Sometimes it is spelled "sabayon"; more often "zabaione" or "zabaglione."

The traditional wine to use is Italian Marsala but a moderately sweet sherry may be used or Madeira or rum. If you use rum—only half as much.

Zabaione is served either warm in warmed stemmed glasses or chilled. Often it is used as a sauce over a cake or a pudding or fruits.

The classic recipes call only for egg yolks. But we learned from no less an authority that Mama Laura (of Mama Laura's own notable restaurant in New York) that adding a couple of whites to half a dozen yolks makes a lighter, more delicate and elegant dessert.

This recipe is close to miraculous because it requires no cooking whatsoever. All you do is heat the wine.

YOU WILL NEED:
    egg yolks   Marsala or sherry
    sugar   egg whites (optional)

To serve 4, heat to boiling point ¾ cup Marsala, sherry or Madeira, or ⅜ cup rum. Place in the glass container of the blender 6 egg yolks or 4 egg yolks and 2 whole eggs. Add 6 tablespoons sugar. Cover and blend just about 5 seconds, just enough to mix the eggs and the sugar. It is important not to blend too much. While the blender is still running, remove cover and slowly pour in the hot wine. As soon as the last drop is added the zabaione should be foamy and thick, ready to use.

If for any reason it should not seem quite thick enough you can go back to the old method and heat it at 200° F. or in the top of a double boiler. Stir constantly! Remove from heat *as soon as it begins to look puffy.*

AT SERVING TIME:

Pour into 4 warmed wine or champagne glasses. Serve with lady fingers or macaroons. Or chill and serve plain or with fruits, i.e., peaches, strawberries or pears, fresh or poached. Can also be used as a sauce—warm or cold, and poured over ice cream, cake or puddings.

Unforbidden Egg Nog   BLENDER AND MIXER

During the holiday season egg nog makes a delightful dessert. And with the new low calorie packaged whipped topping that approximates whipped cream in everything except calories—a taste for egg nog must be indulged.

YOU WILL NEED:

packaged dessert topping mix	vanilla
	noncaloric sweetener
egg yolks	egg whites
bourbon or American blended whiskey	milk
golden rum	nutmeg or cinnamon

Prepare whipped topping mix as directed on the package. This must be done with an electric mixer, otherwise it takes practically forever.

In the blender place 4 egg yolks, blend about 10 seconds or until thick and lemon colored. While blender is still running pour into the center ¾ cup bourbon or American blended whiskey and ⅓ cup golden rum, 1 teaspoon vanilla and enough noncaloric sweetener to equal ⅔ cup sugar.

Turn to the beater again and beat 4 egg whites until stiff. Place the egg whites into the large serving bowl, fold in the whipped topping, then the sweetened egg yolk mixture, add 2 cups milk and beat well with the mixer. Allow to chill and mellow in the refrigerator for at least 24 hours. The old recipes used to suggest two or three days of mellowing but the mechanical blending and mixing shortens the time necessary for mellowing.

AT SERVING TIME:
Serve in sherbet, champagne or wine glasses. Sprinkle with freshly grated nutmeg or cinnamon. Recipe makes 14 servings of about 4 ounces each.

VARIATION: If calories are no problem use ⅔ cup sugar instead of a substitute.

Crème Brulée (Broiled Cream)   BLENDER, SAUCEPAN, AND BROILER

This is a rich custard which gets a topping of crackling crisp brown sugar. The old recipes call for scalding the cream, cooking over warm water, setting the pan into cracked ice, using an iron salamander, but we translate it into the blender, the thermostatically controlled frying pan or saucepan, the freezing compartment of your refrigerator and the electric broiler. This recipe should serve 6 to 8.

YOU WILL NEED:
eggs   light cream
brown or white sugar   nutmeg

In the blender place 6 eggs, ¾ cup light brown sugar or 6 tablespoons white sugar, 3 cups light cream, a pinch of salt and a sprinkle of freshly grated nutmeg. Blend until light and creamy, but not too frothy, about 15 seconds. Cook at 200° F., stirring constantly until the mixture coats a silver spoon. Pour into 6 to 8 custard cups or ramekins and set on a cookie sheet in the freezing compartment until cool, stirring once or twice. Sprinkle at least ¼-inch deep with light brown sugar so that no custard shows.

Set under the broiler until sugar melts, watching every second to be sure it does not burn. Put back into the refrigerator. The top will congeal into a shiny crust like the clear part of peanut brittle.

AT SERVING TIME:
It is customary to give the crust a slight whack with a fork or knife to shatter it in the center, probably to make it easier to get at the lovely cream underneath.

VARIATIONS: CREAMLESS CREME BRULEE   Instead of light cream you may use 3 cups milk and 3 tablespoons butter— all of it goes into the blender together.

EASIEST CREAM BRULEE   Instead of basic ingredients, use an instant vanilla pudding and blend in 2 egg yolks. You do not need to bother to cook anything. Simply follow package directions. Chilling is unnecessary, of course. Simply cover the pudding with light brown sugar and proceed as above.

P.S. In all Crème Brulée recipes it is important not to have any lumps for they make large dark blotches. Some people sieve the sugar, but it isn't necessary. If sugar is lumpy, give it a whirl in the blender.

Quickest Crème Brulée   BROILER

Instead of making a custard you can get by with our wonderful American cultured sour cream. Simply sprinkle it to the depth of ½ inch with brown sugar (no lumps) and set under the broiler.

YOU WILL NEED:
sour cream   brown sugar

Place cultured sour cream in shallow serving dish. Sprinkle with brown sugar. Place under broiler, watching very carefully, until the sugar is melted and bubbly. Chill.

AT SERVING TIME:
Crack the top with a fork or spoon. Serve.

Skillet Custard   SKILLET

To bake custard in the electric skillet simply place the cups in the preheated skillet. Surround with 2 cups warm water, cover, and cook at 200° F. from 15 to 20 minutes, if milk has been scalded, or about 10 minutes longer if it has not been scalded.

Pressure-Cooked Custards   PRESSURE COOKER

Some of the best custards you ever tasted can be made without bothering to scald the milk and within 3 minutes in your pressure cooker.

YOU WILL NEED:
    egg yolks or whole eggs   vanilla
    milk or thin coffee cream   nutmeg (optional)
    sugar

In the blender or with a fork beat until just evenly blended 3 cups milk or thin coffee cream, 4 eggs or 6 egg yolks, ½ cup sugar, ¼ teaspoon salt, 1 teaspoon vanilla or 1½ inches of vanilla bean.

Butter 6 custard cups or French pot-de-crème ramekins. Pour the milk mixture into the cups, leaving at least a half inch at the top. Sprinkle lightly with nutmeg or finely ground vanilla bean. Cover with 2 thicknesses of wax paper and tie around the custard cups, or use aluminum foil and press down around the edges and hold firmly with rubber bands. Place cups on rack in pressure cooker. Add 1 cup boiling water to cooker and cook under pressure 2 minutes. Bring down pressure immediately, and as soon as pressure is down remove the custard cups.

AT SERVING TIME:
Custards may be served warm or cooled. If desired, they may be sprinkled with brown sugar and glazed under the broiler.

VARIATION: To make coffee custard, add 2 teaspoons instant coffee to the milk and flavor with rum to taste. Omit the nutmeg.

Cantaloupe Sherbet
BLENDER AND ICE CREAM FREEZER

This is particularly well adapted to the small refrigerator freezer. Really delicious.

YOU WILL NEED:
cantaloupes   lemon juice
sugar   Angostura bitters

Scoop out the fruit of two ripened melons (about 4 cupfuls) and place in blender. Whir 20 seconds. Add sugar, ⅓ to ½ cup depending on how sweet melons are; 3 tablespoons lemon juice; several dashes of Angostura bitters, blending another 10 to 15 seconds. Pour into freezer can and freeze like ice cream. Makes 8 servings.

AT SERVING TIME:
Serve in scooped-out melon shells or well-chilled champagne glasses.

VARIATION: *WATERMELON SHERBET* Substitute 4 cups watermelon for cantaloupe. Add a little red vegetable coloring if desired.

Instantaneous Fruit Sherbet   BLENDER AND ICE CRUSHER

YOU WILL NEED:

frozen lemonade,   crushed ice
  limeade, or cranberry   egg whites
  juice   sugar (optional)

Put 1 6-ounce can frozen lemonade or limeade, partially defrosted,
or ½ cup cranberry juice with 2 heaping cups finely crushed ice
and 2 egg whites into the blender. Add sugar if needed. Cover and
blend on high speed for 1 minute or until sherbet is consistency
of fine snow.

AT SERVING TIME:
Serve immediately in chilled sherbet glasses or keep in trays in
the freezer. Makes 6 to 8 servings.

The Simplest Old-Fashioned Vanilla Ice Cream   ICE CREAM FREEZER

For this recipe you do not cook anything. You don't put in eggs
or cornstarch or gelatine. It is not very rich but it does have that
wonderful old-fashioned taste that some of us remember, and it
is not filled with strange fillers which keep it from melting. It does
melt on the plate and, incidentally, on the tongue.

YOU WILL NEED:

milk   vanilla extract or vanilla
evaporated milk   bean
sugar

Combine 1 quart of milk with 1 can evaporated milk. Add 1 cup
sugar and 2 tablespoons vanilla and 2 inches of vanilla bean. Put
the vanilla bean into the blender with 1 cup of milk and blend

until it is in fine flecks. Then add to the milk mixture. A tiny bit of salt may be added if you like. Follow the general directions for making freezer ice cream.

VARIATION: *RICHER ICE CREAM* Substitute 1 or 2 cups cream for an equal quantity of the milk called for in the recipe above. The more cream you use, the richer and smoother the ice cream will be, but do not dispense with the evaporated milk. For some strange reason it does something very good to the ice cream. Probably because so much of the water has been removed from the milk. Incidentally, if you don't like the taste of evaporated milk, don't be alarmed, for the taste is covered up by the vanilla and the freezing.

Another Old-Fashioned Vanilla Ice Cream
SAUCEPAN, BLENDER, AND
ICE CREAM FREEZER

This recipe achieves a beautiful smoothness through the use of dehydrated milk.

YOU WILL NEED:

whole milk	heavy cream
dry milk powder	pure vanilla or vanilla
egg yolks	bean
sugar	

Heat 2 cups milk to 190° F., not boiling. In the blender put 4 egg yolks, ½ teaspoon salt, 2 cups granulated sugar, blend until light and frothy. Pour hot milk over the egg mixture, slowly, mixing well. Cook in automatic saucepan at 200° F. about 3 minutes or until mixture coats a silver spoon. While this is cooling, blend 1 cup dry milk solids with 4 cups fluid milk.

Whip 2 cups heavy cream and add 2 tablespoons pure vanilla extract or 2 inches of vanilla bean to the cooled custard. Combine the custard and the cream. Pour into a 4-quart freezer can and freeze according to directions (page 67).

AT SERVING TIME:
Sprinkle with vanilla bean that has been grated in your blender.

Vanilla-Flecked Ice Cream   BLENDER

The rarest and finest of all vanilla ice cream, the kind that brought fame to the Main Line hostesses of old Philadelphia, was flecked with tiny bits of vanilla bean. In those days the chefs in the great houses used elaborate equipment to make this ice cream but today it can be done almost instantaneously in the blender. Simply use your favorite vanilla ice cream recipe (pages 277–279) but put a piece of vanilla bean stock about 2 inches long into the milk in a blender and blend until there is nothing left but specks.

"Boughten" vanilla ice cream can be lifted to new heights by sprinkling it with a little vanilla-flecked sugar made in the blender. Other flavored sugars may be used in the same way to garnish ice cream.

Mrs. Pennington's Boiled Custard
Ice Cream   SAUCEPAN, BLENDER, AND
                                  ICE CREAM FREEZER

YOU WILL NEED:

milk	salt
eggs	cornstarch or flour
sugar	vanilla

Scald 2 quarts milk in an automatic saucepan. Set at 190° F. You want to get it hot but you don't want it to boil. Meanwhile place in blender 6 eggs, 1½ cups sugar, 2 tablespoons cornstarch or flour, ½ teaspoon salt, 1 tablespoon pure vanilla extract. Blend until well mixed. Slowly add egg mixture to the hot milk. Cook in the automatic saucepan, set at 200° F., until the mixture coats a silver spoon. Freeze according to general directions (page 67).

VARIATION: *EVEN RICHER CUSTARD* Add 1 cup heavy cream to the custard mixture after it has cooled and before it goes into the freezer.

VARIATION: *STRAWBERRY, RASPBERRY, BANANA OR PEACH CUSTARD ICE CREAM* can be made by adding to the eggs in the blender 2 cups of bananas broken into small pieces or 2 cups fresh or frozen peaches cut into dice. Or 2 cups halved strawberries fresh or frozen or 2 cups raspberries fresh or frozen. If frozen, the juice may be used but you may want to cut down a little on the sugar, using only about 1 cup sugar instead of 1½ cups. Taste the mixture before you put it into the freezer can. But remember that it will taste a little less sweet after freezing. If you feel that a fruit mixture needs a little extra zip, use a touch of lemon juice.

Puerto Rican Coconut Ice Cream
BLENDER AND ICE CREAM FREEZER

Desserts made from freshly grated coconut are a delight. Perhaps you will remember from a trip to Puerto Rico the delicate melting of lime-scented coolness spooned from a coconut shell and garnished with the toasted curls of coconut.

The recipe we found in San Juan was slightly dismaying. "Crack open a couple of coconuts," it says. "Grate on the finest of graters. Scald milk in a double boiler and stir in coconut. Keep on stirring without flagging for 45 minutes. Add sugar. Stir some more. Add the juice and grated rind of a lime; stir some more. Place in a strong loose-woven linen bag; wring hard with your hands until the milk has come through and what is left is dry as saw-dust."

This easy modern version uses the blender.

YOU WILL NEED:

coconut	sugar
milk	heavy cream (optional)
lime	

Crack and remove meat from a coconut or use 1 cup moist-pack coconut. Place in the blender with 2 cups of hot but not boiled milk. Cut I unpeeled lime into pieces, remove seeds. Cut in small pieces and add, along with ½ cup sugar. Blend 1 full minute.

Some people dearly love the textured taste of the fine coconut meat, but if you prefer a perfectly smooth ice cream, line a sieve with a piece of cheesecloth and pour the mixture through it. Freeze according to general directions (page 67). If desired, 1 cup heavy cream whipped may be stirred into the ice cream after it is frozen. This makes about 1 quart.

AT SERVING TIME:

Serve in small coconut shells or orange shells. Sprinkle with grated coconut and pour on a little rum if you like.

Banana Ice Cream

BLENDER AND ICE CREAM FREEZER

This is a particularly delicious ice cream. If you want to enhance the color add 2 or 3 drops of yellow vegetable coloring before freezing.

YOU WILL NEED:

lemon juice	light cream
bananas	sugar

Place in blender 3 tablespoons lemon juice, 6 bananas broken into small pieces, ¾ cup sugar, a few grains of salt. Blend until bananas disappear. Add 5 cups light cream, stir and freeze. Makes 2 quarts of ice cream.

AT SERVING TIME:
Garnish with fresh fruits and chopped nuts and, if desired, make a small depression on the top of the ice cream and pour on a little bit of golden rum.

Georgia Peach Ice Cream
BLENDER AND ICE CREAM FREEZER

YOU WILL NEED:

milk	eggs
vanilla extract or	heavy cream
vanilla bean	peaches

Place in the blender 3 cups milk, 1½ cups sugar, ¼ teaspoon salt, 6 egg yolks, 1 tablespoon pure vanilla extract or 1 inch piece vanilla bean. Whir just until blended. Cook in theromstatically controlled saucepan 200° F. until thick and smooth, stirring constantly. Allow to cool. With electric beater whip 1 quart heavy cream. Fold into custard.

Pour into 4-quart freezer and freeze to soft mush about 10 minutes. Remove from freezer into large bowl. Add 3 to 4 pounds ripe peaches or 3 packages frozen peaches coarsely blended or cut into very small pieces. (If you use frozen peaches, substitute part of juice for milk so you have perhaps 2 cups of milk and 1 cup peach juice and syrup). After blending peaches into partly frozen mixture, fold in 6 egg whites beaten to the peak stage. Return mixture to freezer and finish freezing. Makes about 3 quarts of ice cream.

AT SERVING TIME:
Garnish with fresh fruit.

Green Gage Plum Ice Cream
BLENDER AND ICE CREAM FREEZER

At first reading this recipe seemed almost too simple. But it works beautifully, if you use an electric freezer. But don't try to adapt it to the refrigerator tray. The original recipe says skin, seed and mask one pint of preserved green gage plums. We say use the solid fruit from a large can (1 lb. 14 ozs.) of peeled whole green gage plums.

YOU WILL NEED:

green gage plums	milk
lemon juice	heavy cream
sugar	

Remove the pits from 1 lb. 14 oz. canned green gage plums, and along with the juice of 2 lemons, whir until just blended. Combine the blended fruit with 2 cups sugar, 1½ quarts milk, 1 quart heavy cream. Add ½ teaspoon salt. Freeze in 4-quart freezer. Allow to ripen at least ½ hour.

AT SERVING TIME:

Garnish with whole green gage plums. Serve with pecan meringues (see page 309).

Strawberry Ice Cream
BLENDER AND ICE CREAM FREEZER

YOU WILL NEED:

milk	evaporated milk
strawberries	sugar
cream	vanilla

Reduce 2 quarts fresh strawberries or 2 16-ounce packages frozen strawberries to liquid in an electric blender. Put into the freezer can, along with 3 cups of milk, 1 pint cream, 1 can evaporated milk. Add 1 cup sugar and taste. It should taste a little sweeter than you want it because when it is frozen, it's slightly less sweet than before. Add 2 tablespoons pure vanilla extract, a tiny bit of salt, if you wish it. Freeze according to general directions (page 67).

AT SERVING TIME:
Garnish with more strawberries.

Strawberry Bavarian Cream
BLENDER AND ICE CRUSHER

It is important that the ingredients be added exactly in this order or else there will be an overflow.

YOU WILL NEED:
strawberries	crushed ice
gelatine	cream
milk	sherry wine or almond
sugar	extract
eggs	

Defrost 1 package (10 ounces) frozen strawberries and drain ½ cup juice into a saucepan. Heat juice just to the simmer. Into container of your blender put 2 envelopes gelatine and ¼ cup cold milk. Add hot strawberry juice, cover and blend for 40 seconds. Add 2 tablespoons sugar, package of strawberries and 2 egg yolks or 1 whole egg, cover and blend for 5 seconds. With motor on, remove cover, add 1 heaping cup crushed ice and 1 cup cream and continue to blend for 20 seconds longer or until dessert begins to thicken. Flavor with 1 tablespoon sherry wine or 1 teaspoon almond extract.

AT SERVING TIME:
Decorate with strawberries and almonds.

Chilled Orange Bavarian   MIXER

YOU WILL NEED:

orange-flavored gelatin dessert	mandarin sections or oranges
orange juice concentrate	orange bitters (optional)
eggs	curaçao
whipping cream	

Add to 1 package orange gelatin dessert, made up according to package directions, 2 tablespoons quick-frozen orange juice concentrate, 2 well-beaten egg yolks, ½ cup whipping cream. Swift-chill in freezer 20 minutes or until set an inch around the edge, quivery in the center. Add 2 egg whites. Whip everything together until light and foamy. Fold in 1 cup drained, canned mandarin sections or cubed oranges. If you like, you might add a touch of orange bitters. Makes 6 servings.

AT SERVING TIME:

Serve with whipped cream flavored with curaçao.

Bittersweet Chocolate Bavarian Cream
BLENDER AND ICE CRUSHER

YOU WILL NEED:

gelatine	Angostura Bitters (optional)
instant coffee	
chocolate pieces	eggs
sugar	crushed ice
	cream

Into blender put ¾ cup hot water, 1 heaping teaspoon instant coffee, 2 envelopes gelatine. Add a dash of Angostura Bitters if you like a bittersweet tang. Cover and blend at high speed for 40 seconds. Add 1 6-ounce package chocolate pieces and 1 tablespoon sugar. Cover and blend for 10 seconds. With motor on, remove cover and add 2 egg yolks or 1 whole egg, 1 heaping cup crushed ice and 1 cup cream. Continue to blend for about 20 seconds or until dessert begins to thicken. Serves 6.

Sauterne Bavarian   MIXER

YOU WILL NEED:
lemon-flavored gelatin   eggs yolks
    dessert   lemonade concentrate
sauterne

Dissolve 1 package lemon-flavored gelatin in ½ cup hot water; add ½ cup cold water, 1 cup sauterne, 2 egg yolks beaten until thick and lemon colored, along with 2 tablespoons lemonade concentrate. Swift-chill in freezer 20 to 25 minutes until firm about 1 inch from the edge and soft in center. Whip with beater until fluffy. Set in freezer about 10 minutes until set. Keep in refrigerator until serving time.

AT SERVING TIME:
Garnish with coarsely chopped or slivered nuts or nut brittle. As contrast to this creamy dessert, you should serve a crisp cookie.

Spanish Cream

BLENDER AND ICE CRUSHER

YOU WILL NEED:
gelatine   crushed ice
vanilla   cream
milk   sugar
egg yolks

Into the container of your blender place 2 envelopes gelatine, 2 tablespoons water and 1 tablespoon vanilla. Add ½ cup hot milk, cover and blend on high speed for 40 seconds. Add ¼ cup sugar and 2 egg yolks, cover and blend for 5 seconds. With motor on, remove cover, add 1 heaping cup crushed ice and 1 cup cream and continue to blend for 20 seconds longer, or until dessert begins to thicken.

AT SERVING TIME:
Garnish with lady fingers and chopped nuts.

Charlotte Russe   MIXER

When extra yolks are added to a Bavarian mixture and it is molded inside a ring of lady fingers, it becomes a Charlotte Russe.

YOU WILL NEED:
Sauterne Bavarian (see   plus 2 egg yolks
recipe page 286)   ginger (optional)

Simply make up the Sauterne Bavarian using 4 egg yolks instead of 2. Fold in 4 whipped egg whites after the mixture has been whipped. A quarter of a teaspoon of ginger adds an exciting flavor note.

AT SERVING TIME:
To save yourself the botheration of unmolding, use a straight-sided glass dish to let the lady fingers show through. Set your garnishes of candied fruits or flowers on top of the pudding.

VARIATION: *CHARLOTTE RUSSE IMPERIALE*   Serve the Charlotte Russe with a sauce, passed separately, of frozen raspberries, flavored with 1 tablespoon orange concentrate, 1 tablespoon Grand Marnier.

Apricot Mousse   BLENDER

For a formal occasion when you want to cut a figure, this is a most luxuriously rich mousse. It requires little preliminary work but the result is quite heavenly.

YOU WILL NEED:
apricots   whipped cream
confectioner's sugar

Blend very ripe peeled apricots with ¼ pound of confectioner's sugar and ½ pint of whipped cream.

AT SERVING TIME:
Turn into a dessert dish and serve ice-cold but not quite frozen. If you wish, you can decorate it with whole fresh berries and/or small macaroons.

Russian Paska   MIXER

This is a traditional dish for Russian Easter but it is delightful to serve as a not-too-sweet dessert with coffee cake or sweet rolls at any time of the year.

YOU WILL NEED:
Philadelphia cream   egg yolks
    cheese   chopped almonds
light cream   mixed glacéed fruits and
cognac   peels

Place in the bowl of your electric mixer 12 ounces of Philadelphia cream cheese, ¾ cup light cream and 2 tablespoons cognac. Mix until very smooth. Add the chopped yolks of 2 hard-cooked eggs, ¼ cup chopped almonds, ½ cup mixed glacéed fruits and peels. Line a pint-size mold with dampened cheesecloth. Pack the mixture into the mold or simply mold into a pyramid with your hands and wrap in waxed paper. Cover. Chill in the refrigerator several hours or overnight.

AT SERVING TIME:
Turn out on a plate and decorate with leaves and flowers. For Easter, the orthodox Greeks set a birthday candle in the center.

Concord Grape Parfait   MIXER

Ready and set in half an hour and pretty as can be.

YOU WILL NEED:
grape-flavored gelatin   vanilla ice cream
port or Dubonnet

Dissolve a package of grape-flavored gelatin in 1 cup of hot water. Add ½ cup ruby port or Dubonnet. Place in mixer bowl and at lowest speed add 1 pint of vanilla ice cream a spoonful at a time and stir until melted. Chill until slightly thickened.

AT SERVING TIME:
Pile into parfait glasses. Makes 6 parfaits.

Whips and Snows

It's no news that chilled gelatine whips as magically as the white of an egg. But it is news to be able to achieve a proper whipping temperature within 7 minutes, or maybe 10, if you put the gelatine mixture into a shallow pan or ice tray and set it in the freezer. You needn't add egg whites to a whip but you'll have more flavor and a more delicate texture if you do.

Snow Pudding   ICE CRUSHER
                                     AND BLENDER

One of the lightest, most delicate, least caloric, and most inexpensive desserts imaginable is whipped gelatin. Formerly this dessert required a knack. The packaged gelatin pudding was made up in the usual manner according to directions, and allowed to "chill until syrupy" (a tricky, ephemeral stage); then it was whipped with an egg beater till it was double in size and very fluffy. Usually this had to be done in a chilled bowl set into ice and water. Even when it was done carefully the pudding often developed a line of clear gelatin at the bottom.

Now all you do is to dissolve a 3-ounce package of flavored gelatin dessert in 1 cup of hot water and blend with 1 cup of crushed ice for 1 minute.

Lemon Snow Pudding   ICE CRUSHER
                                     AND BLENDER

This is one of the most popular of all snow puddings, but other flavors may be used.

YOU WILL NEED:
    lemon-flavored gelatin   finely crushed ice
      dessert

Dissolve 1 package lemon gelatin dessert in 1 cup hot water. Place in blender. Add 1 cup finely crushed ice. Blend 1 minute.

AT SERVING TIME:
Spoon into 6 chilled champagne glasses or sherbet glasses and serve either plain, with cake, or with Instant Vanilla Custard Sauce (page 206).

Apple Snow   MIXER

YOU WILL NEED:

lemon snow pudding   applesauce
(see page 290)   cinnamon

Fold into lemon snow pudding after it is whipped, 1 cup applesauce. Flavor with ¼ teaspoon cinnamon.

For variety use strained prunes or apricot purée instead of
applesauce.

Lime Whip   BLENDER AND ICE CRUSHER

One of the prettiest, easiest desserts imaginable. Why not make
it at the table to serve immediately? Or it can be molded to serve
later.

YOU WILL NEED:

gelatine   crushed ice
sugar   green coloring (optional)
quick-frozen limeade
  concentrate

Put ⅔ cup hot water and 2 envelopes gelatine into the blender.
Cover and blend on high speed for about 40 seconds. Add ¼ cup
sugar, cover and blend for 2 seconds. Add 6 ounces frozen limeade partially defrosted and 2 heaping cups crushed ice, cover
and blend for 30 seconds or until dessert begins to thicken. Four
drops green coloring may be added if desired. Pile into 6 sherbet
or wine glasses or champagne saucers. Or pour into an icy cold
quart-size mold that has been rinsed with ice water or painted
ever-so-lightly with peanut oil.

AT SERVING TIME:
Garnish with paper-thin slices of lime and mint leaves.

Tipsy Snow Pudding   MIXER

YOU WILL NEED:
orange-flavored gelatin   sherry
dessert   egg whites

Dissolve 1 package orange-flavored dessert in ½ cup hot water.
Add 1 cup cold water and ½ cup sherry. Swift chill until slightly
thickened. Add 2 egg whites. Set bowl in a pan of ice cubes and
water; whip until fluffy and thick like whipped cream. Makes
8 servings.

Coeur Flottante à la Ritz   MIXER

At the old Ritz Carlton and now at the new Carlton House in
New York floating hearts are a favorite dessert.

YOU WILL NEED:
lemon snow pudding   apricots, strawberries,
wine-flavored custard   peaches or other
sauce   fruits

AT SERVING TIME:
Simply mold snow pudding in a heart shape. Chill. Unmold upon
a wine-flavored custard sauce in which you have hidden halved
apricots, strawberries, sliced peaches or any other delicate fruit.

Pecan Pie from Kings Arms Tavern
PORTABLE OVEN

Trying to describe a pecan pie to someone who has never tasted
it is not too easy. For this is a thoroughly American invention
with no direct European ancestors. It has in older versions char-
acteristics of a custard but made without milk. The traditional

Virginia recipe in "The Williamsburg Art of Cookery" calls for corn syrup as well as sugar, but at Kings Arms Tavern nowadays the syrup is omitted and only sugar is used.

YOU WILL NEED:

eggs   vanilla
brown sugar   pecans
butter

Beat 3 eggs lightly as for custard, then add slowly 2 cups brown sugar and ¼ cup butter which has been melted. Flavor with a touch of salt and a teaspoon of vanilla. Pour into an 8-inch pie plate lined with pastry and sprinkled with ½ cup pecans chopped. Pour the egg, sugar and butter mixture over the nuts. Sprinkle another ½ cup of pecans over the top, bake in a 350° F. oven for 35 to 40 minutes or until the pie is almost set. Reduce the heat to 225° F. and bake for 15 minutes longer or until the pie is thoroughly set.

AT SERVING TIME:

The pie is so buttery rich and sweet that an 8-inch pie should make 8 servings, especially if you serve it with ice cream.

Egg Nog Pie   MIXER

A quick, easy way to achieve a great American favorite.

YOU WILL NEED:

lemon-flavored gelatin   vanilla ice cream
   dessert   pie shell
rum   pralines or peanut brittle
nutmeg

Make up 2 packages of lemon-flavored gelatin dessert with 2 cups hot water. Add ⅔ cup rum, ½ teaspoon nutmeg, 1 quart vanilla ice cream. Swift-chill in freezer until thickened but not set about 10 minutes. Turn into 9-inch baked pie shell or crumb crust. Chill until firm, about 10 minutes longer. Remove to refrigerator and leave until serving time. This pie cuts better if it is allowed to rest for several hours.

AT SERVING TIME:
Crushed New Orleans pralines or peanut brittle make the most perfect garnish. If you can't find them use crushed sugared almonds.

Orange Chiffon Pie in Crumb Crust

BLENDER AND ICE CRUSHER

YOU WILL NEED:

For the crust:

graham crackers	cinnamon
sugar	butter

For the filling:

eggs	sugar
gelatine	crushed ice
orange concentrate	heavy cream
or apricot nectar	

Break 5 graham crackers into blender and blend to crumbs by switching motor on and off high speed 5 times. Empty crumbs into a bowl and repeat until a total of 16 graham crackers have been crumbled. Stir in 2 tablespoons sugar, ½ teaspoon cinnamon and ¼ cup melted butter. Butter an 8-inch pie plate and press crumbs against sides and bottom to make an even coating. For a browned crust, bake in a 400° F. oven for 10 minutes.

Beat 2 egg whites until stiff and beat in 2 tablespoons of sugar. Set aside. Into the blender put 2 envelopes gelatine and ½ cup orange concentrate or apricot nectar. Add ¼ cup sugar and 2 egg yolks, cover and blend for 5 seconds. Remove cover, add 1 heaping cup crushed ice and 1 cup heavy cream and continue to blend for about 20 seconds. Immediately pour the cream into the beaten egg whites and fold gently until mixed. Pile into prepared pie shell.

AT SERVING TIME:
Garnish with chopped or slivered nuts or slices of fruit to match the flavors.

Lime Chiffon Pie   MIXER

YOU WILL NEED:
lime flavored gelatin
eggs
limeade concentrate

crumb crust of chocolate
wafers, graham crackers
or ginger wafers

Dissolve 2 packages lime flavored gelatin dessert in 2 cups hot water. Beat until light and lemon colored 3 egg yolks and one 6-ounce can limeade concentrate. Combine with the gelatin. (Your electric blender is perfect for the job.) Swift-chill about 15 minutes or until set around the edge, still quivery in the center. Add 3 unbeaten egg whites and whip with electric beater at low speed until very light and fluffy. Place in a crumb crust made of chocolate wafers, graham crackers or ginger wafers. Swift-chill 10 to 15 minutes longer in the freezer. Keep in the refrigerator until needed. Makes 8 to 10 servings.

AT SERVING TIME:
Cover with a thin layer of whipped cream, shaved or grated chocolate or chocolate shot.

Nesselrode Pie   MIXER

Once it was frozen pudding made with 8 eggs, a quart of cream, a fortune in candied marrons. Now it's one of the favorite pies in New York's best steak houses. This one is made from ice cream and flavored gelatin. *Very* easy.

YOU WILL NEED:

lemon and orange
   flavored gelatin
brandy
vanilla

vanilla ice cream
ice shell
glacéed diced fruit

Dissolve together 1 package lemon and 1 package orange flavored gelatin in 2 cups hot water. Add ½ cup brandy, 1 teaspoon vanilla, 1 quart vanilla ice cream. Use the same method as for Egg Nog Pie (see page 293), but before turning into the pie shell fold in 1 cup glacéed diced fruit. Chill until firm.

AT SERVING TIME:

Cover with a thin blanket of sweetened whipped cream and grated chocolate.

Half-Moon Pies of Mincemeat

DEEP FAT FRYER

All through the South during plantation days, half-moon pies glowed on party tables, especially in the wintertime. Filled with cooked dried peaches, apples, apricots or raisins, preserves or mincemeat, they were sometimes baked in the oven—but only by iconoclasts. The results never equalled the gold-blistered, melt-in-your-mouth delicacy of fried pies.

YOU WILL NEED:

pie crust mix

mincemeat

Make up a package of pie crust mix according to directions. Roll out and cut into 4-inch circles with a bowl or glass. Place a heaping tablespoon of mincemeat on one side, fold over, press down edges with fork to seal. Fry in deep fat at 360° two or three minutes until flaky blisters appear. Drain on paper towels. To make 8 pies, use 1 package pie crust mix, 1 cup mincemeat.

AT SERVING TIME:
Serve warm with or without a spoonful of vanilla ice cream.

Wisconsin Refrigerator Cheese Cake   MIXER

Cheese cake is a magic word all over America, and cheese cake recipes are legion. Some are rich and close-textured; others are light and fluffy. Most of the old recipes require quite a bit of doing, as well as special equipment such as a spring form. This version, which has its origin in the cheese country of Wisconsin, dispenses with pastry or crumb crust. It does away with those hours of baking—another hour of cooling in a 200° F. oven. In fact, it does away with the cooking altogether.

We discovered that though the original recipe called for cooking the egg yolks and warned ominously against overcooking, it is unnecessary to cook at all. Beating is all the "cooking" that is necessary.

YOU WILL NEED:
lemon-flavored gelatin   cream cheese
    dessert   zweiback or graham
eggs   crackers
lemonade concentrate   cinnamon
whipping cream

Dissolve 1 package lemon-flavored gelatin in 1 cup hot water. Add ½ cup cold water. Stir in with beater 2 egg yolks which have been beaten until light and lemon colored, 2 tablespoons quick-frozen lemonade concentrate, ½ cup whipping cream. Swift-chill in freezer 15 to 20 minutes, until mixture is firm about an inch from the edge, quivery in the center.

Meanwhile, stir until light and fluffy, with fork or hand-beater, 12 ounces (4 3-ounce packages) cream cheese. (To soften cream cheese quickly, just knead the silver foil package in your hands for a minute or two). A good trick to remember! Beat fluffy cream cheese with chilled mixture, using hand beater, until light and fluffy. Fold in 2 stiffly beaten egg whites.

Butter a 1-quart cake pan or mold, bottom and sides, using at least a tablespoonful softened butter. Sprinkle in ½ cup finely grated zwieback or graham cracker crumbs flavored with 1 teaspoon cinnamon. Pour into mold. Cover top with ¼ cup crumbs. Return to freezer for ½ hour. Remove to refrigerator until needed. Good and rich, it makes 8 to 10 servings.

AT SERVING TIME:
Loosen edges with blunt knife. Place a plate over the mold and turn upside down.

Instant Cheese Cake   ICE CRUSHER AND BLENDER

YOU WILL NEED:

gelatine	cream cheese
lemon	crushed ice
milk	heavy cream
sugar	zwieback crumbs
eggs	

Put 2 envelopes gelatine, juice of ½ lemon and a thin strip of lemon peel into the blender. Add ½ cup hot milk, cover and blend on high speed for 40 seconds. Add ¼ cup sugar, 2 egg yolks and 8 ounces of cream cheese, cover and blend on high speed for 10 seconds. Remove cover, add 1 heaping cup crushed ice and ½ cup heavy cream and continue to blend for 15 seconds. Immediately pour into a 4-cup spring-form pan and sprinkle with zweiback crumbs. Serves six.

AT SERVING TIME:
Serve as is (which is wonderful) or top with sour cream and pieces of fruit or the following glaze:

FRUIT GLAZE FOR CHEESE CAKE, FLANS, FRUIT TARTS

YOU WILL NEED:

raspberry, cherry or strawberry flavored gelatin	currant jelly fresh strawberries (optional)

Dissolve 1 package of raspberry, cherry or strawberry flavored gelatin in 1 cup hot water. Add 2 tablespoons currant jelly. Swift-chill in freezer for 10 minutes or until thick as unbeaten egg whites. Spoon on top of cheese cake. If you like, put 1 pint whole or halved fresh strawberries or other berries on chilled glaze. Chill in refrigerator.

Ginger or Chocolate Rolls   MIXER

A fine easy dessert to make ahead of time for parties.

YOU WILL NEED:

whipping cream confectioner's sugar	ginger or chocolate cookies

Whip 2 cups whipping cream stiff and sweeten with ¼ cup confectioner's sugar. Spread a spoonful on a cookie. Place another cookie on top—continue until there are 6 piles of 5 cookies with whipped cream between. Lay piles crosswise on serving platter. Cover roll evenly with remaining whipped cream. Chill at least 6 hours.

AT SERVING TIME:

Garnish a chocolate roll with walnut or pecan halves. Offer a chocolate sauce.

Garnish a ginger cream roll with bits of candied ginger and a touch of apricot jam.

Eclairs   PORTABLE OVEN

A cream puff mix and a pudding mix are put together knowingly to make the most epicurean of pastries.

YOU WILL NEED:

cream puff mix   instant coffee
vanilla pudding   coffee liqueur (optional)

Use the cream puff mixture given in Profiteroles au Chocolat recipe (see page 301).

The classic way to shape the eclairs is with a pastry bag, fitted with ½-inch flat tube. But it is not at all difficult to do without the tube. Simply place the dough on a pan in strips, 1 inch wide and about 4 inches long. Bake in a hot oven 400° F. one half hour. Reduce to 350° F., bake 4 minutes longer.

Before they are quite done, you will notice tiny beads of dew upon them, but these must have completely disappeared before the puffs are taken from the oven. To test for doneness, take one eclair out of the oven. If it has not been cooked long enough it will fall and be soft rather than crisp as it should be.

AT SERVING TIME:

Cool, split and fill. For filling: Use a vanilla pudding flavored with 2 good teaspoons of instant coffee and perhaps a bit of coffee liqueur. Or try making up a vanilla pudding according to package directions, but use 1 cup milk, 1 cup thin cream and flavoring with a couple tablespoonfuls of Grand Marnier. Ice with a thin frosting, stirred up with liqueur, rum or brandy instead of the usual moistening with water.

Profiteroles au Chocolat   PORTABLE OVEN

These are very small cream puffs filled with ice cream. These may be made up at any time and kept in the freezer for weeks. There is a cream puff mix on the market or see the recipe on page 302.

YOU WILL NEED:

cream puff recipe   rum or sherry (optional)
ice cream   orange bitters (optional)
canned chocolate sauce

To make mite-size cream puffs drop by very small spoonfuls two inches apart on a buttered cookie sheet. Bake in a hot oven 450° F. a half hour. Reduce to 350° F., bake 5 minutes longer. Before they are quite done, you will notice tiny beads of dew upon them, but these must have completely disappeared before the puffs are taken from the oven. To test for doneness, take one puff out of the oven. If it has not been cooked long enough it will fall and be soft rather than crisp as it should be.

AT SERVING TIME:

Cut a slit on the side. Fill with ice cream. Serve with heated canned chocolate sauce, to which I like to add a little rum or sherry and a dash of orange bitters. (Puffs filled with ice cream may be frozen and kept for weeks.)

VARIATION: Fill puffs with flavored whipped cream or custard and sprinkle with vanilla sugar (see page 210).

Cream Puffs   PORTABLE OVEN

YOU WILL NEED:
butter   eggs
flour

Heat to a rolling boil in saucepan 1 cup water, ½ cup butter. Stir
in all at once 1 cup sifted flour. Stir vigorously over low heat until
mixture leaves the pan and forms into a ball (about 1 minute).
Remove from heat and beat in thoroughly, one at a time, 4 eggs.
Beat mixture until smooth and velvety. Drop from spoon onto
ungreased baking sheet. Bake until dry at 400° F. about 45 to 50
minutes. Allow to cool slowly.

AT SERVING TIME:
Cut slit in side. Fill with flavored custard, sweetened whipped
cream or ice cream. Makes 8 puffs.

Orange Chiffon Cake   BLENDER AND MIXER

The chiffon cake is an American invention quite dissimilar in
technique to any other. It is made with salad oil instead of shortening and has some of the quality of the old-fashioned sponge or
sunshine cake.

YOU WILL NEED:
salad oil   sugar
eggs, separated   baking powder
grated orange rind   cake flour
orange juice   cream of tartar

Place in the electric blender ¼ cup salad oil, 2 egg yolks, 1 tablespoon grated orange rind, ⅜ cup orange juice, ¼ cup sugar, ¼
teaspoon salt, 1¼ teaspoons baking powder, 1 cup plus 2 tablespoons sifted cake flour.

In the bowl of your mixer place 4 egg whites or enough to make one-half cupful and ¼ teaspoon cream of tartar. Beat egg whites until frothy (at medium speed). Continue beating until egg whites are stiff, gradually adding an additional half cup of sugar.

Cover and blend the ingredients in the blender until very smooth, about 1 minute. Pour blended ingredients over the beaten egg whites, gently folding with a rubber spatula until there are no streaks. Bake in an ungreased 9-inch tube pan (which should be at least 3½ inches high) in a slow oven, 325° F., about 50 minutes or until cake springs back at the touch of a finger.

Place upside down on cake rack immediately. Allow to cool thoroughly. Frost if desired or simply sprinkle with confectioner's sugar or vanilla or orange-flavored sugar (see page 210).

AT SERVING TIME:
Serve like angel cake as an accompaniment to ice cream, sherbets or fruit. Very good with chilled zabaione (see page 271).

Banana Chiffon Cake   BLENDER AND MIXER

The blender and the mixer combine to produce this deliciously light and airy but wonderfully moist chiffon cake. It may be served plain or lightly sprinkled with sugar or topped with a luscious glaze.

YOU WILL NEED:

cake flour or all-purpose flour	salad oil
	eggs
double acting baking powder	bananas
	lemon juice
sugar	cream of tartar

Measure 2¼ cups sifted flour or 2 cups of sifted all-purpose flour.

Add 1½ cups sugar, 3 teaspoons double acting baking powder, 1 teaspoon salt. Sift again.

Place in the blender ½ cup salad oil, ½ cup egg yolks (6 or 8), 2 large or 3 small bananas cut into ½-inch slices, 1 tablespoon lemon juice. Blend until smooth, about 10 seconds. Add the sifted dry ingredients. Stir down and blend 5 seconds longer.

Meanwhile in the mixer place 6 to 8 egg whites and ½ teaspoon cream of tartar. Beat at high speed until stiff peaks form. It is important not to underbeat. Gradually and gently by hand fold the banana mixture into the stiff whites. Fold only long enough to incorporate but do not mix and do not stir.

Pour into an ungreased 10-inch tube pan or angel cake pan. Bake in a preheated oven at 350° F. 40 to 50 minutes or until the cake tester comes out clean and dry.

To cool cake, invert the pan and elevate it about 1 inch above the table by placing the tube of the pan over an inverted funnel or a small-necked bottle. Let the cake hang until cool. Then remove from pan.

AT SERVING TIME:

Serve plain or with zabaione sauce (see page 271) or, if you like, you may frost with a glaze like the following:

Banana Glaze   MIXER

A delicious glaze to serve on a chiffon cake or ginger bread or spice cake.

YOU WILL NEED:

small ripe banana	sifted confectioner's sugar
lemon juice	

Break banana into pieces and place in the mixer along with 1 tablespoon lemon juice and 1 pound sifted confectioner's sugar, the kind that is marked 10-X. Beat at low speed until smooth.

AT SERVING TIME:

Spoon on top of cake or serve like a hard sauce on a piece of cake. This makes about 2 cups of glaze.

Hazelnut Torte with Fruit

BLENDER AND MIXER

This is a St. Louis version of the traditional Viennese recipe. When made in the blender the nuts do not need to be ground ahead of time. The blender does the job for you all at once.

YOU WILL NEED:

egg yolks	pecans or walnuts
sugar	egg whites
hazelnuts	whipped cream

Into the blender place 6 egg yolks (about ¾ cup). Blend about 10 seconds. Gradually add ½ cup superfine sugar (not confectioner's). When the mixture is very light and creamy add 2 ounces shelled hazelnuts and the same amount of pecans or walnuts. You can use nuts all of one kind if you like. Blend until the nuts are in fine little pieces; only a few seconds is enough.

With your electric mixer at medium speed beat 4 egg whites and a speck of salt, until stiff but still moist and shiny-looking.

Gently, little by little with a rubber spatula, add the blended ingredients to the whipped egg whites.

Bake in an 8-inch layer pan with a removable rim in a moderately cool oven, 325° F., about 40 minutes.

AT SERVING TIME:

Garnish with ½ cup heavy cream, whipped and slightly sweetened, and flavored with vanilla, rum flavoring or sherry. If desired, top with about one pint of strawberries or sliced, sweetened peaches. Serves 8.

Pecan Torte

Pecans are an American nut and the tortes given here are typically German or Viennese recipes. But put the two together —use pecans instead of almonds in the almond torte—and you will have an extraordinarily rich and moist cake. Gloriously, almost sinfully delicious!

Almond Torte   BLENDER AND MIXER

In the original German recipes for this cake (known as Mandeltorte) you are warned that the nuts must be put through a special nut grinder, "not a meat grinder which crushes them." In this recipe neither is used. There is no danger of crushing or bruising the nuts when they are done in the blender.

YOU WILL NEED:

eggs, separated
superfine sugar
a lemon or orange
cinnamon

unblanched almonds
toasted bread crumbs
almond extract

Into the blender put 6 egg yolks. Blend about 10 seconds. Then gradually add 1 cup superfine sugar. Blend until ingredients are very creamy. Add a well-washed but unpeeled lemon cut into half inch pieces (remove the seeds, of course) or use one small orange. Add also 1 teaspoon cinnamon, 1 cup unblanched, shelled almonds, ½ cup toasted bread crumbs. (Packaged bread crumbs will do.) For flavoring use ½ teaspoon almond extract or 1 teaspoon vanilla extract. Blend until the almonds practically disappear. With your electric beater at medium speed beat until stiff but still shiny 6 egg whites and ¼ teaspoon salt.

Gently and gradually add the blended material to the egg whites, working lightly and using a rubber spatula.

Bake in an 8-inch tube pan with removable rim in a moderate

oven, 350° F., for about 40 minutes. Invert and allow to cool thoroughly in the pan or else you may have considerable difficulty getting the cake out of the pan.

AT SERVING TIME:
Sprinkle with flavored sugar and serve in pie-shaped wedges with whipped cream and chopped nuts. Serves 6 to 8.

Almond Torte for a Party

The preceding recipe may be doubled for a party, in which case a lemon or orange filling is often used between two layers. The top can be frosted with white or chocolate icing. Or you can simply use whipped cream as a filling and flavored sugar as a topping. Both ideas are good. The second is easier and perhaps more traditional.

Singed Angel Wings   BROILER

Slightly aging angel cake makes a fine comeback this way.

YOU WILL NEED:
angel food cake   melted butter

For orange sauce:
sugar   lemon juice
cornstarch   grated orange and lemon
orange juice   rind

Brush cut sides of wedges of angel food cake with melted butter. Lightly brown both sides under broiler (1 minute each side).
    Serve with orange sauce: Mix in saucepan 1 cup sugar, ¼ teaspoon salt and 2 tablespoons cornstarch. Stir in 1 cup orange juice, ¼ cup lemon juice and ¾ cup boiling water. Boil 1 minute,

stirring constantly. Remove from heat. Stir in 1 tablespoon butter and 1 teaspoon each grated orange and lemon rind.

AT SERVING TIME:
Pour sauce over cake or pass in separate bowl.

Meringue   MIXER

A packaged meringue mix makes life almost too easy, but if you want to start from scratch (egg whites) this one, too, is practically failproof.

YOU WILL NEED:
    egg whites   sugar
    cream of tartar

Beat 6 large egg whites with ½ teaspoon cream of tartar until frothy. Beat in gradually 1 cup sugar. Continue beating until meringue is stiff and glossy. Place in a very hot oven (500° F.) for 3 to 5 minutes (just until meringue is delicately browned.)

Fruit Meringue   BLENDER

YOU WILL NEED:
    gelatine   egg whites
    lemon juice   frozen fruit

Put 1 envelope gelatine, 2 tablespoons lemon juice and ½ cup boiling water into blender. Cover and blend on high speed for 40 seconds. Add 2 egg whites, cover and blend for 10 seconds. Cut 1 package of frozen fruit into 16 pieces. With motor on, remove cover and drop pieces of frozen fruit, a few at a time.

AT SERVING TIME:

Spoon into 4 serving glasses. Garnish with fruit and mint leaves, if they are handy.

Williamsburg Pecan Confections   MIXER

A type of nut meringue.

YOU WILL NEED:

egg white	flour
light brown sugar	pecans, chopped

Beat 1 egg white to a stiff froth and add gradually 1 cup light brown sugar, 1 pinch salt, 1 level tablespoon flour. Stir in 1 cup of chopped pecans, drop on buttered cookie tins by spoonfuls far apart. Bake in a very slow oven (225° to 250° F.) for about 15 minutes. Remove from the tin with a spatula when partly cooled. Makes about 24 confections. If you should be short of cookie tins, heavy-duty aluminum foil makes an admirable substitute.

AT SERVING TIME:

Serve with ice cream. In Williamsburg this is traditional with green gage ice cream.

Meringue Torte   MIXER

A charming Minneapolis hostess has a special way of serving meringues at her delightful luncheon parties. She bakes little rounding handles of meringue to use with individual meringue shells (baked on the same paper) then fashions meringue baskets of ice cream and fruit for individual servings.

YOU WILL NEED:

egg whites or meringue   cream of tartar
    mix   sugar

Make up a package of meringue mix according to directions or beat together until frothy 3 egg whites, ¼ teaspoon cream of tartar. Gradually beat in, a little at a time, 1 cup sugar. Beat until very stiff and glossy. Tint, if desired, with food coloring. Bake and cool (275° F.) for 60 minutes. Turn off oven and leave in until cool.

AT SERVING TIME:

Serve filled with ice cream topped with fresh berries or cut-up fruit, or chocolate or butterscotch sauce. Makes 8 to 10 servings.

Crullers from Ready-to-Bake Biscuits

DEEP FAT FRYER

If you'd rather, you can make doughnuts, round doughboys, mite-size wonders—any shape, any size.

YOU WILL NEED:

oven-ready biscuits   granulated sugar or cinna-
     mon sugar

Start with a package of oven-ready biscuits. Separate biscuits; roll long and twist (or cut out the center with the top of a ketchup bottle). Let stand at room temperature 10 minutes. Deep fry at 380° F. 2 or 3 minutes till brown on both sides, turning once. Shake in a bag with granulated sugar or cinnamon sugar. One package makes 10 crullers.

AT SERVING TIME:

Serve warm with coffee or hot chocolate.

Lumberjacks   MIXER

Most tantalizing of all the specialties at Sturbridge Village in Massachusetts are the fresh-baked, ineffably fragrant cookies, warm from the oven. There are Hobnails, Quakers, Walnut Patties, and almost always, there are Lumberjacks—big, soft, tender, spice-dark molasses cookies, fully half an inch thick, with the texture of cake. All Sturbridge cookies (close to half a million a year) are baked by a learned lady with smiling eyes dressed in the cap and kirtle of long ago. She is Elinor Genung Allen, who earned her Master's degree in English at Vassar in 1916 and has devoted a busy lifetime to the study and adaptation of antique recipes.

This recipe, which makes a batch of 48, is the result of years of experimenting. It is a drop cookie and "to all intents and purposes completely fail-proof."

YOU WILL NEED:

flour	lard or vegetable
baking soda	shortening
salt	sugar
ginger	molasses (dark)
cinnamon	eggs

To 3 cups flour, measured after sifting, add 1½ teaspoons baking soda, 1 teaspoon salt, 1 teaspoon powdered ginger, 2 teaspoons cinnamon. Sift again.

Cream in mixer 1 cup lard or vegetable shortening with 1 cup sugar. Add 1 cup dark molasses, 2 slightly beaten eggs. Blend the dry and the liquid ingredients together to make a dough stiff enough to handle. Have on hand a small bowl of granulated sugar. Dip your fingers into the sugar. Pinch off a small hunk of dough about the size of a walnut. Dip the hunks into sugar and arrange them about 2 inches apart on greased cookie sheets. Bake in a moderate 350° F. oven for 12 to 15 minutes.

AT SERVING TIME:

Lumberjacks should be slightly warm. They go wonderfully well with milk, tea or coffee, or a cold fruit drink. The dough can be kept indefinitely in the refrigerator and the cookies baked as needed. Dough or baked cookies can also be frozen.

Fraulein's Brandy Wafers   MIXER

Years and years ago columnist Doris Fleeson's sister, Elsie, was doing post-graduate work in chemistry at Yale. On one wintry morning, eons before we were anything but mildly interested in cooking, she brought to me on a Haviland china plate some cinnamon-dusted wafers, thin as a veil of dew, ever so crisp, and showing around the edges a pencil line of gold.

It was a recipe, she told me, that had come from the family of a German housekeeper and each year, at the holiday season, the Fleesons always made it. Perhaps they still do.

In Fraulein's time it was, of course, made up in huge quantities by hand. But the beater (not the blender for some peculiar reason) does it quickly and easily. Either the dough or wafers can be stored well covered in the refrigerator or kept in the freezer. Makes 8 dozen.

YOU WILL NEED:

butter	flour
sugar	cinnamon
brandy, rum or bourbon whiskey	

Into the bowl of the mixer put ¼ pound (1 stick) of butter, preferably at room temperature. Beat at low speed till creamy; add ½ cup sugar and continue beating until well mixed. Then add alternately 4 tablespoons brandy, golden rum or bourbon whiskey and 1 cup sifted flour. Beat just until well mixed. Drop on an ungreased cookie sheet in tiny dabs 2 inches apart, using a ¼ teaspoon measuring spoon or a demitasse spoon. Bake at 375° F. 5 to 6 minutes or until a thin rim of gold-brown appears. The tops will still be pale. The wafers are slightly puffy when removed from the oven but they flatten out in moments. Allow to cool slightly. Place a pinch of cinnamon in the center of each. Then remove with a spatula.

AT SERVING TIME:
These are glorious to serve with tea, coffee or wine or to go along with fruits or sherbets or ice creams. They will keep for a week or so in a well-covered tin box or you can arrange them on wax paper in layers and keep them indefinitely in the freezer. They thaw in seconds.

Bourbon Balls   BLENDER

There are families including ours where Christmas wouldn't be Christmas without these balls.

YOU WILL NEED:
vanilla wafers	cocoa
chopped pecans	white corn syrup
powdered sugar	bourbon

Blend 12 to 15 vanilla wafers until they make fine crumbs. Measure to be sure you have 1 cupful vanilla wafer crumbs (graham crackers or other cookies may be used).

Place in a good-sized bowl, along with 1 cup chopped pecans, 1 cup powdered sugar, 2 tablespoons cocoa. Then add to these dry ingredients ½ tablespoon white corn syrup which has been stirred up with about ¼ cup bourbon. The mixture should be moist enough to form readily into a ball. If it isn't, another dribble of bourbon! To lend an extra aromatic savor, moisten your hands with bourbon when making the balls. Roll balls in powdered or confectioner's sugar. Keep cool until ready to serve. This recipe makes at least 48—each about the size of a big aggie marble.

Coffee

Coffee for a Throng ROASTER OVEN

YOU WILL NEED:
    drip-grind coffee   string
    cheesecloth

Remove load and lift rack and pour 10 quarts of water into inset pan of roaster oven. Set temperature control at 250° F. Tie 1 pound drip-grind coffee loosely in two cheesecloth bags and place in the 10 quarts of water. Cover roaster. When light goes out turn control to 160° F. Let stand 10 minutes. Remove coffee bags. Stir and serve or keep hot at 250°.

AT SERVING TIME:
Dip into coffee cups or pour into heated coffee pots.

Coffee for Gourmets BLENDER

All over the world there are people who swear "on the sacred beards of their Ancestors even" that coffee must be ground at the moment you use it. Of course there are grinders and grinders, hand and electric power. The blender does an excellent job if, and this is a large *if*, it is one of the big and let's admit it, one of the most expensive so-called custom multi-speed blenders with extra large blades and plenty of power. The smaller, lighter blenders are quickly ruined if you use them for coffee grinders.

With the proper blender you need buy only one type of coffee in the bean and you can grind it fresh for any kind of coffee making just by timing. Naturally large amounts of coffee take longer to grind but here are approximate timings:

1—for the old-fashioned, open-pot method known as boiled or steeped coffee—¾ cup whole coffee beans will be properly ground in about 10 seconds.

2—for the percolator—12 to 15 seconds.

3—drip coffee—35 to 40 seconds.

4—very fine drip for Chemex, etc.—50 seconds.

5—pulverized coffee for making Turkish coffee—60 to 65 seconds.

MENUS

Menus

The luncheon and dinner menus in this section are made up entirely of recipes in this book and are intended as basic menus on which to build your own variations. For example, a crisp green salad can be substituted for one of the vegetables; fluffy mashed or baked potatoes are easy and delicious with chicken and meats; homemade bread or rolls with lots of butter are always good and sometimes may substitute for potatoes. And, of course, steaming coffee or fragrant tea gives the finishing touch to any meal.

Luncheons

Chicken and Carrot Loaf Nivernaise

Bacon Bread Baked in a Casserole

Apple Snow

Kentucky Hambone Soup

Superior Corn Bread

Lime Whip

Omelet Fines Herbes

Popovers from a Mix

Instantaneous Fruit Sherbet

Chilled Beet Top Soup or Botvina

Sour Dough Pumpernickel

Sweet Whipped Butter

Cantaloupe Sherbet

Beef Bouillon

Heroes Trinacria

Skillet Custard

Sweet and Sour Pork Sandwiches

Mable Stegner's Apple Sauce

Spanish Cream

Cottage Cheese Mold

Deviled Bread

Concord Grape Parfait

Oxtail Soup

Old-Fashioned Whole Wheat Bread

Strawberry Ice Cream

Chicken Broth

New York Style Egg Sandwich

Bittersweet Chocolate Bavarian Cream

Spinach Timbales

Old-Fashioned Vanilla Ice Cream

Lumberjacks

Broiled Hamburgers

Saratoga Chips

Crème Brulée

Cream of Clam Soup

Onion Rolls

Lemon Snow Pudding

Duck Soup from Bones

Anadama Bread

Half-Moon Pies of Mincemeat

Salmon Mousse

Sour Rye Ponies

Pineapple Fritters

Dinners

Frosted Bisque

Sautéed Scallops

Texas Style Potato Chips

Cole Slaw

Ginger Soufflé

Charleston Crab Soup

Broiled Chicken with Wine and Tarragon

Pommes de Terre Soufflés

Spinach with Sesame Dressing

Strawberry Bavarian Cream

Chicken Bouillon

Baron of Lamb

Risotto au Gras

Grilled Zucchini

Lime Chiffon Pie

Essence of Shrimp

Steak Maxim

Pommes de Terre Anna

Artichokes

Banana Chiffon Cake

Consommé

Crown Roast of Pork

Tart Green Apple Sauce

Scalloped Potatoes

Baked Sliced Beets

Sauterne Bavarian

Curried Shrimp Bisque

Blue Grass Ham

French Fried Sweet Potatoes

Spinach Soufflé

Profiteroles au Chocolat

Aspic

Lamb Shish Kabob

Grilled Eggplant and Zucchini

Brown 'n' Serve Rolls

Instant Cheese Cake

Cream of Avocado Soup

    Broiled Fish Japanese

        Chrysanthemum Turnips

        Grilled Tomatoes

        Pecan Torte

Vichyssoise

    Chicken Martinique

        Asparagus Duet Amandine

        Watermelon Sherbet

        Fraulein's Brandy Wafers

Mushroom Broth

    Noisettes of Lamb

        Rotisserie Potatoes

        Russian Scallions

        Chilled Orange Bavarian

Japanese Soup

    Teriyaki Steak Sticks

        Pommes de Terre au Gruyère

        Carrots Vichy

        Fruit Meringue

Cucumber Soup

Boiled Beef

Potato Pancakes

Escarole with Pine Nuts

Georgia Peach Ice Cream

Essence of Crab

Chicken Baked in Clay

Grilled Sliced Potatoes

Soufflé de Tomates à la Napolitaine

Hazelnut Torte with Fruit

Gazpacho

Flaming London Broil

Yam Chips

Cauliflower with Sauce Aurore

Zabaione

Special Occasions

OLD-FASHIONED KITCHEN SUPPER

Raw Vegetable Platter with Sour Cream Dip

Blue Grass Ham   Wilted Greens

Popovers with Lingonberry Butter

Old-Fashioned Vanilla Ice Cream

Lumberjacks   Coffee

PARTY FOR TEENAGERS

Homemade Popcorn with Chives

Hot Heroes Trinacria

Corn Roast   Finger Vegetables

Ice Cream Stacks on Sticks

Crullers from Ready-to-Bake Biscuits

Ice-Cold Cider or Brown Cows

327

SUNDAY BRUNCH ON THE TERRACE

Orange Juice with Melon Balls and Mint Sprigs

Assorted Breads, Toasted

Home Churned Sweet Cream Butter

Eggs Hollandaise

Barbecued Canadian Bacon on Spit

Apple Sauce Croûtes

Coffee for Gourmets

RUSSIAN BARBECUE

Your Own Consommé with Lime

Lamb Shish Kabob

Pilaf of rice

Russian Scallions

Homemade Pumpernickel Bread

Coeur Flottante à la Ritz with Green Gage Plums

Coffee

SIT-DOWN DINNER FOR FOUR

Jellied Mushroom Broth

Noisettes of Lamb   Bearnaise Sauce

Pommes de Terre Anna

Artichokes

Chocolate Soufflé

Demitasse

AFTER-THE-BENEFIT BUFFET SUPPER

Caviar of Eggplant

Buttered Tissue-Thin Pumpernickel Bread

Hungarian Goulash   Poppy-Seed Noodles

Brown 'n' Serve Rolls and Brioche

Whipped Butter

Tomato Aspic

Green Mayonnaise

Almond Torte

Espresso Coffee

Index